Play and
Early Childhood
Development

Play and
Early Childhood
Development

Play and Early Childhood Development

James E. Johnson
The Pennsylvania State University

James F. Christie
University of Kansas

Thomas D. Yawkey
The Pennsylvania State University

Photographs by **Francis Wardle**

Scott, Foresman and Company
Glenview, Illinois London

Library of Congress Cataloging-in-Publication Data

Johnson, James Ewald, 1947–
  Play and early childhood development.

  Includes index.
  1. Play. 2. Child development. I. Christie,
James F. II. Yawkey, Thomas D. III. Title.
HQ782.J63 1987 155.4'18 86-21954
ISBN 0-673-18203-7

678910 – EBI – 92919089

CREDITS

Page 16, Figure 1–2: From Sylva, K., Bruner, J.S., & Genova, P. (1976). The role of play in the problem-solving of children 3–5 years old. In J.S. Bruner, A. Jolly, & K. Sylva (Eds.), *Play: Its role in development and evolution* (pp. 244–257). New York: Basic Books. Used with permission; **28,** Figure 2–1: Adapted from Collier, R.G. (1985, March). *Preschool teachers and children's play.* Paper presented at the Annual Meeting of the Association for the Anthropological Study of Play, Washington, DC. Used with permission; **52,** Figure 3–1: From Rosenblatt, D. (1977). Developmental trends in infant play. In B. Tizard & O. Harvey (Eds.), *The biology of play.* Philadelphia, Lippincott. Used with permission; **75,** Table 4–1: Based on Lieberman, J.N. (1977). *Playfulness: Its relationship to imagination and creativity.* New York: Academic Press. Used with permission; **96–97,** Adapted from *How to play with your children (and when not to)* by Brian and Shirley Sutton-Smith. Copyright © 1974 by Brian and Shirley Sutton-Smith. A Hawthorn book. Reprinted by permission of E.P. Dutton, A Division of NAL Penguin Inc.; **102–103,** Adapted from Giffin, H. (1984). The coordination of meaning in the creation of a shared make-believe reality. In I. Bretherton (Ed.), *Symbolic play: The development of social understanding* (pp. 73–100). Orlando, FL: Academic Press. Used with permission; **112,** Figure 6–1: From LaFreniere, P., Strayer, F., & Gauthier, R. (1984). The emergence of same-sex affiliative preferences among preschool peers: A developmental ethological perspective. *Child Development, 55,* 1958–1965. Used with permission; **152,** Figure 8–1: Adapted from pp. 90, 100, 102, 105, of "Designing a Play Environment for Toddlers" by Doris (Bergen) Sponseller and Matthew Lowry, published in *Play as a Learning Medium,* D. Sponseller (Ed.), by National Association for the Education of Young Children. Copyright 1974. Reprinted by permission of the copyright holder, Doris Bergen; **162,** Figure 8–3: Adapted from Smilansky, S. (1968). The effects of sociodramatic play on disadvantaged preschool children. New York: Wiley. Used with permission; **193,** Figure 10–1: From Kritchevsky, S., & Prescott, E. (1977). *Planning environments for young children: Physical space* (2nd ed.). Washington, DC: National Association for the Education of Young Children. Used with permission; **195,** Figure 10–2: From Kritchevsky, S., & Prescott, E. (1977). *Planning environments for young children: Physical space* (2nd ed.). Washington, DC: National Association for the Education of Young Children. Used with permission; **200,** Figure 10–3: Used with permission of the artist, Francis Wardle; **225,** Figure 11–1, Used with permission of the Children's House, State College, PA; **227,** Figure 11–2: From Hohmann, C. (1985). Getting started with computers. *High Scope Resource, 4*(3), 11–13. Used with permission.

Preface

Perhaps more than with other behaviors, we have mixed feelings about play. These feelings are difficult to describe because their causes are often obscure. Why do we have what can perhaps best be called a love-hate relationship with play? On the one hand, we see child's play as precious—important for the child and enjoyable to watch. At the same time, however, we express ambivalence or resentment toward play. Why?

Positive attitudes toward play are easy enough to understand. After all, watching children at play is enjoyable. We may wonder how they might be as grown-ups, since children reveal their personalities through play. At other times we may remember our own childhood and how we played as a child of the same age. In addition, most of us see the play of children as important for growth and development. As we watch children play, we can feel satisfied that we are somehow assisting in their development by, if nothing else, allowing the play to go on.

Negative attitudes toward play are not so easy to understand. Still, we all can recognize a dark side of play. Children can become mean during play, teasing others or doing dirty tricks in the name of fun. We frown upon such play.

Furthermore, we disapprove of play that is inappropriate. We may view play in the classroom as a form of resistance to authority. We may feel hostile toward play because it is spirited behavior, purposeless and free. Play, after all, rubs against the grain of the Protestant Work Ethic. It is all right to play, but only after the work is done and we have earned it.

Scholars have suggested that we may show hostility to play (and even to those who study or encourage play in children or animals) because play symbolizes not only liberation, but also the loss of our own childhood. The disappearance of childlike play in our lives forebodes our mortality. Our resistance to fate can become directed toward play and those involved with it, scientifically or in applied ways. Such feelings—conscious or unconscious—contribute to our emotional ambivalence about play.

Ambivalent feelings about play held on both personal and social levels have helped create divisions within the research and the teaching ranks. On the practical side, consider the mixed feelings and opposing views about the role of play in different early childhood curricular models (see Chapter 12). Similarly, this ambivalence has affected the research literature. On the one hand are researchers whose studies are largely concerned with the so-called generative functions of play—the worth of play to other developmental functions and processes such as cognition, language, or the development of impulse control. On the other hand there are researchers whose studies are concerned mainly with the so-called expressive functions of play—how play constitutes expressive social and cultural behavior. Play is seen to possess intrinsic worth in the second research concern but not in the first.

This book asserts that it is desirable for early-childhood educators and parents to move away from simple slogans and beliefs about play and toward a more comprehensive awareness and a more thoughtful appreciation of the topic. To that end we have attempted to integrate and share with the reader contemporary views of leading scholars and researchers concerned with play, early-childhood development, and education.

Our primary goal is to integrate with as much fidelity as possible current play research and theory to disseminate the results to the adult practitioner—early-childhood teachers and parents of young children alike. We have tried to do this in such a way as to be not only understood, but also helpful. We have made a deliberate attempt to embody empirical and conceptual insights with practical ideas, methods, anecdotes, and helpful suggestions.

The chapters of this book cover selected major areas of the extant play literature relevant to the play practitioner. Listed below are the chapter titles with the names of the co-authors responsible for the content of each chapter: Chapter 1, "Play: Nonessential or Educational?" (Professor Christie); Chapter 2, "The Role of the Adult in Children's Play" (Professor Christie); Chapter 3, "Development of Play" (Professor Johnson); Chapter 4, "Personality and Play" (Professor Johnson); Chapter 5, "Play and Social Development" (Professor Christie); Chapter 6, "Gender Differences in Play" (Professor Johnson); Chapter 7, "Social Class and Culture" (Professor Johnson); Chapter 8, "Observing Play" (Professor Christie); Chapter 9, "Toys and Play Materials" (Professors Christie and Yawkey); Chapter 10, "Physical Environment and Play" (Professors Christie and Yawkey); Chapter 11, "Play and the Electronic Media" (Professor Johnson); and Chapter 12, "Curriculum and Play" (Professor Johnson). Summaries are provided at the end of each chapter, as are extensive references. Special featured topics, tables, figures, and photographs are found throughout the text. Special thanks go to Francis Wardle for his suggestions regarding Chapters 9 and 10 and for his expert photography. We would also like to express our gratitude to the following persons for their assistance in preparing the manuscript: Betty Ayres, Donna Meek, Lori Mowery, and Edie Sodergren.

Although the topics in the chapters are diverse, at least three common themes run throughout the text. One is the issue raised at the beginning of this introduction concerning our underlying values and ambivalent feelings about play. We believe that differences in Western belief systems operate on both personal and social levels, producing the opposing positions seen in the research literature as well as in the applied literature of child-rearing and early-childhood educational practice. We believe, moreover, that by being aware of this tension we are better able to comprehend and more intelligently evaluate alternative and often conflicting reports and theories.

Our second common theme is the importance of recognizing and understanding distinctions between play and other related phenomena, such as exploration, social interaction, and adult tuition. This goal is central to the book's basic mission of successfully combining research, theory, and practical information. Understanding distinctions promotes not only further research and theory, but also ideas for useful applications—applications that can be subjected to further research necessary for theory construction. Research, theory, and practice in this way are viewed as functionally and reciprocally related.

Our third theme is that however one views specific research findings, theoretical conceptions, or practical ideas, the phenomenon of play is indeed necessary for development. The adult does have an important role in children's play behavior. Accordingly, in each chapter following the first two, which present conceptual and historical background, we discuss the role of the adult in relation to play, child development, and early-childhood education. Chapters 8, 9, and 10 in their entirety illustrate this dimension of the book by the nature of the topics discussed. In the remaining chapters a special section on adult roles in children's play is found just before the chapter summary. We hope that teachers and parents of young children, day care specialists, children's librarians, hospital play group leaders, and other adults who have frequent contact with children find these suggestions and recommendations useful.

For thoughtful review suggestions, the authors would like to thank Susan Kontos, Purdue University; Mary Louise Burger, Northeastern Illinois University; Maryann O'Leary; and Mary Fauvre.

Contents

4 Personality and Play   70

5 Play and Social Development   90

6 Gender Differences in Play   109

7 Social Class and Culture   129

8 Observing Play   148

9 Toys and Play Materials   168

10 Physical Environment and Play   187

11 Play and the Electronic Media   211

Play: Nonessential or Educational?

Everyone knows that children's play is fun and exciting. The smiles and laughter that accompany play attest to its enjoyable nature. But is play educational as well as pleasurable? There are sharp differences of opinion on this issue. Some adults consider play trivial and nonessential, while others believe that play makes important contributions to all aspects of child development.

We will use examples of two important types of play—sociodramatic play and constructive play—to illustrate these contrasting viewpoints. Both types of play are common during the preschool and kindergarten years. *Sociodramatic play* occurs when two or more children adopt roles and act out a make-believe situation or story. For example, three preschoolers are enacting a domestic scene in their classroom's housekeeping corner. John takes the role of the father, Wendy is the mother, and George, the youngest of the three, reluctantly agrees to be the baby.

WENDY:	Baby looks hungry. Let's cook him some food.
JOHN:	Okay.
WENDY:	(addressing George) Cry and say that you're hungry.
GEORGE:	But I'm not hungry.
WENDY:	Pretend that you are!
GEORGE:	(using a babyish voice) I'm hungry.
WENDY:	(addressing John) Father, what should we have for dinner?
JOHN:	How about eggs?
WENDY:	I'll go get some eggs from the 'frigerator. (She goes to a wall shelf and takes several cube-shaped blocks.)
GEORGE:	Aah! I'm hungry!
WENDY:	(pretending to scold George) Be quiet! (She puts the blocks in a toy pan and places the pan on the toy stove.) The eggs are cooking. Father, you'd better set the table.
JOHN:	Okay.

GEORGE:	Let me help, Daddy.
JOHN:	No! Babies don't set tables! You're just supposed to sit there and cry.

John then sets the table using miniature plates and cups. There is no silverware or coffeepot, so popsicle sticks and an empty can are used as substitutes. George pretends to cry from time to time, and Wendy continues cooking. Finally, Wendy puts a block on each child's plate, and John pretends to pour coffee from the empty can. The children then act like they are eating the make-believe eggs and drinking the invisible coffee.

Constructive play involves using materials like blocks or Tinkertoys to build something. Five-year-old Megan is playing with unit blocks on the floor of her bedroom. She first makes a base with a double-unit block in the center and unit and half-unit blocks on either side. She then makes a bridge in the center using three more double units. Next, Megan uses unit and half-unit blocks to make graduated steps up each side of the bridge. She finishes by adding small triangles to both ends and to the center of her structure.

Megan admires her bridge for a few moments and then gleefully knocks it down. She then begins building a new, entirely different structure.

Some adults would argue that the two play episodes are unimpressive and of little importance. The children in the first example are only engaging in trivial make-believe, and the girl in the second example thought so little of her block structure that she immediately tore it down. People with such opinions regard play as frivolous and believe that it would be better if children spent their time in more serious activities, such as receiving academic instruction or playing organized sports. They oppose school time being used for play activities because they feel that children spend more than enough time playing outside of school.

FIGURE 1-1

Megan's Block Structure

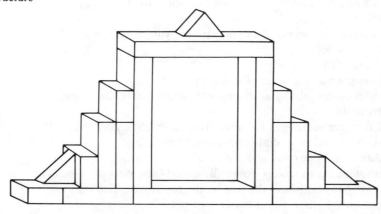

Other people would contend that the two episodes illustrate some of the important ways play contributes to child development. The children in the sociodramatic play example have to use social skills such as cooperation and turn taking to keep the play episode going. They must use precise language to plan and carry out their story lines. They are learning to use and interpret symbols (e.g., a block represents an egg). By enacting various roles, the children learn to view things from different perspectives. Megan, the girl in the constructive-play example, is gaining valuable experience with the concepts of symmetry and sequence. The deliberate manner in which Megan went about building the structure implies that she may have been following a mental plan. Children in both episodes are learning to persist at the task at hand.

The past two decades have witnessed a tremendous increase in research on play. Sutton-Smith (1983) reports that more than 200 scholarly journal articles and dozens of research books were published on the topic of play during the 1970s. Most of these research studies fall into four categories: (a) *definitional studies,* which attempt to distinguish play from nonplay behaviors, (b) *correlate studies,* which investigate the effects of play on social, emotional, and cognitive development, (c) *individual difference studies,* which examine the effects of factors such as differences in age, sex, and cultural background on play, and (d) *ecological studies,* which investigate the effects of settings and materials on play behavior.

This chapter reviews recent developments in play theory and the first two areas of play research (definitional and correlate studies). We begin by briefly summarizing the major theories of play. These theories are important because they reflect changing attitudes toward play and have motivated much of the research on play. We then examine recent progress in defining play, in order to better understand exactly what play is and what it is not. This is followed by a review of the research on play and child development. Finally, we attempt to answer the question: Is play nonessential or educational?

THEORIES OF PLAY

The theories described below attempt to explain and, in some cases, predict play behavior. They help define what play is and what causes it. We have divided play theories into two groups: (a) classical theories, which originated in the nineteenth and early twentieth centuries, and (b) modern theories, which were developed after 1920. The increased sophistication of the modern theories demonstrates the progress that has been made in understanding the phenomenon of play.

Classical Theories

The classical theories of play all originated before World War I. They try to explain why play exists and what purpose it serves. Ellis refers to them as "armchair" theories, based more on philosophical reflection than on experimental research. The four theories can be grouped into two pairs: (a) surplus energy and recreation theories, which view play as a means of energy regulation, and (b) recapitulation and practice theories, which explain play in terms of instincts. It is interesting to note that the members of each pair have opposite explanations of how play affects energy or instincts. Table 1-1 summarizes the four classical theories of play. A more detailed discussion of these theories are presented in Ellis' (1973) book *Why People Play*.

Surplus Energy Theory. The surplus energy theory of play can be traced back to Friedrich Schiller, an eighteenth century German poet, and to Herbert Spencer, a nineteenth century British philosopher. According to this theory, each living thing generates a certain amount of energy to meet survival needs. Any energy left over after these needs have been met becomes surplus energy. This extra energy builds up pressure and must be expended. Play, which is viewed as otherwise purposeless behavior, is how humans and animals get rid of this energy.

The surplus energy theory has a commonsense appeal that may explain why it is still popular today. Anyone who has seen young children run out to the playground after a long period of sedentary work in a classroom can see that there is an element of truth to this theory. It also neatly explains why children play more than adults (adults take care of children's survival needs, leaving children with lots of surplus energy) and why animals higher on the evolutionary scale play more than lower animals (the

TABLE 1-1

Classical Theories of Play

Theory	Originator	Purpose of Play
Surplus energy	Schiller/Spencer	Eliminate surplus energy
Recreation	Lazarus	Regenerate energy expended in work
Recapitulation	Hall	Eliminate ancient instincts
Practice	Groos	Perfect instincts needed for adult life

higher animals meet their survival needs more efficiently, resulting in more energy being left for play).

Recreation Theory. In direct opposition to the surplus energy theory, the recreation theory proposed by the German poet Moritz Lazarus stated that the purpose of play is to restore energy expended in work. According to Lazarus, work uses up energy and creates an energy deficit. This energy can be regenerated either by sleeping or by engaging in an activity which is very different from the work that caused the energy deficit. Play, being the opposite of work, is the ideal way to restore lost energy.

As with the surplus energy theory, there is a certain commonsense quality to the recreation theory. If one gets tired doing one type of activity, it helps to switch to something completely different. This theory explains the popularity of adult recreational activities. After a long day of stressful mental activity at the office, a period of physical activity (such as handball) can be rejuvenating. Early childhood educators have long recognized the principle behind the recreation theory, and the school day is structured so that periods of sedentary mental work alternate with periods of active play.

Recapitulation Theory. Prior to the turn of the century, scientists discovered that as the human embryo develops, it appears to go through some of the same stages that occurred in the evolution of the human species. At one point, for example, human embryos have structures similar to fish gills. This discovery led to the theory that ontogeny (the development of the individual) recapitulates or reenacts phylogeny (the development of the species).

G. Stanley Hall, an American psychologist, extended recapitulation theory to children's play. According to Hall, children reenact the developmental stages of the human race in their play: animal, savage, tribal member, and so on. These stages of play follow the same order that they occurred in human evolution. Thus children climb trees (our primate ancestors) before engaging in gang play (tribal man). The purpose of play is to rid children of primitive instincts that are no longer needed in modern life. For example, sports like baseball enable children to "play out" and eliminate ancient hunting instincts such as hitting with a club.

Practice Theory. Philosopher Karl Groos believed that, rather than eliminating instincts from the past, play serves to strengthen instincts needed for the future. Newly born humans and animals inherit a number of imperfect, partially formed instincts that are essential for survival. Play offers a safe means for the young of a species to practice and perfect these vital skills. The purpose of play is to exercise and elaborate skills required for adult life.

The best example of play as a means of practicing survival skills is the play fighting of young animals such as lions. Groos believed that his theory applied to humans as well. For example, when children take on roles as parents during sociodramatic play (as in the example at the beginning of the chapter), Groos would contend that they are practicing parenting skills that will be needed in adult life.

Outdoor play provides many opportunities for physical exercise and social growth.

All of the classical theories of play have serious weaknesses. They are very limited in scope and explain only a small segment of play behavior. There are numerous exceptions to each theory. The surplus energy theory offers no reason why children continue to play when exhausted. The recreation theory falsely predicts that, because adults work more, they should play more than children. The recapitulation theory cannot explain why children like to play with toys, such as cars and spaceships, that reflect modern technology. All four theories are also based on outdated, discredited beliefs about energy, instincts, and evolution. The surplus energy theory assumes that energy has hydraulic properties similar to those of water, and the practice theory contends that children inherit a knowledge of which specific skills will be needed in adult life.

However, in spite of their limitations, the classical theories are still important. First, they give historical perspective to adult attitudes about play. Notice that the current debate about the importance of play is evident in these old theories. While the surplus energy theory holds that play is purposeless, nonproductive behavior, the practice theory argues that play is vital for the survival of the species. Second, several of these theories are still very much with us. Many of today's adults, without being aware of the fact, believe in the surplus energy theory. Third, a number of the modern theories of play discussed in the next section have their roots in the early theories. Hall's recapitulation theory, with its different stages of play, stimulated interest in systematically observing children's play and was the forerunner of modern stage theories of play (for example, Piaget's theory). Groos' practice theory held that many play behaviors have adaptive significance, an idea that is reflected by Bruner (1972) in his recent theory of play and evolution.

Modern Theories

Modern theories of play attempt to do more than simply explain why it exists. They also try to determine play's role in child development and, in some cases, to specify

Table 1–2

Modern Theories of Play

Theory	Play's Role in Child Development
Psychoanalytic	Masters traumatic experiences
Piaget	Practices and consolidates previously learned skills
Vygotsky	Promotes abstract thought by separating meaning from objects and actions
Bruner/Sutton-Smith	Generates flexibility in behavior and thinking
Arousal modulation	Keeps arousal at optimal level by increasing stimulation
Bateson	Promotes ability to comprehend multiple levels of meaning

antecedent conditions that cause play behavior (Ellis, 1973). These modern theories are summarized in Table 1–2.

Psychoanalytic Theory. Sigmund Freud, the founder of psychoanalytic theory, believed that play has an important role in children's emotional development. According to Freud (1961), play can have a cathartic effect, allowing children to rid themselves of negative feelings associated with traumatic events. Play allows the child to suspend reality and switch roles from being the passive recipient of a bad experience to being the one who gives out the experience. For example, after being spanked by a parent, a child might spank a doll or pretend to punish a playmate. By reversing roles and becoming the active party, a child is able to transfer negative feelings to a substitute object or person.

Repetitive play is another mechanism through which children deal with unpleasant events. Repeating a bad experience many times in play divides the experience into small segments the child can handle. In this manner, the child can slowly assimilate the negative emotions associated with the event. Brown, Curry and Tittnich (1971) give an excellent example of the therapeutic value of repetitive play. Their preschoolers had the misfortune to watch a worker fall 20 feet to the ground and sustain serious injury. They watched while the man was given first aid and then taken away by an ambulance. Initially, many of the children were deeply disturbed by the incident. They frequently, almost compulsively, engaged in dramatic play themes related to the accident (falling, death and injury, ambulances, hospitals). After many weeks the frequency of such play diminished, and the children no longer appeared to be bothered by the accident.

Erikson (1950) extended the psychoanalytic theory of play by examining its contribution to normal personality development. According to Erikson, play progresses through stages that mirror children's psychosocial development. Through play, children create model situations that help them master the demands of reality.

Cognitive Theories. Swiss psychologist Jean Piaget (1962) proposed a detailed theory of children's intellectual development. According to Piaget, children go through a series of different cognitive stages during which their thought processes

TABLE 1-3

Piaget's Theory of Play

Approximate Age	Cognitive Stage	Dominant Type of Play
Birth–2	Sensorimotor	Practice play
2–7	Preoperational	Symbolic play
7–11	Concrete operational	Games with rules

become increasingly similar to those of adults. Children engage in the type of play that matches their level of cognitive development (see Table 1–3). For example, children under two years of age can only engage in practice play (*e.g.*, repeated physical movements). They cannot participate in dramatic or make-believe play because they do not yet have the cognitive abilities needed for symbolic representation.

Play does more in Piaget's theory than merely reflect a child's level of cognitive development; it also contributes to that development. Piaget stipulated that in order for learning to take place there must be adaption. Adaption requires a balance between two complementary processes: assimilation (modifying reality to fit one's cognitive structures) and accommodation (changing those structures to conform with reality). Piaget viewed play as an imbalanced state in which assimilation dominates over accommodation. Because play is nonadaptive, children do not learn new skills when they play. They do, however, practice and consolidate recently acquired skills. Take, for example, the sociodramatic play episode described at the beginning of this chapter. When Wendy used several symbolic transformations (*e.g.*, using a wooden block as an egg), she was not learning a new skill. But she may have been practicing representational skills learned earlier in a nonplay context. Piaget considered this practice/consolidation role of play very important because, without practice, many newly acquired skills would be quickly lost.

Vygotsky (1976), a Russian psychologist, believed that play has a more direct role in cognitive development. According to Vygotsky, young children are incapable of abstract thought because, for them, meaning and objects are fused together as one. As a result, young children cannot think about a horse without seeing a real horse. When children begin to engage in make-believe play and use objects (*e.g.*, a stick) to stand for other things (*e.g.*, a horse), meaning begins to become separated from objects. The substitute object, the stick, serves as a pivot for separating the meaning "horse" from the horse itself. As a result, children soon become able to think about meanings independently of the objects they represent. Symbolic play therefore has a crucial role in the development of abstract thought.

Other cognitive theorists emphasize how play promotes creativity and flexibility. Bruner (1972) points out that in play the means are more important than the ends. When playing, children do not worry about accomplishing goals, so they can experiment with new and unusual combinations of behavior they never would have tried if they were under pressure to achieve a goal. Once these new behavioral combinations occur in play, children can use them to solve real-life problems. Thus play promotes flexibility by increasing children's behavioral options. Sutton-Smith (1967) believes that the symbolic transformations (*e.g.,* using a stick as if it were a horse) that occur in make-believe play have a similar effect on children's mental flexibility. According to Sutton-Smith, these "as if" transformations allow children to break free from conventional mental associations and put ideas together in new and unusual ways. This results in an enlarged collection of creative ideas and associations that can later be used for adaptive purposes. Both Bruner's and Sutton-Smith's theories are related to Groos' practice theory in that they argue that play prepares children for adult life. However, the modern play theories contend that children do this by developing flexibility rather than by practicing specific skills.

Arousal Modulation. The arousal modulation theory, which was developed by Berlyne (1960) and modified by Ellis (1973), contends that play is caused by a need or drive in our central nervous system to keep arousal at an optimal level. When there is too much stimulation, arousal increases to uncomfortably high levels and causes us to engage in stimulation-reducing activities. For example, if arousal has been elevated because of the presence of a strange object, arousal can be reduced by exploring the object and becoming familiar with it. On the other hand, if there is not enough stimulation, arousal falls to unpleasantly low levels, and we become bored. Ellis views play as a stimulus-seeking activity which can elevate arousal to its optimal level. Play increases stimulation by using objects and actions in new and unusual ways. If, for example, children get bored sliding down a slide in the conventional manner, they can increase their level of stimulation by sliding down (and up) the slide in as many unusual ways as they can imagine. Play is therefore a stimulation-producing activity caused by low levels of arousal. As will be explained in later chapters, this theory has important implications for the design and use of playgrounds and play materials.

Bateson's Theory. Play, according to Bateson (1955), is paradoxical. Actions performed during play do not mean what they normally mean in real life. When children engage in play fighting, the blows delivered denote something very different from actual hitting. Before engaging in such play, children must establish a play "frame" or context to let others know that what is about to happen is play, that it is not real. This is usually done by smiling and laughing. If a play frame is not established, the other children will interpret the mock blows as a real attack and respond accordingly. When children play, they learn to operate simultaneously at two levels. At one level, they are engrossed in their pretend roles and focus on the make-believe meanings of objects and actions. At the same time, they are aware of their own identities, the other players' real identities, and the real-life meanings of the objects and actions used in the play.

Bateson's theory has stimulated interest in communicational aspects of play, prompting psychologists such as Garvey (1977) to examine the messages that children use to establish, maintain, terminate, and reinstate play episodes. This research has led to the discovery that children constantly shift back and forth between their pretend roles and their true identities while engaging in sociodramatic play. When problems arise during the make-believe portion of the play, children "break frame" and resume their real-life identities to resolve the difficulties. Note that several frame breaks occur in the play episode at the beginning of this chapter. For example, when George inappropriately asks to help set the table, John breaks the make-believe frame by reminding George that babies do not do that sort of thing.

Bateson contends that play does not occur in a vacuum. Play *texts,* the play activities themselves, are always affected by *contexts,* the surroundings in which the play occurs. Schwartzman (1980), for example, has demonstrated how children's social status affects their play. The fact that George, in the play episode, is low on the classroom's pecking order helps explain why he had to take the role of baby and why the other two children order him around. We are just beginning to realize the impact that context has on play.

Bateson's text/context distinction has also stimulated interest in play texts. Fein (1975) and others have investigated developmental trends in the symbolic transformations that children use in make-believe. One consistent finding is that two-year-olds must use symbols that physically resemble the objects they represent (*e.g.,* a small, rectangular piece of wood stands for a comb), whereas older children can use symbols that are increasingly dissimilar to what they depict (*e.g.,* a toy car or rubber ball can be used to represent the comb). Wolf and Grollman (1982) have examined age trends in the narrative organization of children's play. Their results showed that as children grow older, the scripts they enact become better integrated and increasingly complex. This type of research is adding greatly to our knowledge of play behavior and how it changes with age.

Modern theories of play have increased our understanding of play both through the explanatory power of the theories themselves and through the research they have stimulated. The arousal modulation theory has led to research on the distinction between play and exploration. This research is reviewed in the next section, which deals with the definition of play. After this discussion of definitions, we will examine the massive amount of recent research on play and child development. Most of this research can be traced back to the theories of Freud, Piaget, Vygotsky, Bruner, and Sutton-Smith. Research generated by Bateson's theory will be discussed in later chapters, including Chapter 9, "Toys and Play Activities," and Chapter 10, "Physical Environment and Play."

THE DEFINITION OF PLAY

Play is easy to recognize but very hard to define. Most adults have little trouble deciding whether or not children are playing. As Ellis (1973) points out, we can even recognize play in other species such as dogs and chimpanzees. Defining play, on the other hand, has proved to be an extraordinarily difficult task. Some scholars have even considered the term undefinable and therefore not worthy of serious study (Schlosberg, 1947).

Fortunately, the current increase in play research has led to progress in defining play. The following section discusses how this research has helped us differentiate between play and exploration and has led to a clearer understanding of the characteristics of play. We will end by clarifying how we intend to use the term "play" in this book.

Play Versus Exploration

Research by Hutt (1971), Weisler and McCall (1976), and others has revealed that play and exploration are similar in that they are intrinsically motivated behaviors that are not directed by externally imposed goals. Recent research, however, has revealed some important differences between play and exploration. Exploration is a "stimulus-dominated" behavior that is concerned with acquiring information about an object. It is controlled by the stimulus characteristics of the object being explored. Play, conversely, is "organism-dominated" behavior, which does not attempt to gain information about objects. Instead, play is concerned with generating stimulation and is governed by the needs and wishes of the child. Hutt (1971) explains, "In play the emphasis changes from the question of 'what does this *object* do?' to 'what can *I* do with this object?'" (p. 246). When children play, they ignore the reality of how an object is supposed to be used and use it in any way they desire. Table 1–4 summarizes the major factors that differentiate play and exploration.

Characteristics of Play

Recent research has done more than simply differentiate play from exploration. It has also led to the discovery that play is usually characterized by a small number of dispositional factors (Garvey, 1977; Rubin, Fein, & Vandenberg, 1983). These characteristics include:

TABLE 1-4

Play Versus Exploration

	Exploration	*Play*
Timing	Occurs first	Follows exploration
Context	Strange object	Familiar object
Purpose	Gain information about object	Create stimulation
Focus	External reality	Internal reality
Behavior	Stereotyped	Variable
Mood	Serious	Joyful
Heart rate	Low variability	High variability

Source: Based on research by Hutt (1971), Hughes & Hutt (1979), and Weisler & McCall (1976).

1. *Nonliterality.* Play events are characterized by a play frame or boundary that separates the play happening from everyday experience. This essential characteristic applies across all play forms—sociodramatic play, doing a puzzle, building with blocks, or playing a game. Within this play frame, internal reality takes precedence over external reality. The usual meanings of objects are ignored, and new meanings are substituted. Actions are performed differently from when they occur in nonplay settings. In the play episode at the beginning of this chapter, for example, the children used wooden blocks as if they were eggs and used the motion of lifting a toy cup to represent drinking. This "as if" stance toward reality allows children to escape the constraints of the here and now and experiment with new possibilities.

2. *Intrinsic motivation.* Play is not externally motivated by drives such as hunger or by goals like power or wealth. Instead, the motivation for play comes from within the individual, and activities are pursued for their own sake.

3. *Process over product.* When children play, their attention focuses on the activity itself rather than on the goals of the activity. In other words, means are more important than ends. This absence of pressure to achieve a goal frees children to try many different variations of the activity and is a major reason play tends to be more flexible than goal-oriented behavior.

4. *Free choice.* Free choice is an important element in young children's conception of play. King (1979) found that kindergartners considered an activity like block building to be play if it were freely chosen but considered the same activity to be work if it were assigned by the teacher. The free-choice factor may become less important as children grow older. A subsequent study by King (1982) revealed that pleasure, rather than free choice, was the key factor differentiating play and work for fifth graders.

5. *Positive affect.* Play is usually marked by signs of pleasure and enjoyment. Even when it is not, children still value the activity (Garvey, 1977). Sometimes play is accompanied by apprehension and mild fear, such as when a child is preparing to go down a steep slide. However, even this fear seems to have a pleasurable quality because the child will go down the slide again and again (Rubin, Fein, & Vandenberg, 1983).

Freedom from externally imposed rules and *active engagement* are also often listed as characteristics of play (*e.g.*, Rubin, Fein, & Vandenberg, 1983). However, we believe that these two characteristics are too restrictive because they exclude two important forms of play: games with rules and daydreaming. Games, by definition, involve following preestablished rules. As will be explained in Chapter 3, games are a form of play that becomes increasingly important as children grow older. Daydreaming also becomes more prevalent as children approach adolescence. Singer (1973) contends that daydreaming slowly replaces dramatic play as the major form of fantasy activity. Adolescents mentally play with ideas rather than playing externally with words and actions.

In this book, we will adopt a rather broad definition of play. We will treat any activity with most of the above five characteristics as play. In addition to the

Among play's most important benefits is the enjoyment it provides.

traditional categories of practice, constructive, dramatic, and game forms, we will consider as play all activities such as art and music which have an element of spontaneity, nonliterality, free choice, and pleasure.

RESEARCH ON PLAY AND DEVELOPMENT

During the past decade, dozens of research studies have investigated the relationship between play and child development. This research has focused on all aspects of children's growth, including cognition, language, social skills, and emotional adjustment. The following section summarizes the evidence linking play with each area of development.

Emotional Development

From 1930 until the mid 1960s, psychoanalytic theory was the dominant theory of play. Most of the research and writing on play during this period dealt with psychoanalytic topics such as play therapy, use of play for diagnostic purposes, and its role in emotional development. The research was primarily nonexperimental, consisting mainly of case studies of individuals. Axline (1964), for example, detailed how play therapy helped a young boy named Dibs solve his emotional problems. The little experimental research that was conducted suffered from methodological weaknesses such as inadequate controls and unreliable or invalid instrumentation (Rubin, Fein, & Vandenberg, 1983). As a result, findings were inconsistent and often contradictory. A number of doll-play studies were conducted to investigate the "displacement" hypothesis, which says that people tend to shift negative emotions onto a substitute. This hypothesis predicts that children who have been severely punished by their parents will be more aggressive in their play with dolls. While half of the doll-play studies supported the displacement hypothesis, half did not (Levin & Wardwell, 1971).

The disappointing results of past research combined with the rising influence of cognitive theories of play has recently resulted in a sharp drop in research on play and emotional development. Sutton-Smith (1983) reports that only five psychoanalytically oriented articles on play were published during the 1970s as compared with sixty-nine studies during the 1950s.

There are little experimental data to back up the contention that play has an important role in emotional development. However, Guerney (1984) has reported that play therapy studies are becoming more sophisticated, and Barnett and Storm (1981) have found physiological evidence linking play with anxiety reduction. If this trend continues and researchers begin to conduct tightly controlled studies of play and emotional growth and adjustment, perhaps such data will become available.

Cognitive Development

As the cognitive theories of Piaget and Vygotsky came into prominence in the late 1960s, attention shifted from play's role in emotional adjustment to its role in cognitive development. Researchers began to investigate the relationship between play and a number of different mental skills. Most of this research falls into three categories:

1. Correlational studies—These descriptive studies attempt to determine the extent of the relationship between play and various cognitive abilities. It is important to note that causality cannot be determined from this research. If a correlational study reveals that make-believe play is related to creativity, this does not mean that the play causes creativity. It is just as likely that creativity is responsible for high levels of pretend play.
2. Experimental studies—These studies use experimental controls in an attempt to determine if play has a causal role in cognitive development. Different groups of subjects are exposed to play and nonplay treatments, and then the effects of these treatments are monitored on different cognitive variables.
3. Training studies—In this special type of experimental study, adults attempt to teach children how to engage in different types of play (usually make-believe). If the training results in higher levels of play and enhanced cognitive performance, it can be assumed that the increased level of play is responsible for the cognitive gains.

In the following sections, we briefly review the evidence linking play with four important cognitive variables: IQ (intelligence quotient) scores, conservation ability, problem-solving skills, and creativity. [For a more complete review of this area of research, see Christie & Johnsen (1983).]

IQ. IQ tests attempt to tap a number of different cognitive abilities including memory, reasoning, abstraction, and understanding of language. Play—particularly make-believe play—may contribute to these skills in several ways. According to Vygotsky, the use of symbols in make-believe play leads to the development of abstract thought. In addition, Piaget contends that play enables children to practice and consolidate newly acquired mental skills.

Recent research supports the possibility that play increases IQ. Correlational studies have revealed a positive relationship between IQ scores and two types of play: sociodramatic (group make-believe) play and constructive play (Johnson, Ershler, & Lawton, 1982). Investigators have also found that play training positively affects children's IQ scores. Children who initially exhibited low levels of sociodramatic play were taught how to engage in this type of play. Results showed that the training resulted in gains in both play and IQ scores (Saltz, Dixon, & Johnson, 1977). Long-term studies have demonstrated that the gains in IQ brought about by play training are lasting (Christie, 1983; Smith, Dalgleish, & Herzmark, 1981).

Conservation. Conservation refers to the understanding that certain properties of objects, such as quantity and number, do not change in spite of perceived transformations. For example, the amount of clay in a ball does not change even when the ball is flattened out like a pancake. Piaget discovered that most preschoolers are not capable of conservation. These children will be fooled by the change in the clay's appearance and will be convinced that the amount of clay has been altered.

Rubin, Fein, and Vandenberg (1983) have argued that the role playing that occurs in make-believe play involves two cognitive operations needed for conservation: (a) decentration, the realization that children can be themselves and enact a role simultaneously, and (b) reversibility, the awareness that they can change from their make-believe role back to their real identity at any time. Research indicates that making children aware of the reversibility inherent in make-believe transformations can help some children perform better on conservation tasks (Golomb & Cornelius, 1977).

Problem Solving. Bruner (1972) contends that play contributes to children's ability to solve problems by increasing their behavioral options. Children try lots of different behaviors in their play, and these behaviors can later be useful in solving problems. Research has generally supported Bruner's theory. Several studies have found that play helps children's problem-solving abilities (Sylva, Bruner, & Genova, 1976; Simon & Smith, 1983). In these studies, children had to solve a problem that involved clamping sticks together to retrieve a marble or piece of chalk that was out of reach (see Figure 1–2). Results showed that children who were allowed to play with the clamps and sticks did just as well at solving the problem as children who were directly trained to solve it.

It appears that the play/problem-solving relationship is affected both by the nature of the play and the problem being solved. Pepler and Ross (1981) make a distinction between convergent problems, which have only one correct solution, and divergent problems, which have a variety of solutions. They found that playing with puzzle pieces and form boards led to better solving of convergent puzzle problems.

FIGURE 1–2

Schematic View of Task Posed by Sylva et al. (1976)

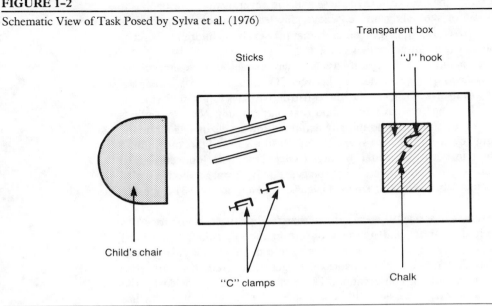

SOURCE: Sylva, Bruner, & Genova (1976), p. 246

Non-task related, divergent play (playing with puzzle pieces as if they were blocks) tended to interfere with the solution of puzzle tasks. Divergent play did, however, result in a wider variety of problem-solving strategies and facilitated the solving of divergent problems such as using blocks to build a make-believe village. This latter finding leads directly to our next topic, play and creativity.

Creativity. Perhaps the strongest link between play and cognition is in the area of creative thinking. A number of correlational studies have established a positive relationship between play and various measures of creativity. Lieberman (1977), for example, found that kindergartners who were rated high in terms of playfulness scored higher on tests of divergent thinking than other children. In addition to such correlational evidence, a series of experimental studies by Dansky and Silverman (1973, 1975) has yielded evidence that there is a causal link between play and creativity. These studies revealed that children who were allowed to play with objects were later able to find more creative, nonstandard uses for them. A series of play-training studies has provided further evidence that play promotes creative thinking (*e.g.*, Dansky, 1980a).

Dansky (1980b) discovered that free play helped divergent thinking only in children who regularly engaged in make-believe. This finding supports Sutton-Smith's (1967) contention that the symbolic transformations that occur in make-believe play are a key factor in play's contribution to creativity.

Language Development

Observational research has revealed that young children frequently play with the different forms and rules of language (Weir, 1962). They play with sounds by repeating strings of nonsense syllables, with syntax by systematically substituting words of the same grammatical category, and with semantics by intentionally distorting meaning through nonsense and jokes. This language play helps children to perfect newly acquired language skills and increases their conscious awareness of linguistic rules (Cazden, 1976).

Children also gain valuable language practice by engaging in sociodramatic play (Garvey, 1974). As depicted in the example of sociodramatic play at the beginning of this chapter, children follow the rules of conversation (*e.g.*, turn taking) and use language precisely to plan story lines and to designate the make-believe identities of objects and actions. Research has shown that sociodramatic play training can result in gains in language development (Smith & Syddall, 1978).

There is growing evidence that sociodramatic play may also improve children's language arts skills. Correlational studies by Wolfgang (1974) and Pellegrini (1980) have revealed a positive relationship between levels of sociodramatic play and reading and writing ability. Other researchers have found that children's story comprehension is enhanced by dramatic play activities (Pellegrini & Galda, 1982).

Social Development

To engage successfully in sociodramatic play, children must work together, take turns, and share props. Group dramatic play thus provides an opportunity for children to practice and perfect their social skills. Research supports this connection between play and social development. A study by Connolly and Doyle (1984) revealed positive correlations between preschoolers' sociodramatic play and several measures of social competence. Training in sociodramatic play has also been shown to result in gains in social skills such as cooperation (Shmukler & Naveh, 1980).

The role playing that occurs in sociodramatic play appears to contribute to another important aspect of social development: the ability to view the world from another person's perspective. When children engage in dramatic play, they enact a variety of roles such as parent, child, firefighter, grocer, and superhero. In order to portray such characters accurately, children must mentally put themselves in other people's places and experience the world from their point of view. Research indicates that dramatic play training enhances children's perspective-taking skills (Burns & Brainerd, 1979). We will examine the literature on play and social development in more detail in Chapter 5, "Social Environment and Play."

SUMMARY

The research reviewed above indicates that certain types of play are linked to cognitive and social development. Correlational studies have revealed that sociodramatic and constructive play are positively related to a number of different cognitive variables including IQ scores and creativity and to social skills such as cooperation. Experimental and training studies have yielded evidence suggesting that these forms of play may actually promote cognitive and social growth.

However, these findings do not indicate that all forms of free play contribute to development. There is little evidence linking gross motor play or nonsocial forms of dramatic play with growth in intellectual or social skills. It should also be noted that, in the play training studies mentioned above, it is not clear which component of the treatment—sociodramatic play, adult involvement, or peer interaction—caused the gains brought about by play training (Smith & Syddall, 1978). It is likely that the play itself was not totally responsible for the benefits. Adult and peer involvement may often be needed for play to have a developmental impact.

Our answer to the question "Is play nonessential or educational?" is that *some* types of play are educational. Play that is optimal for development is play that reflects or slightly stretches the current social or cognitive abilities of the child. Some play experiences devised by teachers and parents may do little more than amuse or entertain children; some play may actually bore or frustrate them. To contribute to the development and education of the child, play opportunities must be appropriate and challenging. The main objective of this book is to acquaint adults with strategies for providing this type of challenging play. In the chapters ahead, we discuss how adults can enrich play by *provision* of appropriate materials and conducive settings, by *observation*, and by direct *participation*. In so doing, we hope to make parents and teachers "play connoisseurs" who can help their children and students obtain the maximum benefits of play.

REFERENCES

Axline, V. (1964). *Dibs: In search of self.* New York: Ballantine.

Barnett, L.A., & Storm, B. (1981). Play, pleasure, and pain: The reduction of anxiety through play. *Leisure Sciences, 4,* 161–175.

Bateson, G. (1955). A theory of play and fantasy. *Psychiatric Research Reports, 2,* 39–51.

Berlyne, D.E. (1960). *Conflict, arousal and curiosity.* New York: McGraw-Hill.

Brown, N.S., Curry, N.E., & Tittnich, E. (1971). How groups of children deal with common stress through play. In N.E. Curry & S. Arnaud (Eds.), *Play: The child strives toward self-realization* (pp. 26–38). Washington, DC: NAEYC.

Bruner, J.S. (1972). The nature and uses of immaturity. *American Psychologist, 27,* 687–708.

Burns, S.M., & Brainerd, C.J. (1979). Effects of constructive and dramatic play on perspective taking in very young children. *Developmental Psychology, 15,* 512–521.

Cazden, C.B. (1976). Play with language and meta-linguistic awareness: One dimension of language experience. In J.S. Bruner, A. Jolly, & K. Sylva (Eds.), *Play: Its role in development and evolution* (pp. 603–608). New York: Basic Books.

Christie, J.F. (1983). The effects of play tutoring on young children's cognitive performance. *Journal of Educational Research, 76*, 326–330.

Christie, J.F., & Johnsen, E.P. (1983). The role of play in social-intellectual development. *Review of Educational Research, 53*, 93–115.

Connolly, J.A., & Doyle, A. (1984). Relation of social fantasy play to social competence in preschoolers. *Developmental Psychology, 20*, 797–806.

Dansky, J.L. (1980a). Cognitive consequences of sociodramatic play and exploration training for economically disadvantaged preschoolers. *Journal of Child Psychology and Psychiatry, 20*, 47–58.

Dansky, J.L. (1980b). Make-believe: A mediator of the relationship between play and creativity. *Child Development, 51*, 576–579.

Dansky, J.L., & Silverman, I.W. (1973). Effects of play on associative fluency in preschool-aged children. *Developmental Psychology, 9*, 38–43.

Dansky, J.L., & Silverman, I.W. (1975). Play: A general facilitator of associative fluency. *Developmental Psychology, 11*, 104.

Ellis, M.J. (1973). *Why people play*. Englewood Cliffs, NJ: Prentice-Hall.

Erikson, E.H. (1950). *Childhood and society*. New York: Norton.

Fein, G.G. (1975). A transformational analysis of pretending. *Developmental Psychology, 11*, 291–296.

Freud, S. (1961). *Beyond the pleasure principle*. New York: Norton.

Garvey, C. (1977). *Play*. Cambridge, MA: Harvard University Press.

Golomb, C., & Cornelius, C.B. (1977). Symbolic play and its cognitive significance. *Developmental Psychology, 13*, 246–252.

Guerney, L.F. (1984). Play therapy in counseling settings. In T.D. Yawkey & A.D. Pellegrini (Eds.), *Child's play: Developmental and applied* (pp. 291–321). Hillsdale, NJ: Erlbaum.

Hughes, M., & Hutt, C. (1979). Heart-rate correlates of childhood activities: Play, exploration, problem-solving and day dreaming. *Biological Psychology, 8*, 253–263.

Hutt, C. (1971). Exploration and play in children. In R.E. Herron & B. Sutton-Smith (Eds.), *Child's play* (pp. 231–251). New York: Wiley.

Johnson, J.E., Ershler, J., & Lawton, J.T. (1982). Intellective correlates of preschoolers' spontaneous play. *Journal of General Psychology, 106*, 115–122.

King, N.R. (1979). Play: The kindergartners' perspective. *Elementary School Journal, 80*, 81–87.

King, N.R. (1982). Work and play in the classroom. *Social Education, 46*, 110–113.

Levin, H., & Wardwell, E. (1971). The research uses of doll play. In R.E. Herron & B. Sutton-Smith (Eds.), *Child's play* (pp. 145–184). New York: Wiley.

Lieberman, J.N. (1977). *Playfulness: Its relationship to imagination and creativity*. New York: Academic Press.

Pellegrini, A.D. (1980). The relationship between kindergartners' play and achievement in prereading, language, and writing. *Psychology in the Schools, 17*, 530–535.

Pellegrini, A.D., & Galda, L. (1982). The effects of thematic fantasy play training on the development of children's story comprehension. *American Educational Research Journal, 19*, 443–452.

Pepler, D.J., & Ross, H.S. (1981). The effects of play on convergent and divergent problem solving. *Child Development, 52*, 1202–1210.

Piaget, J. (1962). *Play, dreams and imitation in childhood*. New York: Norton.

Rubin, K.H., Fein, G.G., & Vandenberg, B. (1983). Play. In P.H. Mussen (Ed.), *Handbook of child psychology: Vol. 4. Socialization, personality, and social development* (4th ed., pp. 693–774). New York:

Wiley.

Saltz, E., Dixon, D., & Johnson, J. (1977). Training disadvantaged preschoolers on various fantasy activities: Effects on cognitive functioning and impulse control. *Child Development, 48,* 367–380.

Schlosberg, H. (1947). The concept of play. *Psychological Review, 54,* 229–231.

Schwartzman, H.B. (1978). *Transformations: The anthropology of children's play.* New York: Plenum.

Shmukler, D., & Naveh, I. (1980). Modification of imaginative play in preschool children through the intervention of an adult model. *South African Journal of Psychology, 10,* 99–103.

Simon, T., & Smith, P.K. (1983). The study of play and problem solving in preschool children: Have experimenter effects been responsible for previous results?. *British Journal of Developmental Psychology, 1,* 289–297.

Singer, J.L. (1973). *The child's world of make-believe: Experimental studies of imaginative play.* New York: Academic Press.

Smith, P.K., Dalgleish, M., & Herzmark, G. (1981). A comparison of the effects of fantasy play tutoring and skills tutoring in nursery classes. *International Journal of Behavioral Development, 4,* 421–441.

Smith, P.K., & Syddall, S. (1978). Play and non-play tutoring in preschool children: Is it play or tutoring which matters? *British Journal of Educational Psychology, 48,* 315–325.

Sutton-Smith, B. (1967). The role of play in cognitive development. *Young Children, 22,* 361–370.

Sutton-Smith, B. (1983). One hundred years of change in play research. *TAASP Newsletter, 9*(2), 13–17.

Sylva, K., Bruner, J.S., & Genova, P. (1976). The role of play in the problem-solving of children 3–5 years old. In J.S. Bruner, A. Jolly, & K. Sylva (Eds.), *Play: Its role in development and evolution* (pp. 244–257). New York: Basic Books.

Vygotsky, L.S. (1976). Play and its role in the mental development of the child. In J.S. Bruner, A. Jolly, & K. Sylva (Eds.), *Play: Its role in development and evolution* (pp. 537–554). New York: Basic Books.

Weir, R. (1962). *Language in the crib.* The Hague: Mouton.

Weisler, A., & McCall, R.B. (1976). Exploration and play: Resume and redirection. *American Psychologist, 31,* 492–508.

Wolf, D., & Grollman, S.H. (1982). Ways of playing: Individual differences in imaginative style. In D.J. Pepler & K.H. Rubin (Eds.), *The play of children: Current theory and research* (pp. 46–63). Basel, Switzerland: Karger.

Wolfgang, C. (1974). An exploration of the relationship between the cognitive area of reading and selected developmental aspects of children's play. *Psychology in the Schools, 11,* 338–343.

The Role of the Adult in Children's Play

Attitudes about the role of the adult in children's play have changed considerably in recent years. Before 1960, most early childhood educators and authors of child-rearing books were schooled in the psychoanalytic theory of play. According to that theory, play's main function was to enable children to work out their inner conflicts (Isaacs, 1930). For example, if a child was jealous of a newborn sibling, play offered a safe means for the child to work off negative feelings toward the baby. The adult's role, as parent or teacher, was to set the stage for play and to observe children's play closely for clues about their emotional problems. The adult was never to enter into or interfere in any way with the children's play. It was believed that adult intervention would disrupt play, inhibit children from revealing their true feelings, and reduce play's therapeutic benefits.

In recent years, this hands-off attitude about adults' role in play has begun to change. In the 1960s, the cognitively oriented theories of Piaget, Vygotsky, and Sutton-Smith became prominent, and attention was shifted to play's role in social-intellectual development (Christie & Johnsen, 1983). As a result, the psychoanalytic theory and its strict prohibition against adult intervention in play had less influence. Furthermore, a series of play-training experiments demonstrated that direct adult involvement in play could have beneficial effects on children's cognitive growth.

This chapter begins with a brief review of play-training research. The benefits of adult participation in children's play are then summarized. Two important prerequisites to adult involvement in play—provision and observation—are discussed. This is followed by a description of four roles that adults can have in play: (a) parallel player, (b) co-player, (c) play tutor, and (d) spokesman for reality. Next, the important issue of when to intervene is examined. Differences between the role of the teacher and parent in facilitating play are also outlined.

PLAY-TRAINING RESEARCH

Interest in play training was initially sparked by a study conducted in Israel by Sara Smilansky (1968). She observed that children from low-income North African and Middle Eastern immigrant families engaged in less sociodramatic play than middle-class Israeli children. Sociodramatic play is an advanced form of make-believe play in which groups of children adopt roles and carry out cooperative dramatizations (for example, several children might take on roles as family members and pretend to eat dinner). As pointed out in Chapter 1, cognitive and social development is most commonly linked with this type of play. Because these low-socioeconomic status (SES) children also experienced academic difficulties, Smilansky hypothesized that their school problems might be caused by the absence of sociodramatic play. She reasoned that if sociodramatic play improves social skills, stimulates language development, and enhances one's ability to use and interpret symbols, then children who do not engage in this type of play might be less prepared to cope with school tasks than those who do.

Smilansky conducted an experiment to discover what causes the lack of sociodramatic play by low-SES children. Large numbers of preschool and kindergarten students were given extra experiences (such as field trips), play training, or a combination of play training and extra experiences. The play training, which was administered by the children's regular teachers, involved two types of intervention: (a) outside intervention, in which the adult remained outside the play episode but made comments and suggestions, and (b) participation in the play, in which the adult took part and modeled desired play behaviors. Results showed that both the play training and combination treatments effectively increased the amount and quality of the children's sociodramatic play. Both treatments also appeared to improve certain aspects of the children's cognitive performance. On the other hand, simply providing extra experiences had no effect on play or on cognitive abilities. Smilansky concluded that it was lack of knowledge of specific play skills rather than inadequate experiential backgrounds that kept many low-SES children from engaging in sociodramatic play.

Smilansky's study took on added significance when it was supported by a series of investigations on social class differences in play behavior. These studies indicated that lower-class children in the United States (Feitelson & Ross, 1973), England (Smith & Dodsworth, 1978), and Canada (Rubin, Maioni, & Hornung, 1976) all exhibited lower levels of sociodramatic play than their middle-class counterparts. These findings raised the possibility that a lack of sociodramatic play inhibits cognitive development and educational progress of low-SES children in many different countries.

During the 1970s, American, British, and Canadian researchers conducted a number of play-training experiments. The motivation behind these studies was twofold: (a) to gain evidence that play was a positive influence on cognitive development, and (b) to determine if play training effectively enhanced the cognitive growth of low-SES children. Most of these studies used variations of Smilansky's "outside intervention" and "participation in the play" training strategies. As already noted in Chapter 1, the results of this research were very positive. Play training not only brought about gains in creativity, verbal IQ, perspective taking, language development, and conservation attainment, it also led to improvement in social skills such as cooperation and impulse control.

However, several design problems prevented these training studies from providing firm evidence that play causes growth in cognitive and social skills. First, most of the studies did little to control for the effects of adult contact that accompanies play training. Experiments in which adult contact has been carefully monitored and controlled (Smith & Syddall, 1978; Smith, Dalgleish, & Herzmark, 1981) suggest that adult instruction, rather than increased levels of play, is responsible for most of the gains brought about by play training.

Moreover, the early play training experiments did not include follow-up assessments to determine if the resulting improvement was lasting. It had not been disproven that play training might have only temporary effects on children's performance. However, several more recent studies using delayed post-tests have had very positive results. Gains in cognitive and social variables were maintained on post-tests administered up to twelve weeks after treatments had ceased (Christie, 1983; Smith, Dalgleish, & Herzmark, 1981), suggesting that play training has lasting effects on children's social and intellectual development.

In summary, it is not known whether play or adult contact is the more influential component of play training. The research clearly indicates, however, that play training is an effective means to foster young children's cognitive and social growth. The first issue can only be addressed by researchers through more carefully controlled experiments that will delineate further the different roles play serves in child development. Parents and teachers, on the other hand, are more likely to be interested in the second point. To them, the fact that play training works is more important than fully understanding why it is successful.

WHY GET INVOLVED IN CHILDREN'S PLAY?

Recent research has revealed that, far from being harmful or disruptive, adult involvement often enriches the quality of children's play and is beneficial in other ways as well. The value of adult participation in play has been demonstrated in play training experiments and observational studies of play in the home and in preschool classrooms. This section summarizes some of the major benefits of adult involvement in play while pointing out the dangers of excessive intervention.

Approval

Adults let children know that play is valuable and worthwhile by showing an interest in that activity. This approval may be communicated even more strongly when parents and teachers actually participate in children's play. On the other hand, if adults ignore play, they may send a message to children that this activity is not worth

Adult participation can often enhance children's play.

pursuing. Manning and Sharp (1977) explain:

> Children's attitude to play in school is related to the teacher's. They are not so likely to concentrate, persevere and devote time to play if they know that the teacher is not interested, or does not find time to participate. It becomes evident to them that play is not a highly valued activity in school. It is generally accepted that a teacher's class will reflect her interests and enthusiasm. If she finds children's play exciting, stimulating and worthwhile, so will they. Teachers who join in children's play find the children are in no doubt that it is a valued activity. (p. 22)

The approval expressed by adult involvement is particularly important in the case of make-believe play. Some parents do not approve of make-believe; some actually believe that it is dangerous to their children's mental health, fearing that the children will become lost in a fantasy world. Children from such families are often hesitant about engaging in pretend play when they start school. An effective way to help these children realize that make-believe is acceptable is for the teacher to join in children's play and model pretend behaviors.

Rapport

Participating in children's play is an excellent way for parents and teachers to build rapport with childen. Brian and Shirley Sutton-Smith (1974) have detailed how parents can get in touch with their babies by playing simple games like pinkie pull and peek-a-boo. As children grow older, a family play time in which parents play pretend games with their children helps to maintain a friendly, happy atmosphere in the home. Participation can also improve teachers' relationships with their students. When a teacher comes down to the children's level and joins in their play, children learn that the teacher is an approachable human being rather than a remote authority figure (Wood, McMahon, & Cranstoun, 1980).

Persistence

When adults participate in children's play, they act as buffers against distractions that can interrupt the play. This results in longer, richer play episodes. Dunn and Wooding (1977) observed the play of two-year-olds at home and discovered that play lasted significantly longer when mothers were involved. Sylva, Roy, and Painter's (1980) observational study of British preschoolers had similar findings. Children's play episodes lasted twice as long when a teacher took part than when the children played only with their peers.

Sylva and her associates (1980) pointed out that persistence in play can lead to the capacity for sustained commitment to tasks. This ability to concentrate on the job at hand is crucial for later success in school. By becoming involved in children's play, parents and teachers can help children develop this important skill.

More Elaborate Play

Recent observational studies indicate that much of the free play that occurs in preschool classrooms is low level. Tizard (1977) reported the findings of her research conducted in British preschools:

> Much of the play in the nursery school tends to be repetitive and of a rather low level. We found that 84 percent of the play in nursery schools involved the child in only one action, e.g., swinging, or digging in the sand or perhaps running round saying, "I'm a Dalek." The kind of elaborate socio-dramatic or constructional play which involves a sequence of relatively integrated activities linked by an idea was really relatively infrequent. (p. 206)

Unfortunately, this situation is not unique to England. Sylva and her colleagues (1980) found that the quality of free play in American preschools was lower than that in British schools.

There does appear to be a need to enhance the level of play that occurs in classrooms. If children are to reap the full benefits of play, it is necessary for them to engage in high-quality sociodramatic and constructive play, the types of play that appear to have the biggest roles in intellectual and social development.

Adult involvement in play is an excellent means for accomplishing this goal. Play-training experiments have shown that adult modeling can lead children to engage in higher levels of play. Observational research in schools and in the home support this finding. Bruner (1980) reported that preschoolers were more likely to move toward higher levels of play and stay there when teachers became involved in their play than when the children played only with their peers. In a study of two-year-olds' play in the home, Dunn and Wooding (1977) discovered that almost half of the toddlers' pretend play was initiated by their mothers. This finding suggests that parental involvement has a major role in the development of sociodramatic play.

Cognitive and Social Development

Research has shown that play training not only leads to higher levels of play; it also promotes children's cognitive and social development. Play-training procedures that involved direct adult participation in play resulted in gains in creativity, verbal intelligence, perspective taking, cooperation, and a number of other skills. A growing body of evidence suggests that adult contact that occurs during play tutoring is primarily responsible for these gains (Smith & Syddall, 1978).

A Note of Caution

We have described a number of benefits arising from adult involvement in play. It should be noted, however, that these benefits will occur only if the adult participation is appropriate both to the ongoing play situation and to the needs of the children who are involved.

Excessive intervention can have disruptive effects on children's play. Bruner (1980) gives an example of a teacher who constantly joined in her children's make-believe play, whether it served any purpose or not. She always took the role of central adult figure, preempting some of the better roles that the children could have enacted. The result of this combination of too much and the wrong kind of intervention was that the children engaged in very little sociodramatic play.

PREREQUISITES TO ADULT INVOLVEMENT

Before intervening in children's play, it is important that parents and teachers first set the stage by providing an environment that is conducive to high-quality play. Often such provision makes direct adult participation in the play unnecessary. Once the stage has been set, the parent or teacher should carefully observe the play that ensues. This observation will reveal whether additional provision or direct involvement is needed to develop the play to its full potential.

Setting the Stage

In order to set the stage for play, adults need to provide four things: (a) time, (b) space, (c) materials, and (d) preparatory experiences (Griffing, 1983). Each of these variables can affect the quality of children's play.

   Time. Children need adequate time to plan and carry out elaborate sociodramatic and constructive play episodes. Ample time also allows children to persist in their play. The exact amount of time required varies, depending on the child's age and play skills. Free play periods of 30 to 50 minutes are usually recommended for preschoolers and kindergarten-age children (Griffing, 1983). Such periods give children time to recruit co-players, select roles, get props, plan story lines, work out

Adults can encourage sociodramatic play by providing dress-up clothes and theme-related props.

differences, and carry out their dramatizations. Once their original plot is exhausted, children can extend their story by adding new elements. If play periods are too short, children will have barely finished preparing for their play when it is time to stop and clean up. After many such experiences, children may simply give up trying to engage in dramatic play and resort to simpler forms of play (physical play) which easily fit into short time periods.

Because increasing amounts of structured academic activity have worked their way into early childhood programs, many teachers may have difficulty fitting lengthy play periods into their daily schedules. In such cases, we believe that it is preferable to schedule several lengthy play periods per week than to have short (ten- to 15-minute) play periods every day.

Space. Adequate space is also required for high-quality play. At a minimum, preschools and kindergartens should have a block area for constructive play and a housekeeping area for sociodramatic play. The addition of a theme area that can be changed to represent different places such as a restaurant, store, and doctor's office can greatly enrich children's sociodramatic play (Woodard, 1984).

A special place for make-believe in the home helps to promote pretend play. Segal and Adcock (1981) discovered that large cardboard boxes were popular places for make-believe play at home. They also found that preschool-aged children preferred having their play spaces in high-activity areas such as the kitchen or family room. Older children did not mind conducting their make-believe play in more remote areas of the house.

Arrangement of space also affects play behavior. For example, children tend to engage in more sociodramatic play in well-defined, partitioned areas than in large, open spaces. This topic is discussed in more detail in Chapter 10, "Physical Environment and Play."

Play Materials. Play materials are another ingredient needed for high-quality play. Research indicates that children's play is heavily influenced by the types of materials available (Rubin, Fein, & Vandenberg, 1983). Theme-related props such as costumes encourage sociodramatic play, whereas blocks, puzzles, and art materials stimulate constructive play. If adults wish to promote these two types of play, it is

---

FIGURE 2-1

Enriching Play: Provision, Observation, and Involvement

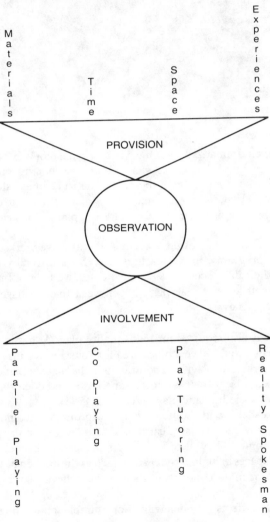

SOURCE: Adapted from Collier (1985) and Manning and Sharp (1977).

important that both types of materials are available. Guidelines for selecting play materials are presented in Chapter 9, "Toys and Play Materials."

Preparatory Experiences. Role playing requires that children draw on their prior knowledge and act out roles as they understand them. If children have had little experience with the roles they are attempting to portray, sociodramatic play can become difficult or impossible to sustain. Most children have had adequate experience with the roles of family members, but they may be unfamiliar with many work-related roles. Woodard (1984), for example, relates how preschoolers became confused when attempting to act out the roles of chef and dishwasher in a restaurant theme area.

Teachers can help clarify children's understanding of themes and roles by providing relevant experiences such as field trips, classroom visitations by people in different occupations, and stories about different jobs. Parents, of course, can provide similar experiences for their children. Smilansky (1968) found that preparatory experiences greatly increased the effectiveness of play training.

Observation

Successful adult involvement in play depends heavily on careful observation. Observation reveals what help, if any, is needed for children to develop and extend their play. As Manning and Sharp (1977) pointed out, observation can serve not only as the basis for provision for play but also as the bridge linking provision with adult involvement (see Figure 2–1). Observation can indicate when additional time, space, materials, and experiences need to be provided. It can also reveal when direct adult involvement in play would be beneficial.

Observation lets adults know what already exists in play, enabling them to base their intervention on the children's current interests and needs. Manning and Sharp (1977) give an example of what happens when an adult intervenes without first carefully observing the ongoing play. A six-year-old girl was playing with some shells in a sand tray, making up a story. The shells represented people and trees, and the girl's finger was a make-believe cat. A teacher aide intervened by trying to draw the girl into a conversation about the pattern she was making with the shells:

> Those shells are very pretty, aren't they? Doesn't the sand feel soft and smooth on your fingers—is it tickling? You have made a lovely pattern. Have you finished or are you going to put more shells or something in it? (p. 18)

This intervention disrupted the make-believe context or frame of the play, causing the girl to stop playing. It also failed to elicit the desired conversation. Unless adults carefully observe play before intervening, their involvement may do more harm than good.

Several systems for observing play are described in Chapter 8, "Observing Play." These systems specify exactly what to look for in children's play, making observation a much easier task.

TYPES OF ADULT INVOLVEMENT

In an observational study of teacher-child interaction in British preschools, Wood, McMahon, and Cranstoun (1980) discovered that teachers became involved in children's play in four different ways and that these four types of involvement had different effects on children. They labeled these kinds of adult involvement: (a) *parallel playing*, (b) *co-playing*, (c) *play tutoring*, and (d) being a *spokesman for reality*. This section describes and gives examples of each of these four roles. The advantages and disadvantages of each type of involvement are also discussed.

Parallel Playing

Parallel playing occurs when the adult is close to the child and plays with the same materials. The adult does not, however, interact with the child or impinge on the child's play. This type of adult involvement usually occurs in functional (sensorimotor) play or constructive play. For example, if a child is sitting on the floor playing with Tinkertoys, the adult would sit near the child and also use the Tinkertoys. The adult might make occasional comments addressed to no one in particular ("Oh, I've made such a pretty house"), but no attempt would be made to directly engage the child in conversation.

Wood and his associates (1980) point out several potential benefits arising from this type of adult involvement in play. The adult's presence can comfort children and indicate to them that play is a worthwhile activity. Children are also likely to persist longer in their play when an adult is present, whether or not there is any interaction (Sylva et al., 1980). Finally, it is possible that children may learn new ways of playing with materials by watching the adult play. Research has yet to show, however, that adult parallel play has any impact on the quality of children's play.

Co-Playing

Co-playing occurs when an adult joins in an ongoing play episode but lets the children control the course of the play. While primarily responding to the children's comments and actions, the adult occasionally asks questions and makes remarks that can extend the play. The children are free to accept or reject these suggestions.

The following episode illustrates adult co-playing. Two children are in the house-keeping corner pretending to make hamburgers out of Playdough. A teacher has been observing this play for several minutes, and now the children invite her to join in the play:

CHILD 1:   Would you like a hamburger?
TEACHER: Yes, I would.
CHILD: Here's a big one. (Gives the teacher a pancake-shaped piece of Playdough.)
TEACHER: Why thank you. It looks very good.
CHILD 2:   Have some mustard.

TEACHER:	Thanks. Do you have any ketchup?
CHILD 1:	Yes. Donald, get it for her.
CHILD 2:	Here's the ketchup. (Hands the teacher a small block of wood.)
TEACHER:	Thanks. How do I get the cap off?
CHILD 2:	Here, I'll show you. (Pretends to screw a cap off the block of wood.)
TEACHER:	Thank you very much. (Pretends to put ketchup on the make-believe hamburger.)
CHILD 1:	How is it?
TEACHER:	Very delicious!
CHILD 2:	Mine's good too!

Notice how the teacher allowed the children to control the play but also subtly influenced its direction by introducing a new element, ketchup. She used three types of conversational moves:

1. Asking for information: "Do you have any ketchup?"
2. Asking for instructions: "How do I get the cap off?"
3. Responding to the children's actions and comments: "Very delicious!"

Wood and his colleagues (1980) found that these three types of comments were frequently used by adults when they were co-playing.

In the absence of a direct invitation from the children, the best way for adults to become a co-player is to do something playful that fits in with the ongoing play. For example, if several children have adopted roles as storekeepers, an adult might pretend to be a customer and inquire about buying some merchandise. This works much better than asking "Can I play?" (Sutton-Smith & Sutton-Smith, 1974).

Co-playing expresses the same approval and encourages persistence just like parallel playing. However, it also allows adults to build rapport with children and be better able to influence the level of play. Actually playing and interacting with the children enable the adult to model more types of play behaviors, to engage the children in play-related conversations, and to draw other children into the play episode.

Co-playing does not involve tutoring; that is, the adult does not teach the children any new play behaviors. For this reason, it is most appropriate for use with children who are already engaging in high-level play (sociodramatic play or constructive play) but who have become bogged down in a repetitious play episode. The co-playing adult can subtly introduce new elements that can extend and enrich the play, as illustrated in the hamburger example above.

Co-playing is usually less successful with children who lack experience in high-level play or who lack the prerequisite cognitive or social skills. Co-playing requires an ongoing dramatic or constructive play episode that the adult can join.

For example, if a child engages almost exclusively in physical play, there will be few opportunities for an adult to enter onto ongoing dramatic or constructive play. Such children may need the types of tutoring described in the next section in order to begin engaging in more advanced forms of play. After they begin to engage spontaneously in dramatic and constructive play, then the adult can join in as a co-player.

Play Tutoring

Play tutoring is the type of adult involvement used in the play-training experiments reviewed earlier in this chapter. It differs from co-playing in three important respects. First, in play tutoring the adult often initiates a new play episode, whereas an adult co-player always joins play already in progress. Second, the adult takes a more dominant role in the play and has at least partial control over the course of the play episode. Third, the adult teaches the child new play behaviors.

Play tutoring is commonly used to teach children how to engage in sociodramatic play. According to Smilansky (1968), fully developed sociodramatic play contains five elements:

1. Role-playing—the child adopts a make-believe role (parent, doctor, or super-hero) and communicates this transformation with verbal declarations and role-appropriate behavior.
2. Make-believe transformations—objects, actions, and words are used as substitutes for other objects, actions, or situations. For example, a child might pretend that a stick is a broom or use the verbal declaration "Let's pretend we're on a boat" to create an imaginary situation.
3. Social interaction—at least two players must interact directly with each other in the play episode.
4. Verbal communication—the children engage in verbal exchanges related to the play episode. These exchanges take two forms: (a) metacommunications, comments *about* the play ("You be the patient and I'll be the nurse"), and (b) pretend communications, comments that are appropriate for the role that the child is enacting ("Now I'm going to give you a shot, Mrs. Peabody").
5. Persistence—the children engage in sustained play episodes. Given suitable provision for sociodramatic play, most preschoolers can be expected to sustain at least 5- or 6-minute episodes (Sylva et al., 1980); kindergartners can be expected to keep an episode going for at least 10 minutes (Smilansky, 1968).

If observation reveals that children are missing some of these elements in their play, play tutoring can be used to help children acquire the missing behaviors. Play tutoring can also be used to promote constructive play. The three most common types of play tutoring are described below.

Outside Intervention. Outside intervention was one of the types of play tutoring used by Smilansky (1968) in her pioneering play-training study. It is so named because the adult remains outside the play episode. From this outside position, the adult makes comments and suggestions designed to encourage children to use sociodramatic play behaviors. Smilansky recommends that these comments be addressed to the roles that children have adopted rather than to their real-life identities. For example, if a child named Suzy has taken on the role of Dr. Summers, then the adult should address her as Dr. Summers. This is done to encourage role playing and to avoid disrupting the make-believe atmosphere of the play.

The following example illustrates how outside intervention works. A teacher observes that a child is sitting by herself engaging in functional play with a doll (*i.e.*, she is simply manipulating the doll). At the same time, other children are engaging in sociodramatic play in a store theme area. The teacher approaches the lone child and says, "Mrs. Phillips, your baby looks very hungry. Why don't you take her to the store and buy her some food?" This comment would encourage the child to take on the role of a parent and to use the doll as a make-believe child. This suggestion would also promote social interaction and verbal communication by getting the lone child involved in the other children's store play. After "Mrs. Phillips" has finished her make-believe shopping trip, the adult could promote persistence by suggesting a way to extend the play. For example, the teacher might say, "Now that you've finished your shopping, your baby needs to be fed. You'd better take her home and fix her some supper." Note that in making these comments the teacher did not get involved in the play itself. She did, however, initiate the play and control the course of the play episode. She also encouraged the child to use new play behaviors such as role playing and make-believe transformations.

Inside Intervention. Inside intervention was the other type of play tutoring used in the Smilansky (1968) study. In this type of intervention, which Smilansky referred to as "participation in the play," the adult takes on a role and actually joins in the children's play. While acting out this role, the adult models sociodramatic play behaviors that the children have not been using. The adult takes on a major role and directs the course of the play by actions and comments. It is the degree of control that the adult exerts over the play that differentiates inside intervention from co-playing.

The following example illustrates how inside intervention can be used to stimulate sociodramatic play. A teacher observes that several children are in the housekeeping corner but are not engaging in group make-believe. The teacher approaches the children and announces that she is a doctor who has come to check on the sick baby. This demonstrates role playing and encourages the children to adopt roles as family members. The teacher then models make-believe transformations by pretending to take a doll's temperature with a small pencil. Verbal communication and social interaction are promoted by getting all the children involved in a single dramatization. The teacher is also modeling the use of verbal exchanges to designate the make-believe identities of objects, to assign roles, and to plan story lines.

"Two Types of Play Tutoring" highlights some important differences between outside and inside intervention. The fact that inside intervention involves modeling gives it a distinct advantage over outside intervention. Modeling is a very effective way to teach young children new skills. Outside intervention, on the other hand, is less obtrusive and is less likely to disrupt children's play.

Singer (1977) gives an example of the positive effects that play tutoring had on one preschooler's play:

A little girl, named Sara, in one of our studies was characterized in the initial pretesting by apathy and unresponsiveness. When other children played happily, she seemed somewhat downcast and withdrawn and clung frequently to the teacher. Following exposure to two weeks of make-believe play modeling [the training was a combination of inside and outside intervention], during which she still continued to be a relative nonparticipant, a change began to take place. Within a few days after the termination of the training, she was observed by raters unfamiliar with the conditions of the study in which the children had participated. Sara had organized a group of boys into a tea party. She had them seated around the table and was serving them pretend tea and cookies, treating them as if she were a mother and they the children; she also fed a make-believe dog under the table. Following the completion of the meal, she took them off to another area where they were going to take their nap for the afternoon in her pretend game. Throughout the game she kept up a lively patter introducing various details of make-believe which seemed to delight the other children. Her mother, who was unfamiliar with the specific nature of the study, later also reported her own pleasure in the increased liveliness and communication that the child was showing. (pp. 139–140)

Thematic-Fantasy Training. Thematic-fantasy training, which was developed by Saltz and Johnson (1974), helps children act out stories like Little Red Riding Hood, Hansel and Gretel, and The Three Pigs. Any fairy tale, folk tale, or short story with a small number of characters and a simple, repetitive plot can be used as the basis for this type of play tutoring.

TWO TYPES OF PLAY TUTORING: OUTSIDE AND INSIDE INTERVENTION

A preschool teacher observes that Bobby, a shy four-year-old, is playing alone with blocks. He is not engaging in constructive or dramatic play with the blocks; instead, he is merely stacking them up in piles and then knocking them down. However, the teacher has observed that Bobby is very proud of his new pair of shoes. Two types of play tutoring could be used to encourage Bobby to engage in more challenging play.

Outside Intervention. In this type of tutoring, the teacher makes comments and suggestions aimed at encouraging sociodramatic play. For example:

TEACHER: Mr. Storekeeper, you certainly have a lot of shoes (pointing to the small blocks). Have you sold any yet?
BOBBY :   No, I haven't.
TEACHER: Why don't you make some shelves out of the bigger blocks so people can see the shoes you have to sell. While you're doing that, I'll see if I can find some customers for your store.

The teacher might then approach some other children who are playing in the

Thematic-fantasy training involves a three-step sequence which can be spread over several days:

Step 1
The adult reads the story and discusses it with the children.

Step 2
The adult assigns roles to the children and helps them do a preliminary enactment of the story by acting as narrator, prompting when needed, and occasionally taking a role in the story.

Step 3
The story is enacted several more times with the children exchanging roles. Adult assistance is phased out.

Saltz and Johnson (1974) recommend that the use of props and costumes be kept to a minimum in order to focus the children's attention on the plot of the story. Detailed examples of thematic-fantasy training and suggestions for using this form of intervention are presented in Chapter 12.

Thematic-fantasy training is more structured than the two previously described methods of play tutoring. The children are assigned simple roles and are given a ready-made plot to follow. Thematic-fantasy training is therefore a good procedure to use with children who have had little or no experience with sociodramatic play. Through practice with role playing and using make-believe transformations, these

housekeeping corner and suggest that they make a trip to Bobby's store to buy some new shoes.

Inside Intervention. This type of tutoring requires that the teacher actually take on a role and join in the play. While engaging in the play, the teacher can model desired play behaviors and skills. For example:

TEACHER:	Mr. Storekeeper, I would like to buy a pair of your shoes (pointing to the small blocks).
BOBBY:	Which ones?
TEACHER:	How about these nice brown ones (picks up two small blocks and pretends to put them on her feet).
BOBBY:	Do you like them?
TEACHER:	No, they're too tight.
BOBBY:	Here, why don't you try these on? (Hands the teacher two more blocks).

The teacher might then offer to become a salesperson and help Bobby try to sell his shoes to other children.

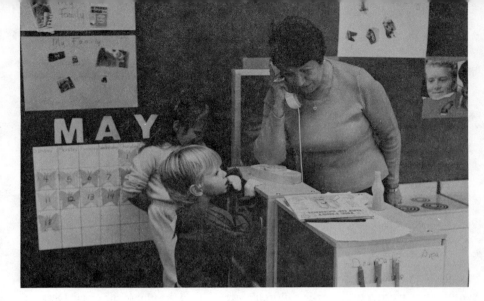

In play tutoring, adults often adopt a make-believe role and model sociodramatic play behaviors. This form of tutoring is known as "inside intervention."

children are better prepared to engage in sociodramatic play. Inside and outside intervention can then be used to extend these skills and to help the children learn to work together to create their own roles and to plan their own story lines.

Advantages and Disadvantages. Play tutoring has two major advantages over less structured forms of adult involvement. First, because the adult initiates the play, play tutoring is better suited for use with children who do not yet engage in sociodramatic play. Such children often do not have sufficient play skills to benefit from adult parallel playing or co-playing. Second, it is the only form of adult participation in play that involves tutorial interactions between adult and child. These tutorial interactions have been found to result in rich adult-child conversations (Sylva et al., 1980) and appear to be responsible for many of the cognitive gains brought about by play training (Smith & Syddall, 1978; Smith, Dalgleish, & Herzmark, 1981). Perhaps the reason that instruction is such an important component of play tutoring is that it provides an opportunity for children to learn how to learn from adults. Tizard (1977) explains:

> ...the human cultural heritage can, after all, only be transmitted to the child by adults—that is by adults talking to the child, explaining things to him, demonstrating how to do things, and by their own activities serving as a model for him to learn from. (p. 206)

Play tutoring is an enjoyable way for children to become accustomed to the teaching process.

The degree of adult structure and control that is inherent in play tutoring is its main disadvantage. Internal control and intrinsic motivation are two qualities that define play (Garvey, 1977). Whenever an adult takes control of a play episode, there is always the danger that the activity will cease to be play for the children involved.

For this reason, it is recommended that adults phase out play tutoring as soon as the children begin to exhibit the desired play behaviors. This can be done by either switching to the nondirective role of co-player or by withdrawing completely from the play situation. This stepping back returns control of the play to the children and helps promote independence and self-confidence (Kleiber & Barnett, 1980). In addition, there is some evidence that phasing out enhances the effect of play tutoring on children's subsequent free play (Gershowitz, cited in Singer, 1977).

Spokesman for Reality

The fourth type of adult involvement, being a spokesman for reality, occurs when play is used as a medium for academic instruction. The adult remains outside the play and encourages children to make connections between their play and the real world. This type of involvement is similar to outside intervention in that the adult does not take a role in the children's play. However, instead of encouraging make-believe, the adult's questions and suggestions are aimed at suspending make-believe and interjecting reality into the play episode. This form of involvement is particularly effective with older children.

The following example illustrates how an adult (A) intervened as a spokesman for reality in two children's play with blocks and cars:

A:	What's that then, umm, Peter? (playing with cars and model village)
PETER:	A gate.
A:	That's a gate? Don't you think you ought to open it before you crash into it, mm? I mean you have to open a gate before you go through with a car don't you?
PETER:	Mm.
A:	Else you'll damage the car.
AMANDA:	Else it will be broke down.
A:	It would be broke down.
AMANDA:	An' the policeman'll crash.
A:	What would the policeman do?
AMANDA:	Mend it.
A:	He'd mend it, would he? I don't think a policeman would mend the car. He'd take it to somebody that would mend it.
AMANDA:	The shop.

(WOOD ET AL., 1980, pp. 143–144)

In this particular example, the adult attempted to get the children to think about the real-life consequences of the actions in their play.

Wood and his associates (1980) found that this type of intervention was used relatively often by teachers but had mixed results. Sometimes, as in the above example, the children's play was not seriously disturbed by the adult's reality-oriented comments and questions. The children would give thoughtful answers to the questions and continue with their play. On other occasions, the adult's intervention would seriously disrupt the make-believe play frame, causing the children to stop playing. The example cited earlier in this chapter in which a teacher aide disrupted a girl's pretend play with seashells by trying to get her to discuss the shells' physical characteristics illustrates the potential negative effects of being a spokesman for reality.

Wood also discovered that being a spokesman for reality often had a restrictive effect on adult-child conversations. The adults tended to ask many closed questions and questions to which they already knew the answers, causing children to give brief one- or two-word responses. In the following example, an adult (A) was co-playing with two children (C and C1) who were pretending to bake a cake:

A: Did you put the cherry on the top of my cake?
C1:   No. I thought, I'm going to make you a sandwich. I'm going to make you...
C: (breaks in) Cream in it this time.
A: Oh, how delicious, I...
C: I'll make me one of with cream; 'cos I've I've sold out of jam.
A: You've sold out of jam, have you? So you're having to use cream instead, are you?
C: Yes.
A: Oh, I see.
C: Like ice-cream, ice-cream.
A: Oh, how lovely...
C: I'm rolling it, making you a nice cake.
C1:   I maked a bigger cake than you.

(WOOD ET AL., 1980, p. 149)

Later, the adult saw an opportunity to teach the children about fractions and switched to the spokesman-for-reality role:

A: Look, can I cut it in half? That's a half, isn't it, I've cut there.
C: Yes.
A: And then I cut it in half again. How many pieces have I cut now?
C: Two
A: No. How many pieces have I got altogether? Now I've cut that one piece in half?
C1:   Ha ha! Look!
C: One, two, three.
A: Three, right. Shall I cut this piece in half as well?
C: Yes.
A: Now how many have I got?
C: Four

(WOOD ET AL., 1980, p. 150)

Note how the children's comments shrank from phrases and sentences to one-word utterances when the adult switched roles. This is not an isolated instance. Wood found the children's conversations were consistently richer when adults were co-playing or play tutoring than when they were acting as spokesmen for reality.

Because of its potentially disruptive effects on children's make-believe play and their conversations, the spokesman for reality role should be used sparingly and its duration kept as brief as possible, particularly at the preschool level. It is also recommended that this type of intervention be used only with children who are experienced at make-believe play. When used cautiously with skilled players, this type of adult involvement in play can be an enjoyable way to improve children's thinking skills and to teach them new concepts. For this reason, the spokesman for reality role is an ideal way for elementary school teachers to infuse academic content into classroom play, thereby justifying play's existence in the school curriculum. Manning and Sharp (1977) have implemented a program to train British teachers to integrate play and learning activities. Their book *Structuring Play in the Early Years at School* gives numerous examples of how, when accompanied by play tutoring and spokesman for reality intervention, play can be used to help kindergarten and primary-grade children learn science, mathematics, and social studies concepts.

WHEN TO INTERVENE

Timing is an important element in successful adult involvement in play. While properly timed intervention can extend and enrich children's play, intervening at the wrong moment can disrupt play or stop it completely.

When to intervene depends both on the type of adult involvement being contemplated and on the nature of the children's play. As mentioned, the adult should carefully observe the activity to determine the latter.

Parallel playing lends itself best to functional (sensorimotor) play and constructive play. It can be used at almost any time. The lack of adult-child interaction in parallel playing makes it unlikely that the adult will disturb children's play.

Co-playing can be used any time children invite an adult to join in their play. Because the children initiate the adult involvement and remain in control of the play episode, there is little chance of disrupting the activity unless the adult remains in the play for too long. A good rule for co-playing is to participate as long as both you and the children are enjoying it (Sutton-Smith & Sutton-Smith, 1974).

Timing is more critical in the case of play tutoring because of the increased amount of adult control. There are three instances when play tutoring is appropriate:

1. When children do not engage in make-believe play on their own.
2. When children have difficulty playing with other children.
3. When children engage in make-believe play, but the play becomes repetitious or appears ready to break down.

In these instances, play tutoring can be used to get make-believe play started or to keep it going.

Being a spokesman for reality is the type of adult involvement most likely to disrupt make-believe play. It should be used only when children are securely involved in their pretend roles and when an opportunity exists for significant learning. Caution and restraint should be exercised.

There are, of course, times when adult intervention is not advisable. The Sutton-Smiths have some good recommendations to parents about when not to join in children's play:

> ...there are times *not to play* with your children—not ever *if* you feel you are intruding (and you may be), or if you feel it is a duty (for their "own good"), or if you are too grumpy, preoccupied, or just plain exhausted to enjoy the fun you are supposed to be having together.
>
> (SUTTON-SMITH & SUTTON-SMITH, 1974, p. 232)

These recommendations also hold for teachers with one exception. It is a teacher's duty to help children engage in high-quality play so that it has a maximum impact on their learning and development. So teachers should participate in children's play even though they feel a duty to do so. However, teachers must trust their judgment and not intervene if they feel they are intruding or if they are too tired or preoccupied to intervene effectively.

ROLES OF THE ADULT

Parents obviously are in quite a different position than are teachers in relation to children's playing. They see their children in many more situations and have many more opportunities to observe their play behavior and to become involved if it seems appropriate. Unlike teachers, parents see children before bedtime, while taking a bath, riding to the grocery store, and going shopping at the mall. At these times, children are often alone or with siblings or friends of different ages. This is quite different from the usual classroom, day care center, or playground situations where teachers see children at play.

Parents have a deep personal relationship with their own children which is quite different from the relationships that teachers develop with children. In addition, while teachers' responsibilities are geared toward educational goals, parents are usually oriented more toward leisure pursuits by the family. One consequence of this basic difference is that parental instruction, when it does occur, is much less formal than teacher instruction. Using play to promote children's well-being or development therefore has quite a different tone and meaning when it involves parent and child as opposed to teacher and child. Teachers' play involvement is more limited and specific in that it is primarily tied to classroom routines and curricular goals.

The significance of the special opportunities that parents have for positively influencing the development of play in their children will be discussed in Chapter 3. The role of the parent versus that of the teacher will also be addressed in Chapter 4, which deals with play and personality formation, and in Chapter 5, which concerns play and social development.

SUMMARY

We have described how adult involvement in play benefits the level of children's play, adult-child rapport, and children's social and intellectual development. In order for adult participation in play to be effective, parents and teachers must first provide an environment that is conducive to high-quality play. It is also important that adults carefully observe the ongoing play before intervening. Only through this observation can parents and teachers know when to intervene and which type of intervention is best. Sutton-Smith (Toy Manufacturers of America, 1982) has suggested a good sequence for adult participation in play:

1. Observe carefully to determine children's play interests and skills.
2. Join in and play with the children.
3. Back away and observe again.

Notice the heavy emphasis on observation. The cycle also includes the phase-out procedure mentioned earlier in connection with play tutoring.

Given the potential benefits of adult involvement in play, it is disturbing to find that recent observations in American and British preschools revealed that the level of teacher participation in play was low (Singer, 1977; Sylva et al., 1980; Tizard, Philps, & Plewis, 1976; Wood et al., 1980). These studies found that teachers spent only between 2 and 6 percent of their time involved in children's play.

Several reasons may account for this lack of teacher-child play. Time is almost certainly a factor. Many teachers are so encumbered with administrative duties that they end up spending the entire free-play period checking worksheets, preparing for the next activity, or handling discipline problems (Sylva, et al., 1980). Other teachers do not believe that play is important or still hold on to the old psychoanalytic belief that adult involvement in play is always harmful. Finally, some teachers are simply embarrassed about playing with children, particularly when other adults are present.

Less is known about the amount of parental involvement in play. The little evidence that exists suggests that there may be social class differences in parents' attitudes about play and in the extent to which they participate in play. Johnson (1984) found that college-educated parents had more positive beliefs about the value of play than less educated parents, and Dunn and Wooding (1977) discovered that middle-class parents joined in their children's play more than low-SES parents.

There appears to be a pressing need to educate parents and teachers about the importance of adult involvement in play and how to do it effectively. Several programs have been created recently to accomplish these goals. Strom (1981) has developed a procedure that uses play themes and related props to help parents become more skilled at playing with their children. Parents are provided with toys (such as miniature dinosaurs) and two-dimensional figures with a play theme written on the front (*e.g.,* "Teach the dinosaur how to cook so that he won't be hungry" and "The dinosaur wants to go to school, but it is not allowed"). Strom found that these props and suggested themes made it easier for many parents to engage in make-believe play with their children. Manning and Sharp (1977) have implemented a program to assist teachers in integrating play with academic instruction. Finally, Singer and Singer (1977) have developed a series of exercises aimed at developing parents' and teachers' sense of playfulness to make them less self-conscious and embarrassed about playing with children. These programs appear promising, but research is needed to evaluate their effectiveness. Such programs may lead eventually to increased adult involvement in play both in the home and at school, with many beneficial effects on children's development.

REFERENCES

Bruner, J. (1980. *Under five in Britain.* Ypsilanti, MI: High/Scope Press.

Christie, J.F. (1983). The effects of play tutoring on young children's cognitive performance. *Journal of Educational Research, 76,* 326–330.

Christie, J.F., & Johnsen, E.P. (1983). The role of play in social-intellectual development. *Review of Educational Research, 53,* 93–115.

Collier, R.G. (1985, March). *Preschool teachers and children's play.* Paper presented at the Annual Meeting of the Association for the Anthropological Study of Play, Washington, DC.

Dunn, J., & Wooding, C. (1977). Play in the home and its implications for learning. In B. Tizard & D. Harvey (Eds.), *Biology of Play* (pp. 45–58). London: Heinemann.

Feitelson, D., & Ross, G.S. (1973). The neglected factor: play. *Human Development, 16,* 202–223.

Garvey, C. (1977). *Play.* Cambridge, MA: Harvard University Press.

Griffing, P. (1983). Encouraging dramatic play in early childhood. *Young Children, 38,*(4), 13–22.

Isaacs, S. (1930). *Intellectual growth in young children.* London: Routledge & Kegan Paul.

Johnson, J.E. (1984, March). *Attitudes toward play and beliefs about development.* Paper presented at the meeting of the Association for the Anthropological Study of Play, Clemson, SC.

Kleiber, D.A., & Barnett, L.A. Leisure in childhood. *Young Children, 35*(5), 47–53.

Manning, K., & Sharp, A. (1977). *Structuring play in the early years at school.* London: Ward Lock Educational.

Rubin, K.H., Fein, G.G., & Vandenberg, B. (1983). Play. In P.H. Mussen (Ed.), *Handbook of child psychology: Vol. 4. Socialization, personality and social development* (4th ed., pp. 693–774). New York: Wiley.

Rubin, K., Maioni, T., & Hornung, M. (1976). Free play behaviors in middle- and lower-class pre-schoolers: Parten and Piaget revisited. *Child Development, 47,* 414–419.

Saltz, E., & Johnson, J. (1974). Training for thematic-fantasy play in culturally disadvantaged children: Preliminary results. *Journal of Educational Psychology, 66,* 623–630.

Segal, M., & Adcock, D. (1981). *Just pretending: Ways to help children grow through imaginative play.* Englewood Cliffs, NJ: Prentice-Hall.

Singer, D.G., & Singer, J.L. (1977). *Partners in play: A step-by-step guide to imaginative play in children.* New York: Harper & Row.

Singer, J.L. (1977). Imagination and make-believe play in early childhood: Some educational implications. *Journal of Mental Imagery, 1,* 127–144.

Smilansky, S. (1968). *The effects of sociodramatic play on disadvantaged preschool children.* New York: Wiley.

Smith, P.K., Dalgleish, M., & Herzmark, G. (1981). A comparison of the effects of fantasy play tutoring and skills tutoring in nursery classes. *International Journal of Behavioral Development, 4,* 421–441.

Smith, P.K., & Dodsworth, C. (1978). Social class differences in the fantasy play of preschool children. *The Journal of Genetic Psychology, 133,* 183–190.

Smith, P.K., & Syddall, S. (1978). Play and non-play tutoring in preschool children: Is it play or tutoring which matters? *British Journal of Educational Psychology, 48,* 315–325.

Strom, R.D. (1981). Learning to play with preschoolers. In R. Strom (Ed.), *Growing through play: Readings for parents & teachers* (pp. 115–130). Monterey, CA: Brooks/Cole.

Sutton-Smith, B., & Sutton-Smith, S. (1974). *How to play with your children (and when not to).* New York: Hawthorn.

Sylva, K., Roy, C., & Painter, M. (1980). *Childwatching at playgroup & nursery school.* Ypsilanti, MI: High/Scope Press.

Tizard, B. (1977). Play: The child's way of learning? In B. Tizard & D. Harvey (Eds.), *Biology of play* (pp. 199–208). London: Heinemann.

Tizard, B., Philps, J., & Plewis, I. (1976). Play in preschool centres—I. Play measures and their relation to age, sex, and I.Q. *Journal of Child Psychology and Psychiatry, 17,* 251–264.

Toy Manufacturers of America. (1982). *Parents are the first playmates.* New York: Author.

Wood, D., McMahon, L., & Cranstoun, Y. (1980). *Working with under fives.* Ypsilanti, MI: High/Scope Press.

Woodard, C. (1984). Guidelines for facilitating sociodramatic play. *Childhood Education, 60,* 172–177.

CHAPTER

3

Development of Play

In Chapter 1 we discussed definitions of play and examined different classical and modern theories about the role of play in development. Up to now we have dealt with play and development from the vantage point of the question "What good is play for the child's development?" As we have seen, there are many different ways to begin to answer this basic question. This chapter is devoted to another major aspect of research—the development of play as a phenomenon of behavior and growth in its own right. Obviously this is an important topic from a practical point of view.

We will first trace the development of play behaviors from infancy through the preschool years within four domains: (a) play with people, (b) play with objects, (c) play with symbols, and (d) motor play. We will deal with the differences in play development between normal and atypical children. Finally, we will suggest some adult interventions for enhancing children's play.

DEVELOPMENTAL CONSIDERATIONS

There are many ways to characterize the nature of play. Agreement can be found in the literature that both emotional and learning factors are involved and that different kinds of play can be categorized or defined in structural terms. For example, there are the games of children and the motor routines of infants. For purposes of this chapter we will divide play into four types: motor play, social play, object play, and play involving symbols. Although these classifications are artificial, they allow us to present a systematic approach. Some studies summarized under one section could have been included in one of the other sections.

Development implies time. How do play structures or processes change over time? And what does change mean? First, change can be over small time spans within a single event—*e.g.*, children first exhibit parallel or side-by-side play as a prelude to socially interactive play, or explore single objects before combining or transforming objects. Tempo, intensity, and style of play also can change within a small time frame, as can response variability. Second, change can mean shifts over much longer periods of time. Here the issue of age-related developmental stages of play enters into the picture. Both types of "change" are discussed in the following sections. It is important to keep in mind the particular meaning of the term when working and playing with children.

DEVELOPMENT OF SOCIAL PLAY

By kindergarten age, children normally possess an array of social play skills. They are expected to be able to engage in complex social exchanges during play. Children must learn to assert their wills to achieve personal goals using behaviors that are acceptable within the peer group.

French ethologist Hubert Montagner (1984) learned from his extensive observations of young children that socially competent youngsters appropriately combine five types of actions: (1) actions to produce attachment or pacify—behaviors that fall into this category include offering toys, caressing another child, and moving or vocalizing in a nonthreatening way; (2) actions that generate fear, flight, or tears—examples are frowning, loud vocalization, showing clenched teeth, and raising an arm; (3) aggressive actions—examples are grabbing objects, shaking another child, and hitting or kicking; (4) gestures of fear and retreat—for instance, a child might widen the eyes, blink, run away, or cry; and (5) actions that produce isolation—such behaviors include thumb-sucking, lying down, tugging at the hair, or standing or sitting apart from other children. These behavioral and social actions and interactions are expressions of the child's cognitive abilities and problem-solving skills. Children who are simply dominant and aggressive are not the most socially adept. In fact, such children tend to become unpopular. The best-liked children, the ones who become social leaders, use affection and power to persuade other children. To what extent are these competencies acquired as a result of social play? How do such social and play skills form? What does the research literature indicate?

Social play development from infancy through the preschool years has not been examined in a single long-range comprehensive study. Rather, we must rely upon cross-sectional and short-term studies covering narrow age ranges.

In general, researchers agree that as a child grows older there is an increase in interactive play. Interactive play skills develop along with a number of social skills within the changing social situations of the growing infant, toddler, and preschooler. For example, as the child's social play becomes more complex, specific social behaviors become more pronounced, such as being able to take turns or initiate, maintain, or end social interactions. Use of language in socially appropriate ways also becomes more elaborate.

Two different research traditions on the social aspects of play have developed. One

Play tends to become more social with age. Solitary play, however, remains a common activity among preschool- and kindergarten-age children.

PRACTICAL APPROACHES TO PROMOTING SOCIAL COMPETENCE IN CHILDREN

Sally's parents are concerned about her. She is almost five years old and wants to play with other children in the neighborhood. However, when Sally goes next door to play on the gym set or in the sandbox, other children ignore her. She wants to play with other children but doesn't seem to know how. Her parents want to help her play and get along better with other children. How can we help?

Teachers and parents can provide ample opportunities for play as well as specific learning activities and coaching to encourage children to make better use of play time. There are a number of techniques possible based on different views of the relationship between social skill development and the development of social play.

From the point of view that play fosters the development of social skills, it follows that through opportunities, encouragement, and support for play, the child will become more skillful in social situations. Adult-guided play and adult co-playing with the young child and infant are important for play development, as are making playthings and peer play partners available in structured situations. Smilansky (1968) refers to two types of identification, general and specific, which are important for play development. Children in their home environment need to form positive attachment with parents or other adults to establish basic trust. Beyond this, however, young children also need to be shown specifically how to play and be encouraged to play with parents in the home. Social skills emerge through playing in social situations.

On the other hand, it is possible that there are social skill prerequisites to being a good play partner. Teachers and parents may have to model and encourage divergent thinking and various social and language skills to improve the child's play skills and foster acceptance by other children. A certain amount of learning and development may be needed to engage successfully in different types of play. For example, children could examines how social play fosters specific social skills; the other focuses on the extent to which social play depends upon and reflects these skills (Strayer, Mosher, & Russell, 1981). Although it may seem that this distinction is merely academic, in fact, the two offer rather different approaches for fostering play and development. "Practical Approaches to Promoting Social Competence in Children" illustrates these approaches.

The social world of the infant is very important for the development of play. Through interacting with caregivers the child acquires several abilities needed in early games and pretend activities. Ross, Goldman, and Hay (1979) conducted a program to identify the characteristics and purposes behind the social play of infants and their caregivers. These researchers point out that because any interaction between the young child and another person can include mutual involvement, alternation of turns, and repetition, those interactions that highlight the difference between literal and nonliteral events are especially important. Often simple

be taught to perform communication or perspective-taking tasks outside of play to help them in subsequent situations. Exercises in inferring what the other person sees on the other side of a two-faced card, for example, could be helpful. Learning outside of play through reading, listening to records, watching television, and other shared activities can help make the child more playful with others in play situations. Parents can help by pointing out good social behaviors in others as well as by rewarding the child for good social behaviors such as greeting others, sharing, and "using your words" instead of physical aggression in social conflicts.

Nonetheless, neither of the above two approaches in extreme form is acceptable. Undoubtedly the relationship between social skills and play is complex and reciprocal. Positive play experience promotes the acquisition and use of social skills; possessing these skills makes the child more likely to achieve satisfying and enjoyable play experiences. What is critical from a practical point of view is to recognize when a negative cycle exists and to attempt to change it for the better as soon as possible, using any number of possible techniques. Since children are different from one another both developmentally and individually, it is obvious that the same technique will not be effective for all children. Perhaps Sally needs to be taught how to listen to and observe what others are playing and then be coached to enter ongoing play gracefully and not disruptively, by assuming an appropriate role for herself in relation to what others are doing. For example, instead of asking "Can I play?" perhaps Sally will learn that it is more effective to assume a complementary part in a pretend episode, such as acting the part of another pupil or the principal in a situation in which others are teachers and students. Perhaps puppet play depicting these strategies would help Sally learn. On the other hand, maybe Sally will learn best from storybooks or discussion with her parents or from some kind of reward system aimed at shaping her overt behaviors through reinforcement and praise.

repetition such as rolling a ball back and forth signals nonliterality or pretense; that is, what is taking place is separate from the usual things that come up in everyday life. After all, why roll a ball back and forth?

Our typical indications that social interaction is to be taken playfully, not literally include gleeful vocalization and other exhibitions of pleasant feelings or levity. Positive affect often is caused by doing something unexpected, in an exaggerated manner, or not otherwise according to the usual routines. For example, instead of holding on to an object, we drop it; instead of approaching the oncoming person, we run away; instead of opening our mouth to receive food, we close it tight. Pretense in each instance is defined by the social context.

Singer (1973) emphasized the importance of games such as "This Little Piggy Went to Market" and peek-a-boo for the baby to get the feel of the special world of make-believe. Such encounters promote not only pretend play skills, but social skills and social play skills as well. The three are interrelated. Learning to communicate the play intent or the make-believe attitude through play signals is an important accomplishment and is a forerunner to later play development.

Social features of play during infancy involve an interaction with an accommodating play partner. This is usually a parent or an older sibling, a relative, or an unrelated older child or adult. The infant and this other person become engaged with each other, attending to and responding to the other. From this mutual engagement comes alternating turns—waiting for the partner to perform an act before reciprocating. Communicational signals such as standing up, shaking a toy, or waving arms often show that one is waiting for a turn. Usually the infant plays with others who are aware of the child's limitations and abilities and who help assure that the play flows smoothly. Repetition extends the sequence of interaction and maintains mutual engagement and attention. These playful early interactions provide the foundation for social development in general and social play development in particular. The purpose behind these early games, routines, or exchanges is simply to be involved in a social interaction with another person.

The one-year-old child usually plays with toys or other objects used as playthings. The baby does this either while alone in the vicinity of others, or while mutually engaged with others (Hay, 1980). During the latter period of infancy and the early toddler stage, there is increased refinement of the social skill used in infant social games or routines.

Researchers have concluded that play with objects is a major factor in the development of social play during this period (Mueller & Lucas, 1975). Toys serve as "social butter," facilitating interactions particularly between peers who, unlike adults, are unable or unwilling to make special accommodations or concessions to keep play going. Toys often serve as entry mechanisms as two toddlers go from parallel to interactive play. Toys mediate social interaction.

Another view is that social interaction increases in its sophistication as a result of accumulating social experiences and that toy use with others is but a by-product of this. Recent studies of social play during the second year of life suggest that children progress to more advanced forms of social play through both toy use with peers and interaction with peers (Jacobson, 1981).

During the preschool years we witness continued increases in interactive play skills as children mature and gain experiences in a variety of social situations. Although there has been general agreement on this point since Parten's (1932) classic observational studies showing a progression from solitary (2 to 2½ years) to parallel (2½ to 3½ years) to associative (3½ to 4½ years) to cooperative (4½ years) play, recent studies have questioned the developmental status of solitary and parallel play and have shed some doubts on the validity of Parten's stages, asking whether it is even helpful to picture changes in play in such broad terms, and recommending a finer analysis of play changes in specific social situations.

Smith (1978) in a longitudinal study of social play during the preschool years found that while many children followed the trend suggested by Parten, others did not. Older children alternated between solitary and interactive play as they outgrew a tendency to engage in simple side-by-side or parallel play. In fact, with development comes an increasing capacity to use parallel play strategically to initiate or terminate play with particular play partners (Bakeman & Brownlee, 1979). Other researchers have reported that perhaps parallel and not solitary play is the least mature social form of play (Moore, Evertson, & Brophy, 1974; Rubin, Maioni, & Hornung, 1976; Rubin, 1982).

A valuable system for observing and coding the social play of toddlers and pre-school children has been developed by Carollee Howes (1980). Every fifteen seconds (with five seconds in between for coding) the teacher or researcher checks one of five categories each representing a social play level.

Level 1 is Parallel Play
Two children pursue similar activities but do not engage in eye contact or social behavior. This is essentially Parten's classic definition of parallel play. The children play beside, but not with, each other. For example two children might fingerpaint side by side, absorbed in their own activity.

Level 2 is Parallel Play with Mutual Regard
The children pursue the same or similar activity as in Level I but they make eye contact and are aware of each other. For example, the two children who are fingerpainting look at each other or one vocalizes and the other looks up.

Level 3 is Simple Social Play
While engaging in the same or similar activity each child directs a social bid to the other. Social bids include smiling, vocalizing, touching, offering an object, receiving an object, comforting a child in distress, helping with a task, taking a toy, or agreeing. For example, as two children are painting, one child vocalizes and the other offers the first a paintbrush. Or two children are playing with blocks. One child takes a block and is screamed at by the other child.

Level 4 is Complementary and Reciprocal Play with Mutual Awareness
Two children engage in complementary and reciprocal activities and show mutual regard or awareness. Complementary and reciprocal activities are ones in which each child's action reverses the other's, demonstrating awareness of the role of the other. Examples include rolling a ball back and forth; chasing the other and then

being chased; going down a slide and watching the other go up the steps of the slide, then going up the steps as the other goes down; one child's offering a toy, the other's receiving it and then offering it back; and engaging in mutually agreed

TABLE 3-1

Categories of Social Play

Parten (1932)	*Erikson (1950)*	*Seagoe (1970)*	*Iwanaga (1973)*	*Howes (1980)*
Developmental stage	**Categories refer to broad stages of development**	**Play report based on structured interviews with child**	**Categories pertain to how an individual child structures the play situation in regard to other children**	**Categories show increases in the complexity of interaction within dyads**
Solitary play—plays alone and independently; different activity; no reference to others	*Autocosmic*—world of self; explores own body and body of mother; repetition of activity	*Informal-individual*—self-directed; not imitative of adults; not formally patterned	*Independent*—no involvement of peers in play	*Parallel*—engaged in similar activities but not paying any attention to one another
Parallel play—plays independently but near or among others; similar toys or activities; beside but not with	*Microcosmic*—world of small, manageable toys and objects; solitary play; pleasure derived from mastery of toys	*Adult-oriented*—adult-directed; formally patterned; not imitative of adult life	*Parallel play*—with peers; undifferentiated roles; roles enacted independently; close physical proximity; awareness of activity of others	*Mutual regard*—similar activities plus eye contact and awareness of each other; no verbalization or other social bids
Associative play—plays with others; conversation is about common activity, but does not subordinate own interests to group	*Macrocosmic*—world shared with others	*Informal-social*—self-directed; imitative of adult life; not formally patterned	*Complementary*—differentiated roles, enacted independently; some cooperation but each child engages in a different activity; little adjustment to others' behavior	*Simple social*—similar activities along with social bids such as talking, smiling, offering toys
Cooperative play—activity is organized; differentiation of roles; complementing actions		*Individual-competitive*—formally patterned; directed toward individual victory	*Integrative*—roles enacted interactively; intense awareness of others; adjustment of behavior to shifts in others' complementary roles	*Complementary*—collaborating in the same activity with mutual awareness but no social bids
		Cooperative-competitive—formally patterned toward team victory		*Complementary reciprocal*—collaborating in the same activity with social bids

SOURCE: Based on Frost and Klein (1979)

Development of Play

upon fantasy play—one child pushes a truck from the block structure to the shelves where the second child loads the truck with blocks.

Level 5 is Complementary and Reciprocal Social Play
Two children engage in complementary and reciprocal activity (as in Level 4), and each child directs a social bid to the other (as in Level 3). For example, two children are at the easel board painting a picture together. One child says, "Use this color for the water," and the other child takes the brush and says, "OK."

Howes' system analyzes social play, particularly parallel play, in a more fine-grained manner than Parten's original formulation of parallel play. Table 3–1 presents categories of social play developed by various authors, including Howes.

DEVELOPMENT OF OBJECT PLAY

The typical kindergarten child shows a great deal of versatility in using objects during play. The normal child is able to use tools, participate in supervised cooking activities, and create elaborate constructions from blocks and other materials. The child can finish rather complicated puzzles and displays considerable problem-solving strategies using objects in play. Furthermore, these skills are frequently exhibited in social settings requiring additional capabilities. Such behavior reflects and requires considerable development—cognitive, social, affective, physical, and linguistic. How does the kindergarten child obtain this level of proficiency in using objects?

As we saw in Chapter 1, the arousal modulation theory of play focuses upon motivating factors inherent in the external world which prompt the child to play. This theory is particularly useful for understanding play with objects in a particular situation at a given time. Stimulus properties such as novelty, complexity, and manipulability motivate the child to interact with objects. This interaction can take several forms. For example, Hutt (1976), based on Berlyne's work on arousal and motivation, distinguishes between exploring and playing with objects.

Exploration occurs when the child seemingly asks the question "What does this object do?"; play happens when the child seemingly asks the question "What can I do with this object?" In either case, there is intrinsic motivation to learn about objects and what can be done to or with them. Important behavioral changes occur in how objects are used in exploration and in play during the first six years of life.

How many objects are played with at one time and how they are played with are two dimensions of object play that have been investigated developmentally. Quality of play has been judged according to how discriminant, sequenced, and appropriate the activity is. Object play has been studied in children before and after the emergence and consolidation of children's symbolic capacities, thus making it important to distinguish between presymbolic object play and symbolic object play.

During the first months of life there are great changes in how babies play with objects. The newborn is equipped with reflexes and sensory capacities but does not know how to play with objects. Play actions develop as a result of experience. Widespread agreement exists that object play during the first year progresses from repetitious and undifferentiated activity to more organized and sequenced action patterns. Piaget (1962) traced the development of presymbolic or mastery or exercise

FIGURES 3–1: QUALITY OF TOY PLAY

From 9 to 24 Months

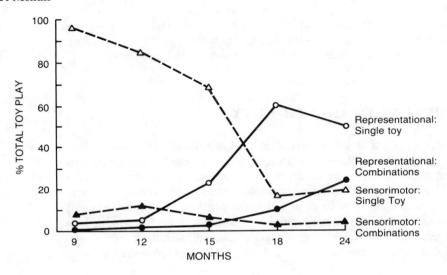

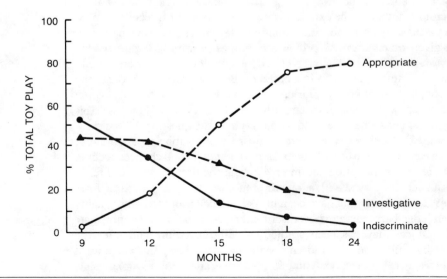

SOURCE: From Rosenblatt (1977)

play while advancing his theories about cognitive development during the sensorimotor period. For Piaget, objects direct the infant's actions at first and then come under the control of the infant—providing the child with an opportunity to employ action schemes. Infants repeat actions on objects and generalize these actions to other objects. Piaget uses the concept of reproductive and generalizing assimilation to describe this behavior. While not goal-directed, these early behaviors are pleasurable, and they define the essence of play for Piaget. During the second year, the child is able to construct new schemes from combinations of past experiences. Ritualization and conventional use of objects increase in frequency.

Rosenblatt (1977) has described major shifts in how infants use objects between their first and second years. Using single objects decreases in frequency. Whereas the child less than one year old typically uses only one toy at a time in an unpredictable manner, the child over one year of age is much more likely to use many objects in play. In addition, the toddler uses toys in a much more predictable way. That is, the toddler uses toys in appropriate or stereotypic ways, paying greater attention to physical characteristics of playthings and showing he knows how different objects are used in daily life.

Several researchers have investigated the developmental transition of object play into symbolic play or presymbolic to symbolic action schemes. For example, Fenson, Kagan, Kearsley, and Zelazo (1976) compared the object play of 9½-, 13½-, and 18½-month-old children. Motor schemes such as mouthing and banging objects predominated in the youngest infants. By 13½ months, infants used objects functionally, grouping or sorting similar objects and making simple pretenses that were self-directed. Like Piaget, these researchers concluded that object play in infancy becomes decentered and more integrated. They also found an increase in combinational play and change from functional or motor use of objects to conventional applications.

During the preschool years, object play progresses from the simple to the complex as children gain increasing ability to order objects and actions in time and space. Smilansky (1968), influenced by Piaget (1962), has defined two types of play, functional and constructive. Together they are the dominant cognitive forms of play involving objects during the preschool years. Functional play refers to manipulative play, motor exercise with or without objects, or the use of objects in a stereotyped manner. This form of play decreases as children develop. Constructive play is organized goal-oriented play and increases in frequency as the child matures. By age four, constructive play becomes the most prevalent form of play, occupying more than 50 percent of free time in preschool settings (Rubin et al., 1983).

The typical preschool classroom or day care center is equipped with interest centers and other play areas designed to encourage more constructive and imaginative play by young children as they grow older. The simpler functional play is seen less and less. Preschoolers become increasingly capable of building complex structures and of producing recognizable products through drawing, painting, arranging designs, and making small constructions.

Toys and play equipment (discussed in Chapter 9) and, more recently, computer-related activities (discussed in Chapter 11) are used more and more in modern preschools and day care centers to challenge young children to interact creatively with the world of objects.

DEVELOPMENT OF SYMBOLIC PLAY

During the second year of life, along with the beginning of conventional uses of objects comes the emergence of representational abilities. There is a transition from the mastery play of the infant to the symbolic play of the preoperational child. The infant becomes able to evoke images or symbols derived from imitative activities. This enables the infant to engage in beginning pretense or make-believe play. This new ability is an outgrowth of the infant's use of objects and the adult and infant game routines previously discussed.

Piaget (1962) discusses the relationship between mastery play and symbolic play:

> In mastery play the schemas follow one another without any external aim. The objects to which they are applied are no longer a problem, but merely serve as an opportunity for activity. This activity is no longer an effort to learn, it is only a happy display of known actions. (p. 93) In pretense the child is using schemes which are familiar, and for the most part already ritualized games...but (1) instead of using them in the presence of objects to which they are usually applied, he assimilates to them new objectives unrelated to them from the point of view of effective adaptation; (2) these new objects, instead of resulting merely in an extension of the schema (as is the case in the generalization proper to intelligence), are used with no other purpose than that of allowing the subject to mime or evoke the schemas in question. It is the union of these two conditions—applications of schema to inadequate objects and evocation for pleasure—which in our opinion characterizes the beginning of pretense. (p. 97)

Piaget (1962) defined three kinds of symbolic play. The first type involves the application of one symbolic scheme to new objects. For example, a child says "cry, cry" to a doll and imitates the sound. What is imitated is taken from the child's own experience. This represents the emergence of symbolic play. The second type involves again only one symbolic scheme, but an object may be substituted for another or the child may act like another person or object. Imitated behaviors are borrowed from other models. For example, the child pretends to shave like daddy. The third kind of symbolic play involves planned combinations of symbolic schemes and a sequence or pattern of behavior. For example, a child takes a doll on a stroller ride saying, "You see this, you see that." According to Piaget's theory, during the preschool years there is a continuing trend toward more coherent and orderly symbolic play, often resulting in a replication of reality that is, most important, performed in a social context (termed "collective symbolism"). Piaget's general account has inspired many researchers who have sought to understand the development of pretend play during the early years. Dimensions or components of symbolic play studied include pretend actions and objects and role enactments and themes.

Pretend Actions

Researchers of infant and toddler play such as Fenson et al. (1976), Lowe (1975), Rosenblatt (1977), and more recently Watson and Jackowitz (1984) have traced the development of presymbolic action schemes. Sequences of actions in pretending are ✓ analyzed in terms of agent and object substitutions. Infants as young as 12 months have been observed engaging in the simplest type of pretend play involving self-as-agent.

Examples of the earliest forms of this behavior include pretending to be sleeping, drinking, eating, or talking on the phone. In pretending to sleep, for instance, the infant does not merely touch its head to a pillow. Instead, the behavior seems to replicate in gestures the fine details of such behaviors as they would occur in ordinary life. The behaviors are not related to real needs and are not characterized by confusion or overgeneralization. Instead, the behaviors are selective and represent-ative of customary practices but are independent of needs. During the second year of life the infant becomes increasingly able to pretend and uses a variety of substitute objects (such as a toy banana or a block for a telephone). These simple pretense activities, although unrelated to real needs or wishes, are all self-directed. Thus they do not represent genuine symbolic play according to Piaget (1962).

It is only after the child is capable of outer-directed symbolic activities, at around 18 months of age, that we see genuine symbolic play sequences unfold, according to Piaget's meaning of the term. Here the child can make a mother or a doll pretend to drink from a cup or talk on the phone. Transforming so-called recipient objects (telephone, banana, block) occurs developmentally before the ability to transform agents of pretending (self-as-agent, mother-as-agent, doll-as-agent). Within each type of transformation it is important to note the level of symbolic substitutions required to judge the relative difficulty of the pretend act (Watson & Jackowitz, 1984). Self-as-agent and a realistic or representational toy such as a prototypical toy phone as the recipient object are simplest in that no real transformation is needed.

The form and function of substitute objects as opposed to the real object are important to note to judge further the complexity of the pretend actions. For example, a toy banana has a shape similar to that of a toy phone suggesting its use as a substitute object for the phone. Substituting a toy car for a toy phone would clearly be a greater symbolic leap because of dissimilarity both in shape and intended function. A third dimension that determines the difficulty of the pretend act is the content of the objects and actions. Jackowitz and Watson (1980), suggest that real telephones may be "off limits" to children in some homes and hence pretend play with phones may be inhibited in the same children who may find pretending with cups and dolls relatively easy. Social conventions that promote sex-typing of toys may be viewed in this vein as limiting the play development of children as we will explain in Chapter 6.

Pretend action during the second year, then, ranges in degree of difficulty

Children's earliest symbolic transformations involve realistic toys that closely resemble their real-life counterparts. Later, they can use substitute objects that bear little or no resemblance to the objects they represent.

according to the type of object transformation, level of transformation, and content. Self-directed or self-as-agent behaviors are the first signs of symbolic play in infancy (pretending to eat, talk on a phone, put on a hat, drink from a cup). Outer-directed pretense occurs when other objects or persons are made the agent of the pretend actions performed on different recipient objects, for example, pretending that toy cows are eating straw. Within both agent and recipient object transformation, transforming things similar to or not conflicting with the thing (either in appearance or intended use) is an easier task for the child than transforming things dissimilar or conflicting with the real object. The nature or content of the pretend play is the third factor to consider to determine whether the child has had positive or negative experiences with the objects involved that would either facilitate or inhibit the pretend play actions.

Thus far we have kept to single pretend-play actions or simple combinations. The older infant or toddler becomes able to engage in more complicated and involved pretend-play sequences (Piaget's third type of symbolic play) in which actions are linked meaningfully while objects are used conventionally and consistently (Fenson et al., 1976).

During the second and third years of life, the child is able to perform two or more consecutive acts that reflect a similar theme or topic, such as pretending to serve tea to dolls or teddy bears seated around a table. A child may at first place each cup on a saucer, then put a spoon in a cup, then pour tea from the pot into the cup, and then place the cup in front of one of the dolls. The variety and diversity of such pretend-action sequences increase as the child leaves toddlerhood. Content of such play is always familiar and comfortable for the child, and the child usually does not interact with a playmate in any reciprocal sense. However, the play can and often does involve a teacher, parent, or other older person who is able and willing to adjust to the child's needs to support the make-believe experience, which, taken together as we have implied, can be viewed as a critical foundation rock for social competence, and indeed, for the child's later mental health.

Role Enactments

Until now we have been examining pretend action-object development and have seen that it becomes more elaborate and organized as the child matures. During the third year for most children, an important change occurs. The child engages in pretend activities while adopting the role of another person—a person with whom the child is intimately familiar. Typically it is the child's mother or another primary caregiving or significant person. Adopting the role of another, or role enactment, is different from the earlier pretend activities with objects in that now the child is able to infer and imagine the role identity behind the pretend actions. This new capacity lends greater coherence, enjoyment, and meaning to the pretend activities of the child. The adoption of the role dictates and controls the actions. Role enactment guides the pretend play. The pretending that results is more planned and persistent.

Role enactment or role play is significant because it indicates not only awareness of others but also the child's knowledge of role attributes, role relationships, and role-appropriate actions (Garvey, 1979). Role-enactment behaviors are influenced by cognitive development and by personality factors (see Chapter 4) as well as by the social situation—the other persons (children as well as adults) who form part of the play or the events surrounding the play. Garvey and Berndt (1977) distinguish four types of roles: (1) functional roles (pseudo-role enactment) are those organized by an object or activity (*e.g.*, pretending to cook dinner is triggered by the presence and use of a toy oven or mixing bowl); (2) relational roles are family roles that suggest real complements (such as mother-child, wife-husband); (3) character roles are either stereotypic (fireman, witch) or fictional (characters with proper names such as He-Man, Princess Leia, or the Big Bad Wolf); and (4) peripheral roles are discussed but not enacted (for instance, real or imaginary friends).

Role enactments typically suggest the theme of the play episode. The development of symbolic play during the preschool years moves away from an exclusive preoccupation with highly familiar themes, such as playing house or doctor, and toward a greater interest in play themes that are more out of the ordinary. Children become more interested in enacting roles of characters from fiction as opposed to familiar occupational roles. Potential themes for role enactments become more numerous as children begin to possess greater linguistic and cognitive abilities and social cognitive abilities and social skills, as well as greater knowledge about the world they live in—both the real world of everyday living and the events transmitted through media that children experience vicariously.

The end point of symbolic play development is seen in the older preschool child who is able to imagine with no objects at all, who is versatile in improvising with props and substitute objects of all types, and who can evoke imaginary situations through words. High levels of symbolic development are seen in the child's being able to take on a variety of diverse roles in collaboration with peers, engaging innovatively and with great enjoyment in sociodramatic and fantasy themes ranging from the most commonplace to the most extraordinary. Concentration, persistence, attention to detail, and seeing the play episode as a whole are other manifestations of symbolic development.

Children at this level will repeat play sequences or start them over again to make them follow a plan. Interest grows in directing and co-directing a play sequence while playing and co-playing the roles in front of real and imagined audiences.

Finally, concerns with reality and peer pressure reduce overt make-believe play as children move toward an interest in games with rules, sports, arts and crafts, and other activities appropriate for school-aged children. Piaget (1962) and Singer (1973), among others, speculate that overt make-believe play goes underground and becomes internalized at this stage of development. There is the speculation that a residual of the preschooler's earlier active fantasy social life persists in exerting a beneficial influence on the child's creativity, imagination, and divergent and operational thinking abilities, all developing in a way that we do not yet understand.

DEVELOPMENT OF MOTOR PLAY

Children by their seventh birthday possess considerable motor-play skill. They may be a far cry from Olympic champions who have reached a zenith in the development of gross- and fine-motor strength and coordination, but children have progressed a great deal since birth. They can ride bicycles, pull wagons, and construct snow forts. What are the motor-development milestones as children progress toward this level of maturity?

Newborns possess rudimentary grasping movements; they can blink and throw out their arms. There are also a number of motor reflexes possessed by the newborn, such as the Babinski or Moro or the automatic waling reflex. That reflex is evoked by supporting the baby in an upright position with the baby's bare feet on a flat surface and moving the infant forward, tilting the child slightly from side-to-side. Motor abilities of newborns form two general categories: first, the general ability to move body parts in an uncoordinated and random way (waving arms or turning the head); second, the automatic and involuntary swift and finely coordinated reflexes.

Healthy human babies progress to gain even better control over their bodies, enabling them to be upright, mobile, and able to explore their surroundings. Often, while there is considerable individual variation in the rate of development, the order of acquisition seems fairly constant.

From one to three months, infants become able to lift their chins and heads while lying on their stomachs. During four to six months infants gain control over their neck muscles and can pull themselves into a sitting position with head remaining erect. The body trunk obtains more muscle control, and at six to seven months infants can sit up for a minute or so.

In the second half of the first year, considerable motor development takes place. Many babies begin to stand holding onto supports such as chairs; they can roll and repeat actions. (As we discussed earlier, playful repetition is significant in many play theories.) Infants play by themselves with body parts and objects. From seven months on, infants begin to have some mobility. From a prone position they can wiggle forward. As babies approach their first birthday some can walk or stand alone, and easily pivot from side to side while sitting. After the first birthday most begin walking. At first they are shaky and fall frequently. They have to concentrate on what they are doing. Very soon, though, walking is a motor skill they can engage in without its being the focal point of their awareness. They can use this new skill as a means to other ends, such as reaching places and exploring objects. By two years, or toddlerhood, the child can run. The sequence of major motor milestones in becoming mobile from birth up to age two includes crawling, creeping or the bear walk, standing, walking, and running.

Progress in gross motor behavior involved in sitting and walking is accompanied by steady improvement in hand skills. To be able to grasp and manipulate objects requires considerable fine-motor or small-muscle strength and coordination. At birth there is virtually no small-muscle control. During the first month of life the limbs, including fingers, act in unison much like a fin. Even at one month infants cannot grasp objects in front of them. In the second month they might hold an object, but only briefly.

Babies begin to pick up objects at four through six months with great effort, often using two hands to trap an object. When they hold a small object it is often between fingers. By the seventh month objects are held between the thumb and several fingers; in the eighth month babies can transfer objects from hand to hand. Hand skills involving grasping and manipulation make play with objects possible and also help babies acquire informal, practical, or intuitive understandings of objects, actions, three-dimensional space, and cause-effect relations. From one to two years, then, infants can walk well and even run, and can turn a few pages of a large picture book.

During toddlerhood (two to three years), there is continual motor-play development. This is evinced both in gross-motor activity involving large objects and use of large muscles for mobility as well as in fine-motor activity involving hand muscles, hand-eye coordination, and the use of small objects. During this period the child walks easily, can run, needs no help in going up or down stairs, and can hold a cup in one hand and a cookie in the other. All of this motor progression depends on physical development, experience, and practice. Motor play occurs in play with objects, people, and symbols.

Preschoolers from three to four years of age demonstrate further developmental progression in motor/physical skills and motor play. They can walk and run easily, surely, and with good balance. They can tiptoe and stand on one foot. Tricycle riding and playing with other vehicles bring great pleasure. In climbing stairs, children at this age can put one foot on each step.

From four to five years old, children achieve further motor mastery, allowing for greater varieties of play. They can skip, climb, hop, and run. They enjoy chasing games and almost any kind of athletic activity, including rough-and-tumble play. Some children are able to ride a small bicycle equipped with supportive training wheels. Children can button clothing and put puzzles and simple constructions together.

From five to six years of age, further physical development makes possible new forms of motor play—jumping rope, doing acrobatics, and trapeze tricks. Because their fine-muscle development has advanced, children can cut, trace, draw, paste,

As children mature, their physical development makes possible new forms of motor play.

and string beads. Many children can use a knife although they cannot cut very well.

Motor play often occurs with the other forms of play. It overlaps with object play to a great extent. It is more distinct in play that involves only body parts—such as in

ROUGH-AND-TUMBLE PLAY: SOME ISSUES

Why do many teachers frown upon rough-and-tumble play and even forbid it? After all, many researchers who have studied the phenomenon suggest that this form of play is valuable in many ways. For one thing, physical contact is important to young children. They need a chance to exercise and release energy. Second, because rough-and-tumble play occurs with other children, it is a form of social communication. It has been noted that rough-and-tumble play is instrumental in children's learning to handle feelings. Children filter out negative from positive feelings and learn to control impulses so as to be able to participate appropriately within a group. Furthermore, pretense saturates the phenomenon. Rough-and-tumble play is play fighting, not real fighting. One special value of this form of play, then, may be that children so engaged, although perhaps especially tempted to cross over the threshold into real fighting, usually hold back because of peer pressure. Isn't this then good for children? And if so, why the objections?

First of all, criticisms of rough-and-tumble play often arise because of failure to adequately define the phenomenon. Many researchers have linked inappropriate acts of aggression with playful aggression to create composite categories which then invariably show that children who engage in rough-and-tumble play are also unpopular with their peers and seem to be deficient in social skills. However, when rough-and-tumble play is distinguished from real fighting or from physical exercise play in general, the behavior can be judged more positively. That is, when properly defined, rough-and-tumble play does not appear to lead to statistically significant negative behavior. Such play may even have running, hopping, and skipping. In this case a body part becomes an "object" of play. Rough-and-tumble play is motor play that overlaps with social play. In rough-and-tumble play, parts of the bodies of playmates and the actions of playmates become a focal "object" of play. Rough-and-tumble play as a special subcategory of motor play also overlaps with symbolic play or pretense. That is, rough-and-tumble play is play fighting, not actual fighting. In rough-and-tumble play, children engage in a form of make-believe in which the body parts and actions of themselves and others take on a symbolic significance which becomes the "object" of play. Criticisms of rough-and-tumble play are discussed in the example "Rough-and-Tumble Play: Some Issues."

To summarize, we have surveyed some important findings from research and some important theoretical ideas about developmental trends in play from birth to six years. We examined trends in social, object, symbolic, and motor play. Table 3–2 depicts some specific behaviors teachers and parents can look for to trace development in each of these four related categories of play.

some developmental virtue (Pellegrini & Perlmutter, 1986).

Nevertheless, many teachers no doubt will remain unconvinced that such play has value. Some may even hold the view that it is downright unethical to permit, let alone encourage, rough-and-tumble play in young children. Why?

The most common answer tends to be that one cannot take any chances that play fighting might turn into real fighting. Accidents can easily happen. Children may fall onto a hard or sharp object and hurt themselves, or may unintentionally hurt another child. Thus, it is much wiser to forbid rough-and-tumble play.

Second, many teachers hold to an implicit threshold theory. Sooner or later children will begin fighting seriously as the intensity increases. As an illustration, Tim, John, and Paul were observed recently in the block area wrestling and roughhousing, playing "Masters of the Universe." As "He-Man" and "Mekanek" were taking on "Skeletor" for supreme command of the universe, Tim's arm unintentionally swung and hit Paul on the nose, hurting him. To retaliate, Paul deliberately poked Tim hard, and John joined in creating a fracas. The teacher quickly separated the children.

A third reason teachers object to rough-and-tumble play is that it symbolizes violent acts of aggression and thereby goes against accepted values. Thus, for the same reason teachers outlaw toy guns and knives in their classrooms, they forbid play fighting. As such actions and objects are desensitizers to violence (making aggression seem more natural or commonplace), teachers certainly do not want children exposed to such influences, just as they do not approve of the exposure of acts of violence in the media.

TABLE 3–2

Play Development Progress Scale

Manipulation/Constructive	*Symbolic*	*Social*	*Physical*
1. Plays with body parts fingers, toes)	1. Imitates in play: a) imitates sounds; b) imitates gestures; c) imitates facial expressions; d) deferred imitation (imitates words/actions that have been heard/seen previously)	1. Touches image in mirror	1. Sits without support while playing
2. Swipes at objects playfully		2. Smiles at image in mirror	2. Stands alone well while playing
3. Plays with other person's body parts (face, hair)		3. Laughs during play	3. Crawls or creeps
4. Plays with water		4. Participates in social games (*e.g.,* pat-a-cake, peek-a-boo)	4. Walks well during play
5. Obtains objects in play	2. Uses sounds in play	5. Solitary independent play (the child plays alone and independently with toys that are different from those used by the children within speaking distance and makes no effort to get close to other children)	5. Throws ball overhead
6. Releases objects in play	3. Uses words in play		6. Climbs in and out of adult chair
7. Brings both hands together such as in clapping or banging objects together	4. Make believe use of objects, ascribing meaning to objects (*e.g.,* block becomes truck, clothes pin becomes doll)		7. Kicks ball forward
			8. Whole body rhythmic response to music
8. Repeats actions that affect environment (*e.g.,* hits object that makes noise)	5. Functional use of symbolic toys (phones, cars, dolls, tea sets, etc.)	6. Independently plays with toys for 15–30 minutes	9. Pedals tricycle
9. Stacks objects			10. Jumps in place (both feet off ground)
10. Scribbles spontaneously	6. Acting out make believe situations using adult clothes	7. Parallel play (independently play but the activity chosen naturally brings the child among other children; play with toys that are like those which the other children are using, but the child plays with the toy as he or she sees fit, and does not try to influence or modify the activity of the nearby children with the exception of taking toys away)	11. Jumps from chair 10 inches high
11. Pulls toys	7. Acting out single make believe events (as drinking cup of tea, driving car down road)		12. Catches a large ball
12. Empties containers			13. Running easily (without falling)
13. Organizes objects in rows			14. Climbs ladder of low play equipment
14. Sand (filling, patting, smoothing, piling, dumping)	8. Acting out make believe situations (sequence of events) (one role for less than 5 minutes) (having a tea party, driving around town to store or gas station, etc.)		15. Jumps rope (two or more consecutive jumps)
15. Plays with puzzles: a) 3 piece form board (circle, triangle, square); b) 4 pieces which are separate (non-touching); c) 4 pieces which are touching; d) 7 pieces which are touching; e) 12 pieces which are touching	9. Acting out make believe situations (one role for more than 5 minutes)	8. Associative play (the child plays with other children. Interest is as much in association with	16. Dare-devil play (somersaults, jumping, swinging, skating, jungle gym play)

TABLE 3–2 (cont'd)

Play Development Progress Scale

Manipulation/Constructive	Symbolic	Social	Physical
16. Fills containers 17. Puts on lids in play 18. Clay: a) clay is crudely shaped, squeezed, and rolled; b) uses tools with clay; c) simple representation through clay and/or sand (constructs recognizable object and/or labels object) 19. Blocks: a) constructions without representations; b) constructions with representation 20. Scissors: a) tears with scissors; b) snips; c) cuts on line; d) cuts out simple shape; e) cuts out picture except for small details 21. Simple representation through drawing or painting (draws recognizable picture and/or labels picture) 22. Result of a play construction become important 23. Crafts assemblies 24. Uses coloring books (coloring in lines) 25. Stencils and tracing	10. Acting out make believe situations (plot line unorganized) 11. Acting out make believe stories (plot line organized) 12. Make believe play with other children	other children as it is in the objects used in the activity. There is communication. Children engage in a common activity. There is no organization of the activity of several individuals around a common goal or product) 9. Cooperative couples play (two children organize around a common goal or product. These common goals may be dramatic situations, competitive and non-competitive games, and/or making material products. The efforts of one child are supplemented by those of another) 10. Cooperative group play (three or more children organize around a common goal or product. These common goals may be dramatic situations, competitive and non-competitive games, and/or making material products. The efforts of one child are supplemented by those of another) 11. Share while playing 12. Can wait turn while playing	

TABLE 3–2 (cont'd)

Play Development Progress Scale

Manipulation/Constructive	Symbolic	Social	Physical
		13. Performs for others	
		14. Child requests to play with another child	
		15. Bragging and name calling	
		16. Child plays with one person frequently and refers to him as best friend	
		17. Observes rules and takes turns in games	

SOURCE: Golden and Kutner, 1980.

NORMAL AND ATYPICAL DEVELOPMENT

As we have seen, the play of normal children progresses during the first six years of life and develops along several dimensions, including social play, object play, and symbolic play. Normal children show progress in social interaction, action schemes, object use, pretend activities, role enactments and themes, and in cognitive and language forms. The child who is atypical in development, who is impaired mentally or physically, cannot be expected to show the same progress.

Mindes (1982) compared the social and the cognitive play of 74 handicapped children who were educable mentally retarded, learning disabled, or behaviorally disoriented. The children ranged in age from 40 to 73 months with a mean age of 63 months. Although no significant differences in play were reported across sex, age, IQ, and diagnosed handicap, it was noted that handicapped preschoolers exhibited higher percentages of nonplay behavior and solitary play behaviors and less cooperative play than normal preschoolers as reported in previous studies.

Earlier research with older children and preschoolers had shown that handicapped retarded children often use playthings in personalized and less organized or ritualistic ways. For example, Hulme and Lunzer (1966) investigated the action plans in retarded children (3 to 12 years old with mental ages of 3 to 5 years) and in normal preschoolers. They reported that retarded children showed constructive and imaginative play abilities similar to those of normal preschoolers but that language abilities of the retarded were below those of normal children. They suggested that the similar play levels of the two groups might be a result of ritualization in the retarded children rather than true symbolic play. Smilansky (1968) found in her observations of retarded children (IQ 50–75) that only functional (manipulative) play occurred and not higher levels of constructive or sociodramatic play.

Research has attempted to evaluate the play behaviors of preschool-aged handicapped children using measures similar to those used in assessing nonhandicapped children. Hill and McCune-Nicolich (1981) studied cognitive play forms in 20- to 53-month-old children with Down's syndrome (mental ages from 12 to 26 months). Results indicated age differences reflecting a developmental sequence progressing from enactment of presymbolic schemes to single pretend acts to symbolic-play sequences and finally to planned pretend acts and sequences. Level of symbolic play was more highly correlated with mental age, as measured by the Bailey Mental Scales, than with chronological age. Children who did not make the transition from single pretend acts to symbolic play sequences also experienced delays in language development. These researchers suggested that an underlying delay in symbolic abilities was evident. Symbolic play did not occur in children with language comprehension and nonverbal mental ages below 20 months, although stereotyped play did.

Johnson and Ershler (1985) compared the toy use and social and cognitive play of nonhandicapped and handicapped preschool children. In different but comparable classroom settings, 21 children in each group were observed for 20 one-minute periods. It was found that nonhandicapped children used tools and scissors more than handicapped children and were allowed to participate in cooking activities more often. Moreover, nonhandicapped children were less predictable in terms of when they engaged in symbolic play. They used a wide variety of playthings or no playthings at all in their make-believe play. When the handicapped children participated in pretend play it was almost always with the same narrow range of toys—little cars on tracks, dolls, dress-up clothes, and other playing-house items. The play of the handicapped children in general was less integrated and less transformational. It appeared to be dominated by stimulus rather than by response as play is supposed to be (Hutt, 1966), and it reminded the researchers of Garvey's (1979) criterion for functional role play—that such role play is triggered by an object or activity.

ROLES OF THE ADULT

The roles of the adult in the play development of children during their first six years are very important, especially in the case of the handicapped child, who is at risk of not being able to benefit from play experiences important for development. Many adults do not know how or have the energy to nurture play behavior in the handicapped child. It is imperative that each child receive stimulation and encouragement for play in accord with his abilities. Adult interventions are critical in enhancing play development and development in general.

We need not think that we must always be playful with children or even enjoy the play of children—even those of us who work with young children. What is needed is a healthy respect for playfulness and spontaneity in children and the importance of play in the child's development. The attitude of the caregiver is all important. We need to recognize that play is response- and not stimulus-dominant behavior. In other words, it is up to the child-as-player what will be played. The child at play must be in control of the situation to a degree. This will require a shift in attitude for some adults who are overly concerned about so-called appropriate play. We need to model and encourage unusual behaviors, as long as they are safe and meaningful in the situation.

We need to be aware of structural changes in play behaviors as the child grows up. We should be familiar with sequences within social play, object play, and symbolic play, as well as physical play. We must know what the next developmental level is for a given child along the sequences traced in this chapter (see Table 3–2). Most important, we must understand the mechanism of play development and help children play to the limits of their existing abilities. We need to be very sensitive to the effect of the environment on different play behaviors, making sure that positive environmental factors are present for all children.

Situations that promote play development are particularly important to create during the first and second years of the child's life. We have underscored the need to provide infants with objects to learn how to play at the very beginning of life. Infants learn from caregivers' play signals and play communications. Especially vital are adult-infant game routines during the first year that will develop social play skills as well as the sense of make-believe. Examples of these games will be presented in Chapter 5, "Play and the Social Environment."

Finally, the limited abilities of the young player must be accommodated to assure smoothly flowing play experiences. Mutual sharing between adult and child is centrally important. Dividends come a little later in the child's life as the peer group, with its demands for mutual accommodations, becomes increasingly relevant and instrumental in each child's growth in play development during the first six years. We prepare the child for later play with others and continue to support it while the child operates more autonomously within the peer group.

SUMMARY

In this chapter, we discussed four dimensions of play development: social, object, symbolic, and motor. *Social* play during the first six years becomes increasingly interactive; it has its origins in the first infant games or routines involving an accommodating partner who compensates for the child's limitations. Objects inspire infant and toddler play but are less important for preschoolers and older children. Social play skills improve with experience in the peer group, where mutual accommodations are required. *Object* play develops from simple and repetitive motor and functional play routines to constructive play and conventional and innovative applications of objects in combinations. Object play becomes more discriminant, sequential, and appropriate as the child matures, and the frequent involvement of other children as well as symbolic representations in the play episodes contributes to the complexity of object play.

Symbolic play advances from earliest imitations of self and then others toward more coherent and orderly symbolic play entailing planning and patterning in a social context. Genuine pretense, according to Piaget, commences when the infant displays outer-directed as opposed to self-directed play behavior. Four dimensions of symbolic play were traced: pretend actions, use of objects, role enactments, and themes. Sequences of pretend actions develop from self-as-agent to outer-directed actions; objects used in early (but not necessarily in later) forms of make-believe play are realistic and representational of the real object. Factors that influence the complexity of pretending during early childhood include the form, function, and content of the substitute object in relation to the real object. Role-enactment improvements during these years reflect growing knowledge of role attributes, relations, and role-appropriate actions and greater linguistic, cognitive, and social skills. The themes of make-believe play move away from an exclusive preoccupation with highly familiar themes and toward the enactment of more adventuresome and fantastic themes. At the end point of symbolic play development during the preschool years, children engage in highly developed sociodramatic or thematic fantasy play characterized by a variety of roles with peers, and by concentration, persistence, and attention to detail.

Motor play development from birth to six years is marked by numerous major motor milestones as children grow physically, become more mobile, and gain greater control, strength, balance, and coordination using their large and small muscles. The child who is atypical in development or impaired mentally and physically does not show the same progress in social, object, and symbolic play. The play of cognitively delayed children tends to be less integrated and transformational.

The role of the adult is to provide an encouraging and a supportive environment with many opportunities for shared play. The adult's accommodation of a child's limited play abilities during game routines and other encounters involving objects and communication prepare the infant, toddler, and young preschooler for later, more independent play with peers when mutual accommodations are necessary.

REFERENCES

Bakeman, R., & Brownlee, J.R. (1980). The strategic use of parallel play: A sequential analysis. *Child Development, 51,* 873–787.

Fagen, R. (1981). *Animal play behavior.* New York: Oxford University Press.

Fenson, L., Kagan, J., Kearsley, R.B., & Zelazo, P.R. (1976). The developmental progression of manipulative play in the first two years. *Child Development 47,* 232–236.

Frost, J.L. & Klein, B.L. (1979). *Children's play and playgrounds.* Boston: Allyn and Bacon.

Garvey, C. (1979). An approach to the study of children's role play. *The Quarterly Newsletter of the Laboratory of Comparative Human Cognition, 1(4),* 69–73.

Garvey, C., & Berndt, R. (1977, September). *The organization of pretend play.* Paper presented at the Annual Meeting of the American Psychological Association, Chicago.

Golden, D.B., & Kutner, C.G. (1980). *The Play Development Progress Scale.* Unpublished manuscript.

Hay, D. (1981). *Interactive play in the second year: The social origins of nonliteral action.* Paper presented at the Society for Research in Child Development, Boston.

Hill, P.M., & McCune-Nicholich, L. (1981). Pretend play and patterns of cognition in Down's Syndrome children. *Child Development, 52,* 611–617.

Howes, C. (1980). Peer play scale as an index of complexity of peer interaction. *Developmental Psychology, 16,* 371–371.

Hulme, I., & Lunzer, E.L. (1966). Play, language and reasoning in subnormal children. *Journal of Child Psychology and Psychiatry, 7,* 107–123.

Hutt, C. (1977). *Towards a toxonomy and conceptual model of play.* Paper presented at the Johnson and Johnson Panel on Play and Learning, New Orleans, LA.

Jackowitz, E.R. & Watson, M.W. (1980). The development of object transformations in early pretend play. *Developmental Psychology, 16,* 543–549.

Jacobson, J.L. (1981). The role of inanimate objects in early peer interaction. *Child Development, 52,* 618–626.

Johnson, J., & Ershler, J. (1985). Social and cognitive play forms and toy use by nonhandicapped and handicapped preschoolers. In J. Neisworth (Ed.), *Topics in Early Special Education: Developmental Toys, 5,* 69–82.

King, N. (1985). *Researching school play.* Paper presented at the Anthropological Association for the Study of Play, Washington, D.C.

Lowe, M. (1975). Trends in the development of representational play in infants from one to three years: An observational study. *Journal of Child Psychology and Psychiatry, 16,* 33–47.

Mindes, G. (1982). Social and cognitive aspects of play in young handicapped children. *Topics in Early Childhood Special Education: Play and Development, 2(3),* 39–52.

Montagner, H. (1984, December) [as reported by Maya Pines]. Children's winning ways. *Psychology Today,* 59–65.

Moore, N.V., Evertson, C.M., & Brophy, J.E. (1974). Solitary play: Some functional reconsiderations. *Developmental Psychology, 10,* 830–834.

Mueller, E., & Lucas, T. (1975). A developmental analysis of peer interaction among toddlers. In M. Lewis & L. Rosenblum (Eds.), *Friendship and peer relations.* New York: Wiley, 1975.

Parten, M.B. (1932). Social participation among preschool children. *Journal of Abnormal and Social Psychology, 27,* 243–269.

Pellegrini, A. & Perlmutter, J. (1986, April). *The Developmental and Educational Significance of Children's Rough-and-Tumble Play* American Educational Research Association. San Francisco.

Piaget, J. (1962). *Play, dreams and imitation in childhood.* New York: W.W. Norton.

Rosenblatt, D. (1977). Developmental trends in infant play. In B. Tizard & O. Harvey (Eds.), *The biology of play.* Philadelphia: Lippincott.

Ross, H.S., Goldman, B.D., & Hay, D.F. (1979). Features and functions of infant games. In B. Sutton-Smith (Ed.)., *Play and learning.* New York: Gardner Press.

Rubin, K. (1982). Non-social play in preschoolers: Necessary evil? *Child Development, 53,* 651–657.

Rubin, K.H., Maioni, T.L., & Hornung, M. (1976). Free play behaviors in middle-and lower-class pre-schoolers: Parten and Piaget revisited. *Child Development, 47,* 414–419.

Schwartzman, H.B. (1978). *Transformations: The anthropology of children's play.* New York: Plenum.

Singer, J.L. (1973). *The child's world of make-believe.* New York: Academic Press.

Smilansky, S. (1968). *The effects of sociodramatic play on disadvantaged preschool children.* New York: Wiley.

Smith, P.K. (1978). A longitudinal study of social participation in preschool children: Solitary and parallel play re-examined. *Developmental Psychology, 14,* 517–523.

Strayer, J., Mosher, M., & Russell, C. (1981). *Social-cognitive skills and play behaviors of toddlers.* Paper presented to the meetings of the Society for Research in Child Development, Boston.

Watson, M.M., & Jackowitz, E.R. (1984). Agents and recipient objects in the development of early symbolic play. *Child Development, 55,* 1091–1097.

4 Personality and Play

W hat does the term "personality" mean? There are a great many definitions in the dictionary. The word is widely used in education and psychology despite disagreements over its definition. Perhaps like "play," the term "personality" is understood by everyone as long as it is employed in a general and vague manner. However, if called upon to give a precise account of what we mean by personality, few of us would be able to agree on its meaning. Nevertheless, the concept of personality is so important that we are unwilling to abandon the term altogether.

All of us employ notions of personality to characterize the behavior of preschool age children. Some children are considered outgoing; others are shy or withdrawn; still others are considered cautious or bold. Descriptive statements abound. But what are we really referring to when we use these terms? And how is personality related to play?

In this chapter we will first present a definition of personality within a broad context of child development in order to approach the topic in a way more relevant to the early childhood educator. We will then review selected research and theory on individual differences in sociability during play and on playfulness as a personality trait, examining playfulness in general as well as the structure and styles of pretend play and object play in particular. Third, we will evaluate the importance of childhood play in the formation of the self-concept and describe the social-intellectual processes involved and the environmental factors that affect play. Finally, we will draw out some practical implications from this area of the play literature for the adult practitioner. We will do this realizing both the relation of play with personality development and the relation of play with children's coping and regulation of stress.

PERSONALITY AND MODELS OF HUMAN DEVELOPMENT

The term "personality" is often cited to explain a wide range of diverse phenomena. What are we doing when we use the term? Within psychology and education the notion of personality has taken on the meaning of personal consistency in certain features of an individual's behavior which persist across a wide range of processes, tasks, or situations. In addition, these differences must be considered and shown to result from differences in personal qualities and not in developmental level. That is, expressed behavior must be stable over time and not caused by differences in cognitive maturity.

We typically employ the concept of personality to attempt to account for some specific social or personal behavior. Social and personal behaviors vary in their expression from individual to individual. How much of this variation in behavior stems from individual personality factors or, in other words, a personal trait? How much of the behavior is caused by situational influences? Finally, how much is based on an individual's level of developmental maturity?

Emmerich, who has observed free-play behavior in Head Start children and middle-to-upper-middle-class students in a number of studies, has proposed six models of behavioral development derived from the ideas of personal consistency (or personality), contextual influence, and developmental change and their two-way and three-way combinations. In one study he observed sixteen nursery school students in free-play periods as well as in teacher-directed small groups over two time periods (Emmerich, 1977). Over time, children learned to exhibit more task-oriented behaviors in the small groups, while socioemotional measures of free play, and to a lesser extent small group behaviors, were fairly stable in their demonstration of personality or individual differences across contexts and time periods. Emmerich suggests that each model by itself is inadequate to account for preschoolers' behaviors and that one should view behaviors within a larger framework. With this more inclusive model of child development and behavior, teachers can better remember that personal and social behaviors are not caused by any one reason or any simple combination or interaction of reasons. "Theory-Guided Observation" gives a good example of the value of this approach.

INDIVIDUAL DIFFERENCES IN PLAY

As we traced in Chapter 3, play behavior is a developmental phenomenon. We have seen this developmental progression in examples of object-dependent play evolving toward increasing independence from props or other play tangibles. Play patterns shift from object manipulation to object transformation and then to object independent play and finally to internalized fantasy. Yet play by definition is open to unlimited forms of expression and content. A comprehensive account of play should adhere to Emmerich's suggestion that we view play and other preschool personal-

social behaviors within a broad framework encompassing developmental considerations, and personality and situation factors. Play is multiply determined. In part, it is
behavior that reveals how different children in the same situation and at the same

THEORY-GUIDED OBSERVATION

Keeping track of how each individual child plays and behaves in a variety of classroom
situations is not an easy task, but it is nonetheless the responsibility of every teacher. Each
child expresses a unique and budding personality. It is fascinating to see such individual
variation at early ages. Noting this individuality becomes particularly important when the
time comes for conferences between parents and teacher or in less formal situations when a
parent can be informed of a child's progress at school. Often teachers collect some
examples of the child's art work, constructions, and other products for the parent. Long-
term projects such as audio-cassette logs, diaries or books of drawings collected over time
may also be included. In addition, observations and anecdotes are a common basis of
information about a child. Some teachers also keep systematic play records to offer more
objective and quantitative information.

The source and kind of observations or information are not as important as what a
teacher makes of them regarding a particular child to pass on to parents. It is at this point
that comprehensive models of child behavior such as Emmerich's can become useful to
analyze what is going on in the classroom. Such models enable teachers to view children
through a discriminating lens to acquire a more sophisticated understanding of each child.
Thus, the teacher is able to give a more thoughtful and valid account or appraisal of how
each child is doing in the classroom.

Consider the following case. Innocently—but harmfully—a teacher told a parent that the
parent's child was very shy at school. This surprised the parent to some extent because the
child was not shy at home and in other situations. The teacher's remarks troubled the
parent. Such labeling, as we know, can influence others and have long-range effects on
children. Personality-trait labeling should be used sparingly. The important point about
this example is that the teacher used a simple model of the child's behavior in deciding
what to say to the parent. It was a "one-factor" model. That is, the child's behavior was
explained by one factor, the individual difference notion of shyness. It would have been
much better if the child's behavior had been considered in terms of a host of reasons. It
happened that the child was the youngest in the class. Tendencies to withdraw or avoid
others, in other words, could be seen as reflecting relative social immaturity or the child's
developmental status as much as anything else. It would also have been smarter for the
teacher to have noted situational variation in the child's behavior. That is, are there times
in the daily schedule of class events when the child appears to enjoy social commerce?
When and under what circumstances does the child seem to avoid social interaction or
seem to display passivity? Theories and models of child development may seem at times a
bit too remote or abstract to be practical, but understood and applied properly they can be
used to great advantage, enhancing the well-being and development of children.

level of cognitive maturity attempt to make sense of their worlds and, in doing so, express their idiosyncratic preferences and unique personalities.

Consider how Anais and Petula engage in the following pretend play. They are from the same family backgrounds and are similar in development level. Each is five years old. The theme is pirates and princesses, and the play occurs during free-play period at nursery school within a larger group of children (C).

ANAIS: Yeah, let's finish this meal and go to the shore. Pirates are near.
C: Where are the pirates? On the shore?
(Anais and C go and crawl on a rug and pretend to watch for pirates.)
ANAIS: Do you see any pirates?
C: Yeah, they are on the boat!
(C points to gym frame laden with boys.)
ANAIS: We can hide in the cave.
C: OK.
ANAIS: Watch for mountain lions up on the hill.
(Anais and C walk across the room.)
ANAIS: Look at Jessie, she is injured. Let's help her.
C: Bring her here.
ANAIS: Put her on this rug.
C: OK.
ANAIS: I'll start warming some soup.
(Anais goes to the domestic center to get some pots and pans and a new play theme begins.)

In contrast, here is a subplot of the same theme in which Petula was involved the same day, but with different children (C).

PETULA: Where is the treasure? Did the pirates get it?
C: No, not now.
PETULA: Bring me the box of gems.
(C bring a box of old jewelry discarded by the teachers and student teachers.)
PETULA: I better get my purse too.
(Petula carries over purse.)
PETULA: Let me see what is in here.
(Petula takes out a number of items and discards them.)
PETULA: I need room for the diamonds. Give them to me.
C: Here.
PETULA: Let's see, these are bigger and these are smaller.
C: Oh.
PETULA: This one is the prettiest one of all. This is gold. This is silver.

Anais and Petula are well-matched in developmental level and background and

Some children tend to prefer play activities that involve lots of social interaction. Such children can be referred to as person oriented.

are playing in the same social and physical situation. Still, their play behavior varies considerably. Anais conjures up a narrative relatively independent of objects. She uses words to transform time and space, and her physical surroundings are less important to her than her social surroundings. Petula, in contrast, seems much more dependent upon her physical surroundings and is more likely to shift attention to particular physical objects during social pretend play.

Object-versus-People Orientation. One of the first ways individual differences in preschool play has been described is in terms of object-versus-people orientation (Emmerich, 1964). Some children are more attracted to activities where there is a lot of interaction with people. Others prefer solitary activities where the focus of attention is on objects.

Jennings (1975), studying the relationship between preschoolers' cognitive abilities and object-versus-social orientation, found a significant difference among the children's abilities to perform cognitive tasks involving physical manipulations of materials. That is, children who spent more time playing with objects performed better on tests requiring organization and classification of physical materials. Also, object orientation or preference was significantly correlated to ability to use objects. For social orientation, children who exhibited more social knowledge were those more effective in social functioning or social competence. Social knowledge rather than preference for social interaction correlated with effectiveness of social interaction. Jennings suggested that object orientation and social knowledge are established early in life and serve to reinforce cognitive skills related to these orientations, thus reinforcing interest in the orientation and knowledge.

Other researchers have examined the relationship between a child's orientation to objects and people as a measure of cognitive style. Cognitive style refers to individual variations in ways of responding to a cognitive task. The most widely researched and generally accepted measure of cognitive style has been field independence-dependence (Witkin, 1954). Subjects who are more field-independent have an easier time finding a simple figure within a complex design. The child's attention and perception, it is assumed, do not get lost in the total design (field). The field-dependent subject apparently gets distracted by elements in the total design and many times cannot find the hidden figure.

Coates, Lord and Jakabovics (1975) found that children who were more field-independent sought out objects to play with while field-dependent children were more people-oriented. The field-independent children's greater success at finding the figure in a design may be due to an analytic style that may make them more likely to learn through observing and responding to physical aspects of the environment. Field-dependent children because of their more global approach, may pay more attention to the social aspects of the same situation.

Playfulness. Researchers have also studied general playfulness as a personality dimension contributing to observed variations in play behavior and divergent thinking (Dansky, Lieberman as cited in Chapter 1). Playfulness according to Lieberman can be understood in terms of five traits: physical, social, and cognitive spontaneity; manifest joy; and a sense of humor (see Table 4–1). Lieberman, using rating scales for scoring the play behavior of 93 kindergarten children, found that four of the five playfulness traits were very highly related, with the remaining trait (physical spontaneity) less related. Lieberman concluded that playfulness is a single personality dimension defined by these traits. She found in her research that playfulness is correlated with divergent thinking scores, mental age, and chronological age.

Further support for the possible association of playfulness with divergent thinking or potential creativity comes from studies by Dansky and Hutt and their associates. Dansky and Silverman (1975) identified players and nonplayers during free-play

TABLE 4–1

Lieberman's Playfulness Construct: Five Aspects

Trait	Manifestation
Manifest Joy	Laughter, expressions of happiness and enjoyment
Sense of Humor	Appreciation of comical events, recognition of funny situations, gentle teasing
Spontaneity	
Physical	Exuberant, coordinated movement of the whole body or parts of the body
Cognitive	Imagination, creativity, and flexibility of thought
Social	Ability to get along with others and to move in and out of groups

SOURCE: Based on Leiberman (1977)

periods and reported that preschool children who were considered players scored significantly higher on tests of divergent thinking. Spontaneous free play enhances divergent thinking, but children are not equally playful. Hutt (1966), in a structured laboratory situation designed to elicit curiosity and exploratory behavior, classified three- to five-year old children as follows: (a) non-explorers, (b) explorers, and (c) inventive explorers. Inventive explorers were those who after investigating a "supertoy" (a complex and novel object consisting of a red metal box on four brass legs and a lever ending in a blue wooden ball with the directional manipulations of the lever registered on four counters which could be left open or covered) proceeded to use the toy in many imaginative ways. Later, in a follow-up study involving the same children, then between seven and ten years old, Hutt and Bhavnani (1972) found that children who were less playful during their preschool years described themselves as unadventurous and inactive, while those who were more playful during their preschool years saw themselves as more assertive and independent, particularly the girls. A correlation was computed between playfulness and originality scores from a battery of creative tests administered when the children were older. It was found to be .516 for boys (significant) and .368 for girls (not statistically significant).

Truhon (1979) has argued that there appear to be two aspects of playfulness, and that it is not the unidimensional construct proposed by Lieberman. One aspect is a cognitive component that may lead to creativity and to the understanding of a joke. The other aspect is the affective component which is seen in the joy of play and the laughter in a joke. Analogous is the distinction Singer (1961) makes between future-oriented or problem-solving daydreams and past-oriented or fanciful daydreams. Truhon used a modification of Lieberman's playfulness scales to observe 30 kindergarten children in solitary play. Each child was also given a battery of creativity tests. Truhon's statistical procedure (path analysis) supported a distinction between affective and cognitive components of playfulness—a playfulness-fun cluster and a playfulness-intelligence cluster. The two related aspects of playfulness (cognitive and affective) have different impacts on play. The playfulness-fun part of the playfulness scale measured manifest joy and sense of humor, while the playfulness-intelligence part measured intelligence and cognitive spontaneity. Truhon concluded that playfulness is a reasonably good predictor of play activities, but that playfulness and play are weakly related to creativity.

Fantasy-Making Predisposition. A third individual difference variable concerning play has been proposed by Singer (1973). Fantasy-making ability (or a predisposition to fantasy-making) and playfulness are related but different concepts. Fantasy-making predispositions refer to playfulness that takes primary expression in overt imaginative play activity or in internalized fantasy; playfulness is more general and can be expressed in more reality-based (constructive) play as well. Research on this individual difference variable has used observation, projective tests, and oral interviews to estimate children's propensities toward fantasy-making. Children high in fantasy-making abilities display higher levels of imaginativeness, positive affect, concentration, social interaction, and cooperation during free play than children with low fantasy-making tendencies. Moreover, children high in this predisposition

are also more likely to report seeing movement in ambiguous stimulus cards (the Barron Movement Threshold Inkblot series) and to report in a play interview (Singer's Structured Interview) that they see "little pictures in their heads" and that they have imaginary companions. Their favorite games and play activities reported in the play interview typically involve some make-believe or transformational behavior.

Children high in fantasy-making tendencies have been reported to be better able to pass long periods of enforced waiting or delays in activity. Thus, these children are less likely to become disruptive or to interfere with others. Instead, they are able to engage in some form of imaginative play or to otherwise entertain themselves without overt acting out. High fantasy is associated with the ability to control impulses and delay gratification (Singer, 1961). Pulaski (1970), among others, has used fantasy-making as an individual difference variable in "aptitude-by-treatment" research. She found that five-year-old children already high in fantasy-making generally scored higher than age-mates low in fantasy-making on various measures of imaginative play with unstructured as well as structured playthings. Less structured toys in general elicited a greater variety of fantasy themes. She suggested that perhaps at younger ages during the preschool period different kinds of play-things may influence imaginative behavior and its underlying fantasy-making predisposition. Both Pulaski and Singer suggested that fantasy-making is linked to cognition and creativity.

Just as was the case in research on playfulness as an individual difference variable, the early work on fantasy-making seemed to indicate that the trait was an isolated one. However, subsequent studies have suggested otherwise. Singer and Singer (1980) analyzed a set of 33 variables relating to imaginative play, language, social interaction, affect, and home television viewing. Three factors emerged. One indexed general good-humored playfulness across a number of behavior domains; a second identified aggressive interaction associated with television viewing; and a third measured *inner* imaginative tendencies and prosocial behaviors. This factor structure was stable over the one-year period of observations. The Singers suggested that both manifestations of fantasy-making tendencies, through play as well as through more inner-directed channels, are the result of a generally positive relationship the child has with the social and physical environment. Shmukler (1977) also reported findings consistent with the hypothesis that during the preschool years one can distinguish between observed overt imaginative play behavior and private forms of fantasy assessed in interviews, tests, and questionnaires. However, as Rubin, Fein, and Vandenberg (1983) point out, it is unclear what the later measures are tapping since method of assessment (free-play observations versus answers to an adult tester's questions) impedes our ability to conclude that there are two subtypes of fantasy-making tendencies in young children. What seems well-established, however, is that there are individual differences during the preschool years; while some children prefer make-believe play activities over other more reality-based play activities, many other children exhibit both forms of play equally.

Types of Imaginative Play Styles. Research conducted at Harvard's Project Zero indicates individual styles of symbolic play in early childhood (Wolf & Gardner, 1979; Wolf & Grollman, 1982). In a long-term study of children's symbolic play, these researchers have delineated styles of symbolic play, or "modes of behavior remaining consistent across a range of materials and situations" (Wolf & Gardner, 1979, p. 119). Symbolic play is defined as the "ability to represent actual or imagined experience through the use of small objects, motions, and language" (Wolf & Gardner, 1979). Two styles of symbolic play are: object-independent fantasy play, in which the child creates imaginary worlds by invoking nonexistent events, roles, and props; and object-dependent transformational play, in which the child creates an imaginary world by ably transforming existing objects and arrangements in the environment (Wolf & Grollman, 1982). Earlier in this chapter Anais and Petula exemplified these contrasting patterns.

Wolf and Grollman propose that these two stylistic differences contrast with developmental differences in that the stylistic differences refer to the quality of an individual's behavior, rather than the developmental level. In addition, these individual styles are stable across time, and are not instances of particular periods within developmental levels. Finally, analysis of free-play behaviors of preschool children support the notion that these stylistic differences persist and characterize children's interactions with materials (Wolf & Grollman, 1982). Stylistic differences in play behaviors have been correlated with children's problem-solving abilities (Jennings, 1975).

What, then, are the characteristics of each play style? By defining the imaginative elements in play, Wolf and associates were able to categorize the elements into those that were object independent and object dependent. Imaginative elements were defined as "vocal or gestural schemes through which a child altered the pragmatic or actual constituents of the ongoing situation" (Wolf & Grollman, 1982, p. 55). Object-dependent instances of imaginative play involved existing or actually present events, objects, or persons. Object-dependent children constructed arrangements or patterns with objects, and substituted items where actions required props. On the other hand, object-independent children evoked nonexistent elements, often incorporating actual events and objects, but in nonappropriate and farfetched substitutions. For example, Anais incorporated a teacher's coughing into play, making it the roar of a mountain lion in the pretend cave. These two styles involve persistent and characteristic modes of play, and are based upon earlier investigations of symbolic development. In their earlier work, Wolf and Gardner (1979) reported consistent patterns of preferences and characteristic ways of organizing responses with materials and tasks in both free-play and test situations, which were the basis for the object-independent and object-dependent styles. "Patterners" displayed considerable skill and interest in making patterns, structures, and orders with objects and materials. These children were interested in an object's mechanical and design possibilities rather than in communication or interpersonal events. "Dramatists" exhibited a strong interest in human surroundings: what others did, felt, and how they could be known. Dramatists preferred and did well in games, sociodramatic play, and storytelling. These children often performed poorly when engaged in tasks demanding close attention to the physical properties of objects. Patterners, however, excelled in visual-spatial tasks and in physical relations between objects. According to Wolf and Gardner (1979), these two distinct styles of play and problem solving are part of children's overall personalities and underlying mental structures.

Matthews (1977) supported the notion of individual differences in play style. In her investigation of transformational modes in make-believe play, Matthews pointed out two modes: material and ideational, which are direct parallels of object-dependent and object-independent play styles. A material transformational mode was characterized by the "child's active manipulation of and transformation fantasy reference to actual material in the play environment..." (Matthews, 1977, p. 214). An ideational mode involved references, ideas, or mental images of things not physically present to the senses. In her study, Matthews stated that familiarity with the play situation had increased the use of ideational modes, and that girls shifted to ideational modes more quickly than boys. This evidence suggests that individual differences in cognitive style may be developmental and sex-related rather than stylistic.

In review of the literature concerning individual differences in play styles, scant research, as well as conflicting results of existing reports, indicates the need for further study to ascertain whether there indeed exist two persistent and characteristic styles of imaginative play. Recent work on the symbolic play of two-year-olds failed to see divergent styles during this developmental period (Franklin, 1985). Perhaps teachers and parents should expect variability within the same child across different play situations and recognize that most preschoolers will exhibit a great deal of behavior characteristic of each style.

Individual Differences in Object Play. Style of play with objects is another variable that can be used to examine individual differences among young children. Fein (1979), in differentiating stylistic from structural or developmental aspects of play, cited three types of style variables: (1) the number of different actions a child uses over a period of time; (2) the number of different objects that a child selects to use over a given period; and (3) the combination and changes of actions and objects over time, called the *tempo* of play. Still other dimensions that can be identified in object play are elaborateness, organizational complexity, and persistence. As we discussed in Chapter 3, object play is a developmental phenomenon. But at the same time, at each level of cognitive maturity, there is wide range of differences in how individual children play with objects—differences that can be described within these object-play dimensions.

Difference in propensities to involve objects in pretend play has been characterized in terms of play patterners versus play dramatists. Motor/manipulative/constructive play with objects is also more likely in preschool children considered task-oriented than in those who seem person-oriented. Some children seem to take advantage of practically every opportunity to engage in play with toys and materials, while other children may engage only rarely in object play unless specifically encouraged by adults. Other than those children with distinct alternative and competing play styles (person-oriented, dramatists), children whose cognitive level and psychomotor developmental levels otherwise match their peers may be reluctant to use toys for a variety of other personal reasons such as anxiety or fear of affiliation with others.

SELF-CONCEPT FORMATION

As indicated in the Preface, views about play and development can be divided into two general camps. First, there is the belief that play serves important purposes in child development. Second, there is the view that play is expressive behavior that does not affect development directly in any positive, or constructive manner. In this second camp, play is seen as serving ego-building functions and is not reducible into component parts to be linked to other developmental phenomena. What is most important to understand about play, according to this view, is that the phenomenon of play is holistic and integrated within the individual personality and self-identity of the player. This position is reflected in the theoretical writings of Erikson (1940), Peller (1952), and Sutton-Smith (1980), among others.

Erikson, for example, addressed the ways in which the psychosexual conflicts of children are reflected in the spatial configuration of their play with toys. While controversial, his ideas deserve some consideration in that they have reinforced the development and use of play as therapy to help children cope with emotional and behavioral difficulties. The belief that play can enable children to better cope with traumatic events, for example, has led to a groundswell of sentiment for providing pediatric patients with play experiences to help alleviate anxieties associated with hospitalization (Lindquist, Lind & Harvey, 1977).

According to Erikson (1963), the adaptive resolution of each stage of psychosocial development (for example, trust vs. mistrust at one year of age) involves the successful integration of social and biological functions. Play creates "a model situation in which aspects of the past are relived, the present represented and renewed, and the future anticipated" (Erikson, 1977, p. 44). Therefore, play as an ego function helps the solutions of the ego contacts (such as anxieties) to be dramatized and played out. For example, playing with toys is a behavior in which children explore and reduce concerns about their competence. Play is a "training ground for the experience of *leeway* of imaginative choice with an existence governed and guided by roles and vision" (Erikson, 1977, p. 78). Erikson has also noted the expressive value of play:

> True, the themes presented betray some repetitiveness such as we recognize as the "working through" of a *traumatic* experience; but they also express playful *renewal*. If they seem to be governed by some need to communicate, or even to *confess,* they certainly also seem to serve the joy of *self-expression.* (Erikson, 1972, p. 131)

Hence, Erikson moves beyond a narrow view on the part play takes in anxiety reduction and compensatory wish fulfillment to a more positive holistic view of play in childhood. Erikson considers the sense of hope as a "prime mover" in human development. Play, and particularly future-oriented role play, reinforces children's intrinsic faith in the future of the human race as well as hopefulness about their own developing personal identities.

Peller (1952) presents a more traditional psychoanalytic view about play, highlighting the diversity of essentially compensatory reasons a child plays. For Peller and the Freudians, play seems to be a substitute for reasoning, and as such, is a "crude kind of test action" (p. 124). Nevertheless, because play enables the child to reexperience past personal events with accompanying moods and emotions, playful repetition is seen as an essential step toward concept formation, including the concept of self.

Sutton-Smith (1980), a scholar who has written extensively on play and relation to the self, highlights the way role reversal in play can foster a sense of control and autonomy in the child. Given that children operate from a position of weakness in relation to adults, it is important for children to know that they have opportunities to turn the tables on adults and on aspects of living that make them feel inferior because of their immaturity and size. Play is a medium that is self-enabling. Play and fantasy give the child a chance to be powerful and the master of circumstances.

Consider how young children might feel, for example, about routine events forced upon them by adults who may or may not think about their consequences for children. Take a child who is dropped off at school or a day care center day after day by a parent who hurries off to work. The child has no choice in the matter. The parent decides what happens and is virtually in total control of the entire situation. But in play the child can reverse roles and pretend to leave dolls or teddy bears at a pretend day care or nursery, thereby recapturing a little of the loss of control experienced in the actual occurrences.

Playing, then, is intimately related to the expansion of a sense of self as an autonomous and functioning person who can influence surrounding events. Through play the developing identity of the child emerges. The child forms a secure position and from this position of strength is able to achieve empathy for others. Playful reciprocity, as noted in Chapter 3, is at first seen in adult-infant and

Playing the role of a powerful adult fosters a sense of control and autonomy.

adult-toddler interactions. From this base, and through later adult-mediated peer role play, the child is able to engage in social play with peers. This process reflects and expresses the child's understanding of self and others, and the relationship between the two.

ENVIRONMENTAL FACTORS

Environmental factors, such as child-rearing styles and family structural characteristics, may influence not only the rate by which children progress through stages of play development, but also individual play styles and expression. Why is it that some children are more playful than others, or that different children acquire different play predispositions? Some children prefer fantasy-based play, while others prefer reality-based play; whereas some children are more interested in dramatic play and storytelling, others may find drawing and clay constructing more to their liking. What do we know about the sources of individual variation in play expression?

The home-life experiences of the young child are vitally important in the development of play behaviors, as we have seen in Chapters 2 and 3. Although our knowledge is limited and not fine-grained in specifics at this time, we know that in general parents and other significant adults in the child's environment exert very important effects on the child's play.

Smilansky (1968) and Singer (1973) have both made the case that young children not only need a generally positive home environment and positive relations with parents to flourish in their imaginative play development, but that children also require specific modeling and encouragement to engage in make-believe play.

Others such as Dunn and Wooding (1977) and Feitelson and Ross (1973) have elaborated upon these arguments. Certainly distinctive play styles, such as being high versus low in fantasy-making predisposition, as well as the quantity and quality of play a child exhibits, emanate in part from patterns of child-rearing, and availability of play space, toys, storage areas, and places for privacy.

Bishop and Chace (1971) and Barnett and Kleiber (1983) are two pairs of investigators who have more recently addressed themselves to identifying home background factors in the emergence of playfulness in children, adapting Lieberman's (1977) use of the term. Both studies used the measure of the home-as-a-play environment developed by Bishop and Chace (1971), which assesses such things as whether parents allow their children to play in unusual ways or in unusual places. An interview questionnaire was used in both studies.

Bishop and Chace reported that mothers' but not fathers' conceptual level of beliefs, measured on a scale from concrete to abstract, related positively and statistically significantly to the home-as-a-play environment. In other words, children deemed more playful in performing specially devised tasks came from home environments that encouraged playfulness, their mother having a more abstract or differentiated belief system. Barnett and Kleiber (1983) found a similar connection when examining each parent in the family separately but not when looking at them in composite. In general these investigators found gender differences when examining additional family structure variables and parental background characteristics. For instance, when birth order, family size, and sex of sibling were analyzed to determine their influence on a child's playfulness in free-play periods at school, the investigators found that, for males only, latter-borns were more playful and that children from larger families were more playful (again males only). Having no sisters reduced the difference between boys' and girls' manifest playfulness, all other things being equal. That is, males with no sisters were less playful but females with no sisters were more playful. Fathers' socioeconomic status was positively and significantly related to playfulness in children; maternal age was negatively and significantly correlated with daughters' playfulness.

These results are complex and research is needed that would evaluate more thoroughly the contribution of family structure variables to play quality, quantity, and style. There is less evidence to suggest the importance of such variables than research evidence pointing to the importance of parental practices, particularly during the first and second years of life when the mother or father provides "scaffolding" that enables the child to engage in play to the margins of his ability (Bruner, 1974). At the preschool level, however, there is little or no evidence suggesting a direct positive link between parental playfulness and the preschool child's playfulness (Barnett & Kleiber, 1983; Johnson, 1978). Parental permissiveness and less family unity may, however, somehow be beneficial to the development of creativity during childhood (Miller & Gerard, 1979). Finally, a number of studies suggest an inverse relationship between anxiety and playfulness. Individual difference in play may be the result of underlying anxiety. Events in the home and the nature of parent-child relations, it is well-known, are related to anxiety in children.

STRESS, COPING, AND PLAY

Elkind (1981) states that play is an antidote to hurrying. Children play to release the stress they build up from all the pressure exerted on them by socialization agents in today's fast-paced society. Children, according to popular current views, are under pressure to grow up fast. Parents, the schools, and the media conspire to pressure children to meet tasks and demands earlier than previous generations. Elkind defines hurrying as "the pressure on children to make social accommodations at the expense of personal assimilations" (p. 195). In other words, children are hurried when forced to learn new things when the time would be better spent playing to reinforce or digest past experiences. Play and work are separate but complementary activities.

Elkind is highly critical of the dictum "play is child's work" because of the way it sometimes gets translated into teaching practice. He gives a poignant example of the inappropriate use of the spokesman-for-reality intervention strategy (Elkind, 1981, p. 196): A teacher interrupted children playing with various toy dinosaurs to try to point out their different sizes. As a result, the children drifted off into other activities to avoid the teacher. Dinosaurs have great symbolic significance—they are big and strong, but as toys small and easy for children to use. Such play gives children a safe way of dealing with the giants in their world—adults. Adults should avoid interrupting this type of play.

Similar examples of inappropriately turning play into a teacher-oriented lesson plan are all too numerous and well-known. Typically, in a classroom or day care center teachers are eager to have children learn. It is easy to become overly enthusiastic. For example, a teacher interrupted a young child during so-called free-play period when the child, who played alone most of the time, was finally beginning to play with other children. The teacher wanted to help the child learn how to spell and write her name!

Children's personal assimilations should not be turned into social accommodation. Elkind (1981) notes that the real work of children is not play but to meet the countless socialization demands placed on them (remembering their phone numbers and addresses and how to get home from school, learning how to brush their teeth, learning to read, learning to deal with conscious and unconscious fears and concerns, etc.). To complement this real work of childhood, children need opportunities to play and use toys for full personal expression. Accordingly, Elkind emphasizes the value of the arts in the elementary schools for obtaining a balance between work and play. In preschool environments the premium certainly should be on play and toys that give the greatest scope to the child's imagination—toys that allow for personal expression. This not only permits personal and autonomous activity and interpretation, but also is assumed to be appropriate cognitive enrichment that prepares the child for later school and life challenges.

ROLES OF THE ADULT

Parents and teachers of young children clearly are important in play development, as we have seen in Chapters 2 and 3. In this chapter we have surveyed the literature on play and personality development. We have shown how individual play behaviors are best viewed within a broader model of child development that takes into account developmental forces (the pull of the future), situational factors (the impact of the present), and individual differences (the push from the past). Parents and teachers influence play development in terms of the second and the third categories.

Given that adults have important roles in the development of play *in general,* what part do they play in the child's adoption of specific play styles *in particular?* Very little research has specifically focused on this question. Most of us would agree, however, that just as adults influence personality development in general, they can affect or change to a great degree play styles or a child's personality as expressed through play. For example, if a parent provides a child with a steady diet of reality-based object and puzzle play at the expense of other kinds of play, we would expect the child to develop an object-based style of play. If a parent enjoys and conveys enthusiasm for music and dance, we would expect that preference to be mirrored in a child's play. If a parent enjoys pretending and sharing a world of make-believe, it is safe to assume that this would influence the child accordingly. In sum, we may speculate that parents continually influence the styles of play behavior of young children, even if by the time the children are preschool age parents no longer play a major role.

As we have seen, researchers have tried to classify play styles and styles of children's personal expression during the preschool years using dichotomies such as visualizers versus verbalizers, patterners versus dramatists, configurational players versus narrational players (see Figure 4–1). Most children in varied settings no doubt show consistent patterns of play styles representative of each of these opposites. Thus, the divisions are artificial and probably are better interpreted as forming a progression, with children somewhere in the middle of each of the scales.

Valid questions remain nevertheless: Should teachers and parents attempt to foster in a child a particular brand of play style? Is it better to be a dramatist than to be a patterner? Although it is quite possible that deliberately promoting a certain style of play is doomed to fail or to backfire in any case, there are at least two reasons for arguing against attempting to modify a child's style of self-expression in play.

First, as we have noted, leading play scholars have cogently stated that play is an ego-building process, the importance of which should not be reduced or tampered with by play theorists and play practitioners. Children at play need to be in control in order for the activity to be playful, enjoyable, and beneficial. The sense of power, mastery, control, and autonomy accompanying play is too integral to play, and too critical to a child's development and well-being to jeopardize through deliberate intrusions by adults trying to cultivate a particular play style.

Sutton-Smith (1979) has discussed the subtlety with which this kind of intrusiveness can take place. For example, a parent may want a child to be more aggressive, domineering, or assertive in play—perhaps particularly if the child is a girl and if the parent seeks to raise a daughter able to succeed in today's corporate, competitive America. This parent may deliberately allow the girl to assume domineering roles in complementary role play with the parent (a child is the doctor and a parent is the subordinate patient). However, a closer examination of what is taking place reveals that the parent is calling all the shots about the play context even if the child is in control of the play text or what occurs within the script. Given the nature of communication as multiple level, even though the parent may feel that one particular play style is being promoted quite a different one may be the result which may become obvious in situations when the child is with peers. The child may be getting the message from the well-intentioned parent that others are to be in control of the play situation although the child is allowed by others to pretend to be in control once the play episode gets rolling. The point is that it is extremely difficult, if not impossible, to infer what the child is experiencing in play, what it means to the child, and what the predicted outcomes may or should be. Hence, any programmatic effort by adults to subtly or not so subtly manipulate play situations and events to foster a particular personality trait in a child cannot be recommended and should probably be avoided.

A second case against deliberately trying to influence personality or play styles is derived from recent work done on symbolic development and multiple intelligences (Gardner, 1983). According to Gardner's theory of multiple intelligences, each child is endowed at birth with specific genetic predispositions that evolve in interaction with environmental events to produce differing levels of talent in specific intellectual domains, or frames of mind as he calls them. He identifies the following intelligences: (1) logical-mathematical; (2) linguistic; (3) spatial; (4) kinesthetic; (5) musical; (6) intra-personal; and (7) inter-personal. The main educational implication he draws from his theory is that each child in early life becomes "at risk" or "at promise" in each domain given the sociocultural opportunities, encouragement, stimulation, or lack thereof, for each category of intelligence as found in the environment in which

FIGURE 4-1

Imaginative Play Styles Continua

Patterners	————————	Dramatists
Visualizers	————————	Verbalizers
Configurationalists	————————	Narrators
Object Dependent	————————	Object Independent

the child is developing. He recommends that, because one cannot prejudge in which areas a child may have latent talent, assuring a general exposure to all kinds of stimulation relevant to each type of intelligence is wiser than providing more limited but intensive exposure to only factors selected to affect a particular intelligence. Purposely attempting to foster a particular style of play in young children could preclude the child's finding the intellectual, expressive, and creative ways of being that are most natural. This is too much to risk, given that spontaneous playfulness in children appears to be so critical for later adjustment and creative expression.

SUMMARY

Play behavior and development are determined by differences in situation, cognitive maturity, and personality. Play during early childhood has been researched in terms of four variables: (1) people-versus-object orientation, (2) playfulness, (3) fantasy-making predispositions, and (4) imaginative play styles. Recent research suggests that the second and third variables are not single characteristics but that each has different aspects. Two aspects of playfulness are a cognitive component that may lead to creativity and humor comprehension and an affective component that is seen in the joy of play and the laughter in a joke. Aspects of fantasy-making predispositions include overt imaginative play tendencies and inner or private forms of fantasy. Styles of imaginative play identified were object-independent versus object-dependent orientations. Dramatists are less focused on objects in make-believe play than are patterners. These differences seem related to overall personality and underlying mental structures. Individual differences in object play have also been researched, showing variation in action-object combinations, play tempo, elaboration, organization, complexity, and attention span or play persistence.

Personality variation in play behavior and development relates to self-concept factors and situation factors. Theories of Erikson, Peller, and Sutton-Smith suggest how play serves ego-building functions to help alleviate anxieties, integrate development processes, cope with stress, and act as a catharsis for past personal events. Through the role reversals that are possible in play children gain a greater sense of autonomy and self-expansion; play is a medium that is self-enabling. For Elkind, play is the antidote to hurrying, or the pressures of growing up. Environmental factors influence individual differences. Home-life experiences, especially during the first and second years, influence play styles and skills. Less evidence exists for the importance of family structure variables than for the importance of parenting practices.

Adults must recognize the ubiquitous effects they have on young children's personality formation and the importance of remaining sensitive to the child's striving for independence and personal fulfillment. Instead of deliberately trying to shape play styles or personality, adults should provide broad support to help children find their own unique talents and preferences.

REFERENCES

Barnett, L.A., & Kleiber, D.A. (1984). Playfulness and the early play environment. *Genetic Psychological Monographs, 144,* 153–164.

Bishop, D., & Chace, C. (1971). Parental conceptual systems, home play environment, and potential creativity in children. *Journal of Experimental Child Psychology, 12* (3), 318–338.

Bruner, J.S. (1974). The nature and use of immaturity. In K. Connolly, & J.S. Bruner (Eds.), *The growth of competence.* London: Academic Press.

Coates, S., Lord, M., & Jakabovics, E. (1975). Field dependence-independence, social-nonsocial play and sex differences in preschool children. *Perceptual and Motor Skills, 40,* 195–202.

Dansky, J.L., & Silverman, I.W. (1975). Play: A general facilitator of associative fluency. *Developmental Psychology, 11,* 104.

Dunn, J., & Wooding, C. (1977). Play in the home and its implications for learning. In B. Tizard & D. Harvey (Eds.), *Biology of play.* London: Heinemann.

Elkind, D. (1981). *The hurried child: Growing up too fast too soon.* Menlo Park, CA: Addison-Wesley.

Emmerich, W. (1964). Continuity and stability in early social development. *Child Development, 35,* 311–332.

Emmerich, W. (1977). Evaluating alternative models of development: An illustrative study of preschool personal-social behaviors. *Child Development, 48,* 1401–1410.

Erikson, E.H. (1940). Studies and interpretation of play. Part I: Clinical observations of play disruption in young children. *Genetic Psychology Monograph, 22,* 557–671.

Erikson, E.H. (1963). *Childhood and society.* New York: W.W. Norton.

Erikson, E.H. (1972). *Play and actuality.* In M.W. Piers (Ed.) *Play and development.* New York: W.W. Norton.

Erikson, E.H. (1977). *Toys and reasons.* New York: W.W. Norton.

Fein, G. (1979). Play with actions and objects. In B. Sutton-Smith (Ed.), *Play and learning,* New York: Gardner Press.

Feitelson, W., & Ross, G.S. (1973). The neglected factor—play. *Human Development, 16,* 202–223.

Franklin, M (1985, March). *Play and the early evolution of social life: Views of two-year-olds at school.* Paper presented at the Anthropological Association for the Study of Play, Washington, D.C.

Gardner, H. (1983). *Frames of mind: The theory of multiple intelligences.* New York: Basic Books.

Hutt, C. (1966). Exploration and play in children. *Symposium of the Zoological Society of London, 18,* 61–81.

Hutt, C., & Bhavnani, R. (1972). Predictions from play. In J.S. Bruner, A. Jolly, & K. Sylvia (Eds.), *Play.* New York: Penguin.

Jennings, K.D. (1975). People versus object orientation, social behavior, and intellectual abilities in preschool children. *Developmental Psychology, 11,* 511–519.

Johnson, J.E. (1978). Mother-child interaction and imaginative behavior of preschool children. *The Journal of Psychology, 100,* 123–129.

Lieberman, J.N. (1977). *Playfulness: Its relationship to imagination and creativity.* New York: Academic Press.

Lindquist, T., Lind, J., & Harvey, D. (1977). Play in hospital. In B. Tizard & D. Harvey (Eds.), *Biology of play.* Philadelphia: Lippincott.

Matthews, W.S. (1977). Modes of transformation in the initiation of fantasy play. *Developmental Psychology, 12,* 211–236.

Miller, B.C., & Gerard, D. (1979). Family influences on the development of creativity in children: An integrative review. *The Family Coordinator,* July, 295–312.

Peller, L. (Ed.). (1952). Models of children's play. *Mental Hygiene, 36,* 66–83.

Pulaski, M.A. (1970). Play as a function of toy structure and fantasy predisposition. *Child Development, 41,* 531–537.

Rubin, K.H., Fein, G.G., & Vandenberg, B. (1983). Play. In E.H. Mussen (Ed.), *Handbook of child psychology, Vol. 4. Socialization, personality, and social development* (4th ed., pp. 693–774). New York: Wiley.

Shmukler, D. (1977). *Origins and concommitants of imaginative play in young children.* Unpublished manuscript, University of Witwatersrand, Johannesburg, South Africa.

Singer, J.L. (1961). Imagination and waiting ability in young children. *Journal of Personality, 29,* 396–413.

Singer, J.L. (Ed.). (1973). *The child's world of make-believe:* Experimental studies of imaginative play. New York: Academic Press.

Singer, J.L., & Singer, D.G. (1980). A factor analytic study of preschoolers' play behavior. *Academic Psychology Bulletin, 2,* 143–156.

Smilansky, S. (1968). *The effects of sociodramatic play on disadvantaged preschool children.* New York: Wiley.

Sutton-Smith, B. (1979). The play of girls. In C.B. Kopp & M. Kirkpatrick (Eds.), *Becoming female: Perspectives on development.* New York: Plenum.

Sutton-Smith, B. (1980). Piaget play and cognition revisited. In W. Overton (Ed.), *The relationship between social and cognitive development.* New York: Erlbaum.

Truhon, S.A. (1979, March). *Playfulness, play, and creativity: A path-analytic model.* Paper presented at the Biennial Meeting of the Society for Research in Child Development, San Francisco.

Witkin, H.A., Lewis, H.B., Hertzman, M., Machover, K., Meissner, P.B., & Wapner, S. (1954). *Personality through perception.* New York: Harper and Row.

Wolf, D., & Gardner, H. (1979). Style and sequence in early symbolic play. In M. Franklin & N. Smith (Eds.), *Symbolic functioning in childhood.* Hillsdale, NJ: Erlbaum.

Wolf, D., & Grollman, S.H. (1982). Ways of playing: Individual differences in imaginative style. In D.J. Pepler & K.H. Rubin (Eds.), *The play of children: Current theory and research.* Basel, Switzerland: Karger, AG.

5 Play and Social Development

As children mature, one of their major tasks is to acquire the skills, values, and knowledge that will enable them to function successfully in society. This process, which is known as socialization, occupies much of children's and their caregivers' energy during the preschool and elementary-grade years. During this period, children learn skills such as cooperation, sharing, and helping that enable them to get along with other people. They develop the ability to solve social problems and learn how to inhibit aggressive and impulsive behavior. These social skills require the ability to understand other people's thoughts and emotions and to see things from others' perspectives.

Play, being a major activity of childhood, is intricately involved in the socialization process. As was explained in Chapter 3, there is a two-way relationship between play and social development. The social environment is an important influence on children's play. Children learn attitudes and skills needed for play from their parents and other children. Parents and peers may also encourage certain types of play behavior and discourage others. At the same time, play acts as an important context in which children acquire social skills and social knowledge. In this chapter we will explore both sides of this relationship. We will begin by discussing how the social environment affects play and will then describe play's role in promoting social development.

SOCIAL INFLUENCES ON PLAY

The social environment influences play through three basic processes: reinforcement, modeling, and instruction. We will examine these three important processes and then explain how they are used by parents and peers to influence children's play.

Reinforcement

Behaviorists such as B. F. Skinner have demonstrated that behavior is often influenced by subsequent events. If a behavior is followed by a pleasurable consequence, the behavior tends to be repeated. Such consequences are known as positive reinforcers. Behaviors followed by negative consequences (punishments) are less likely to occur again.

Reinforcers are classified as being either primary or secondary in origin. Primary reinforcers are related directly to biological needs and are inherently reinforcing. Examples of primary positive reinforcers include food, water, and sexual activity. Pain is, of course, a primary punishment. Secondary reinforcers are initially neutral stimuli that acquire reinforcing qualities through repeated association with primary reinforcers. For example, if a bell were rung every time a baby was fed, the bell would soon become a secondary positive reinforcer. The baby would then tend to repeat actions that were followed by the sound of the bell. Verbal reproaches, such as "no" and "bad," quickly acquire punitive power because they often occur along with painful events such as spankings.

Social interactions that have acquired secondary reinforcing power are known as social reinforcers. Positive social reinforcers include (a) attention, (b) approval, and (c) affection. These reinforcers are the means through which parents and peers exert (often unconsciously) most of their influence on children's social behavior. For example, attention is often coupled with primary reinforcers (mothers pay attention to babies while feeding them). Attention soon comes to acquire reinforcing power of its own, sometimes with unforeseen consequences. If a child's parents always reprimand him for aggression during play, they may inadvertently be reinforcing the aggression by paying attention to it. It is often more effective to ignore the misbehavior. This lack of attention probably will cause the negative behavior to cease (a process known as extinction). The parents can assist this process by paying more attention when the child exhibits desirable behaviors during play and linking such behaviors with expressions of approval and affection.

Punishment can suppress behavior. It is not, however, a very reliable means of controlling the way children behave. As noted above, the attention that accompanies punishment may reinforce the behavior. In addition, punishment tends to be ineffective when not accompanied by new learning. If children are simply punished and not also taught an acceptable means of avoiding the punishment, they will tend to revert to the undesirable behavior as soon as the punishment is removed. For example, if a child is punished for hoarding toys when playing with siblings but is not taught how to share and why sharing is important, the selfish behavior will soon return because it the only behavior the child knows.

Modeling and Imitation

Parents, peers, and teachers also influence a child's social learning by acting as models. They demonstrate a variety of behaviors that children have a strong tendency to imitate. Research has documented that children learn many new behaviors, including play, through social imitation.

Children, of course, do not imitate every behavior that they observe. Bandura (1977) has developed a theory to explain when a child will imitate a particular model and the form in which the behavior will be imitated. Four component processes are involved: (a) *attention*—stimulus that causes the child to notice the behavior and the child's ability to perceive the action; (b) *retention*—the child's ability to interpret the behavior in terms of existing cognitive structures; (c) *motor reproduction*—the child's physical ability to reproduce the behavior; and (d) *motivation*—reinforcement that the child receives for imitating the behavior. Take, for example, a young girl watching her father cook dinner. If the behavior catches the girl's attention and she has previously been rewarded for copying her father, she may try to imitate what she sees. However, the girl probably will enact only a rough approximation of the actual activity. Her observational skills are limited, causing her to miss many important details. In addition, the child does not possess many of the concepts (such as measuring) needed to interpret some aspects of cooking, and she does not yet possess sufficiently developed motor skills to perform some of the more intricate techniques. What results is a series of actions, such as putting pans on the stove and stirring a spoon in a bowl, which match the child's cognitive and physical capabilities.

Bandura also investigated conditions that foster imitation. He found that children tend to imitate models who are powerful and who have control over things that the children desire. In a preschool setting, for example, children are more likely to imitate adults who distribute toys and snacks than they are to imitate other adults in the classroom. A second factor is the warmth and affection generated by the model. Children tend to imitate adults who are nurturant rather than cold and unresponsive. This finding points out the importance for parents and teachers to establish a warm, caring relationship with children.

Instruction

Adults also use instruction to teach children social behaviors. They give directions on how to behave and explain why particular behaviors are desirable or undesirable. For example, if a parent observes that Suzy is crying because Barbara will not let her play with a ball, the parent might instruct the children to roll the ball back and forth to each other. In this manner, the parent directly teaches sharing and cooperative behavior. Note, however, that no explanation was given about why these behaviors were preferable to hoarding.

One particular form of instruction, which is referred to as reasoning or induction, appears to have a vital role in children's acquisition of good social behaviors and attitudes. Induction involves appealing to children's positive feelings toward other people and explaining the reasons particular behaviors are desirable or undesirable. Hoffman (1983) contends that parents unconsciously adapt their induction explanations to fit children's developing social and cognitive abilities. When dealing with very young children, parents tend to emphasize the direct consequences of children's actions to others. In the example above, the parent might say to Barbara, "If you keep the ball all to yourself, Suzy won't have anything to play with and she'll cry."

Children enjoy imitating adult models whom they like and respect.

With older children, parents tend to focus on the psychological rather than the physical consequences of actions, taking advantage of the children's recently acquired perspective-taking skills. For example, the parent might explain to Barbara, "Suzy feels bad because she doesn't have anything to play with. Would you like to feel that way?" Research has shown that induction is more successful in permanently changing children's social behavior and attitudes than withdrawal of love or threats of punishment because induction helps children develop social understanding as well as knowledge of social norms.

Another useful concept for characterizing methods of instruction is the notion of distancing (Copple, Sigel, & Saunders, 1979). Distancing refers to the use of questions, statements, or changes in the environment that encourage children to think. Distancing stimuli (*e.g.*, questions) are directed toward separating the child from the concrete "here-and-now" reality. For example, a teacher or parent may ask a child to solve a social problem, or to plan ahead for a future social encounter, or to remember a past event such as what happened on the visit to the zoo last Saturday. Distancing strategies energize and channel the child's thinking and problem-solving abilities through the introduction of discrepancies between the child's current mental state and the sought-after end. Distancing stimulation must be followed up for the child to benefit from the use of this teaching strategy. "Use of Distancing Strategies and Children's Play" illustrates how it can be used to help children solve social problems during free play.

There are many different techniques of instruction; however, not all techniques work equally well in influencing the growing child. Effectiveness varies depending upon the child and upon the subject matter of learning. When is direct instruction— lecturing and giving directions—most effective? When is the use of induction or distancing more appropriate?

Script writers of Children's Television Workshop, the producers of "Sesame Street," employ a useful guide for selecting instructional methods based on the area of learning. When the goal is to help children master academic subject matter such as letters, words, and numbers or other specific content such as shapes, colors, and seasons of the year, a fast-paced format featuring repeated presentation of material is the chosen (*i.e.*, a very direct method of instruction). When the goal is to help children realize the right thing to do or say in a social situation, the learning message is presented in a vignette or script involving the popular "Sesame Street" characters (*i.e.*, an indirect method). By viewing such dramatizations, children infer appropriate and inappropriate behaviors and their rationales. For example, they see what happens to Cookie Monster and realize why it is better to share than be stingy.

Teachers and parents can employ this general strategy when selecting instructional methods for teaching young children. Indirect methods work best for social lessons, like showing a child the value of cooperation or why it is not nice to tease others. Formats used can include vignettes or scripts involving storybooks, puppets, or dramatic play. In contrast, direct instruction is more effective to help children learn academic subjects. Adults can tell children about words and letters associated with everyday activities (pointing out and pronouncing the words on signs to a child while on a shopping trip). By asking the child to repeat the content, it becomes natural and automatic. Such instruction is, to be sure, less fast-paced than "Sesame Street" but nevertheless exemplifies a direct method of teaching.

Effects on Play

During infancy, parents are the primary agents of socialization. As children grow

---

USE OF DISTANCING STRATEGIES AND CHILDREN'S PLAY

Dr. Irving E. Sigel, the creator of the distancing theory of the development of representational competence, was the director of experimental early childhood programs at the University of Buffalo and then at Educational Testing Service (ETS) during the 1970s and 1980s. He shares many anecdotes about teachers' use of distancing strategies, not only to instruct but also to use with children in classroom management. One example concerned a dispute over the use of the large building blocks in the preschool classroom at the ETS Child Care Center. The boys felt they had sole rights to the blocks—at least they behaved that way until the girls brought their complaint to the teachers. The teachers decided to devote part of the time after a free-play period to discuss the issue. After the children, boys and girls alike, agreed that indeed there was a block-area monopoly by the boys, the teachers used "distancing strategies" to try to lead the children to a solution of the conflict. The teachers began by asking if it was fair for the boys to monopolize the blocks, and, if not, whether some way could be worked out to share the use of blocks.

The childrens' responses to this line of questioning were innovative. To defend their block monoply, some of the boys let it be known that girls (and women) are not strong enough to lift the large blocks. This rationalization was quickly disproved when one of the girls demonstrated her block-lifting prowess. When the teachers asked the children for older, peers begin to have a larger role in the social learning process. Teachers become another important influence as children start school. In the following sections, we will examine how each of these groups use the processes of reinforcement, modeling, and instruction to influence play. The impact of another important social influence, the society in which the child lives, will be discussed in Chapter 7, "Social Class and Culture."

Parents. Parents indirectly affect play by teaching children social skills needed for playing with other children. Research has shown that parents use modeling, reinforcement, instruction, and induction to promote the development of sharing, cooperation, helping, and other forms of altruistic behavior (Radke-Yarrow, Zahn-Waxler, & Chapman, 1983). These skills help children become good play partners and increase the chances that they will be able to engage successfully in sociodramatic and other forms of group play.

Parents directly influence play by encouraging certain types of play. During infancy, much of this encouragement occurs in parent-child games. These games are characterized by mutual involvement, turn alternation, repetition of activities, and pretense (Hay, Ross, & Goldman, 1979). During such games, parents use reinforcement, rewarding desired play behaviors with praise and attention. Modeling is another key component in these initial parent-child games. By actually playing with the child, the parents model important play behaviors such as turn taking and the use of make-believe. A number of researchers, including Smilansky (1968) and Singer

possible fair ways to use the blocks, one child answered that on every other day girls could use them but not boys. One boy piped up that on his "off" day he wouldn't come to school! Other children agreed that this solution might not be best. Another suggestion was splitting the free-play period in half and having the boys and girls take turns using the large blocks. Finally, it was decided that the real problem was the number of children in the block area, not the composition of the group based on gender. Accordingly, the teachers and children voted to post a sign by the block area to remind the group that only four children at a time could use the large blocks.

There are many other ways to use distancing questions to manage and instruct children at play time in homes or schools. To give another example, asking children what they will be doing next in the daily schedule often helps to quiet and reorient youngsters who are too intensely involved in a play session. Such distancing techniques may facilitate smooth transitions through clean-up time or re-entry into the larger group after exciting play in a small group. One teacher remarked after observing how effective distancing strategies were in this regard, "It's much better than before, when it was like you were shooting kids out of a cannon after their thematic fantasy play tutoring!" The use of distancing strategies is strongly recommended.

(1973), contend that this early parental modeling is crucial to the development of pretend play.

Research has revealed the following developmental trend in early parent-child games: (a) at first, the infants have a passive role and exhibit amusement and attention when their parents play with them; (b) at approximately eight months, infants begin to assume an active role; and (c) by twelve months, the infants begin to initiate their own games with their parents (Ross & Kay, 1980). This trend implies that it is important for parents to take the initiative and start playing with their babies soon after birth. The babies will watch the play and will soon learn to play themselves. The Sutton-Smiths (1974) have described an effective procedure parents can use to initiate games with young babies outlined in the example "Parent-

PARENT-CHILD GAMES

In their book, *How to Play with Your Child (and When Not to)*, Brian and Shirley Sutton-Smith describe a very effective strategy that parents can use for initiating play with their babies. Parents should begin by imitating the baby's actions whenever possible. For example, if a baby makes a funny noise, the parent should make a similar sound. Eventually the baby will repeat the sound the parent imitated, and a game of repetitive noisemaking will begin. The Sutton-Smiths explain the principle behind this game-initiation strategy: "By responding to babies in terms of what they can do, you give them a chance to respond to you with what they have" (1973, p. 12).

The Sutton-Smiths also describe large number of games which parents can play with children from birth to age thirteen. The following are some of the games they recommend for use with infants and toddlers:

Birth to Three Months

1. Imitate baby, make baby noises
2. Alternate noises with baby (gurgles)
3. "Baby talk" (long vowels and high pitch)
4. Make clown faces
5. Poke out your tongue
6. Let baby pull your pinky

Three to Six Months

1. Make baby laugh (very regular behavior)
2. Do gymnastics with baby (bounce on bed, turn upside down)
3. Blow raspberries on baby's body
4. Play "pretend" walking, "pretend" standing
5. Let baby pull your hair
6. Play "This Little Pig" (induce anticipation)

Child Games." In addition, a number of games for playing with infants and toddlers are listed.

By the time children have reached two years of age, the parents' role tends to shift from that of a direct participant in play to that of an attentive spectator (Dunn & Dale, 1984). From this spectator role, parents encourage play by reinforcing it with their attention. They also teach play skills to their children. For example, Miller and Garvey (1984) found that mothers frequently used direct instruction to assist their two-year-old daughters' dramatic play:

> Caregivers provided support for the children's portrayals, helping them to achieve fuller realizations of mothering. This support took various forms, including a great

---

Six to Twelve Months

1. Rough-house
2. Grab and give up (give and take)
3. Play peek-a-boo (locate object or person)
4. Bury baby under blanket
5. Ride camel (parent on all fours, baby on parent's back)
6. Make baby laugh (sound, touch, social, and visual stimuli)

One to Two Years

1. Chase, be chased (one at a time)
2. Hide thimble (object permanence)
3. Empty, fill
4. Play catch
5. Play phony birthdays
6. Have tug-of-war

Note how the later games take advantage of the child's developing cognitive and motor abilities. Instructions for playing these and many other parent-child games are contained in the Sutton-Smiths' book.

SOURCE: Adapted from Sutton-Smith & Sutton-Smith (1974, pp. 253–254).

deal of explicit instruction and direction. Caregivers identified or explained props (e.g., "Here. Here. Use this baby bottle"), told the child how to behave with baby (e.g., "Pat the baby"), what to say to baby (e.g., "Say 'chew it up.' Tell the baby, say 'chew it up' "), and how to say it (e.g., "Go 'aw' "). In addition, caregivers explicitly demonstrated mothering behavior. (pp. 115–116)

The mothers only occasionally joined in their daughters' play and modeled mothering play. It appears that, from age two onwards, direct instruction becomes an important factor in parent-child play.

Peers. As children grow older, their play becomes increasingly social (see Chapter 3). By the time they reach the ages of three and four, children usually engage in a considerable amount of group play. As a result, their play becomes much more dependent on other children.

Peers use two of the same basic processes to influence play as do parents: reinforcement and modeling (Hartup, 1983). There is, however, an important difference in how these processes are used. Whereas parents primarily influence play from the outside (at least after children have reached age two), peers usually affect play by direct participation (Dunn & Dale, 1984). From this role of co-player, peers often use selective reinforcement and modeling to shape their partners' play behaviors.

One area in which peers have a particularly strong impact is in the encouragement of sex-typed behavior. Fagot (1977) recorded preschoolers' reactions to their peers' sex-typed activities during free play. She found that boys received more peer criticism than girls when engaging in doll play and make-believe with domestic themes but more positive reactions when engaging in sandbox play and hammering. Conversely, girls received more positive reactions than boys when engaging in domestically oriented pretend play. This selective reinforcement and punishment of sex-typed behaviors by peers has been found to increase the duration of preschoolers' sex-typed behaviors (Lamb & Roopnarine, 1979).

Researchers have investigated how peer characteristics such as age, sex, and familiarity affect children's play. For example, children have been found to engage in more dramatic play with same-age peers and familiar peers than with younger, older, or unfamiliar children (Doyle, Connolly, & Rivest, 1980; Roopnarine & Johnson, 1983).

Other studies have examined how the play of handicapped children is influenced by the opportunity to play with nonhandicapped peers. The results of this research have been mixed. Some investigators have reported that handicapped children engage in more social play with nonhandicapped peers, while others have found that the presence of nonhandicapped peers has no effect on the social level of handicapped children's play (McHale & Olley, 1982). In an interesting offshoot of this line of research, several investigators have taught nonhandicapped peers how to play with handicapped children, with positive results (Strain, 1981).

Teachers. Young children who attend day care centers or preschools come into contact with teachers, who influence their play behavior through the three processes of reinforcement, modeling, and instruction. However, the teacher's role in children's play is more varied than that of parents or peers. As diagrammed in Figure 2-1 (see p. 28), providing for, observing, and involving oneself in children's play all entail specific responsibilities. Teachers need to arrange time and space for play and provide play materials for groups of children who are usually heterogeneous in age and gender. Teachers must develop a skilled eye for observing play and know when it is appropriate to join, assist, or train children at play.

Teachers, more than parents or peers, make decisions that influence children's play. Planning and problem solving are used to design and implement a play environment for a group of children. As we shall discuss in Chapter 12, dimensions of the early childhood educational curriculum have an impact on children's play, and teachers are typically responsible for the curriculum and its implementation.

PLAY'S ROLE IN SOCIAL DEVELOPMENT

We have described how the social practices of parents, peers, and teachers can affect children's play. Conversely, play has a key role in social development by providing a context in which children can acquire many important social skills such as turn taking, sharing, and cooperation, as well as the ability to understand other people's thoughts, perceptions, or emotions. Thus, while the social environment influences play, play also affects children's ability to get along in the social environment.

In this section, we will begin by reviewing the evidence linking play with the growth of social skills and perspective-taking ability. Next, we will discuss the current controversy over which aspect or component of play training is responsible for gains in social competence. We will then suggest how parents and teachers can best use play to promote children's social development.

Social Skills

Studies by Garvey (1974) and others have provided detailed descriptions of the social abilities underlying group play. The most fundamental of these is the ability to understand the rules of play. All social play is rule-governed. Even simple parent-infant games such a peek-a-boo require the establishment of the rule that participants take turns. In sociodramatic play, the rules become much more complex. For example, once children adopt a role, their behavior must be consistent within that role. If their behavior becomes inappropriate, such as a baby acting like an adult, the other players will usually issue a sharp reprimand. Unlike formal games with rules, rules for play are not set in advance; rather, the rules are established by the players during the course of the play. This conscious manipulation of rules provides an opportunity for children to examine the nature of rules and rule making. Therefore, play is a context in which children not only learn specific rules such as turn taking but also learn about the meaning of rules in general.

Children must also be able to construct and vary the theme of the play activity together (Garvey, 1974). This joint planning ability is particularly important in sociodramatic play. To successfully engage in group dramatizations, children must first agree on who will adopt each role and on the make-believe identities of objects and actions. For example, they might agree that Janice will be a doctor, Judy a nurse, and Joey a sick patient. It might then be decided that a pencil will be used as if it were a thermometer and a cylindrical block will be a syringe. The children must also make cooperative decisions about the story sequence. Janice, Judy, and Joey might agree that first, the doctor will take the patient's temperature; next, the nurse will administer a painful injection; and finally, the doctor will perform an operation. These initial plans can be altered during the course of the play. The children may decide, for example, that a second injection is needed before the operation can be performed. This type of joint planning requires give-and-take and cooperation. Children who do not go along with the group's consensus are often excluded from the play. On the other hand, cooperation is rewarded by inclusion in a successful dramatization.

Descriptive studies have provided evidence that social play requires a number of abilities such as turn alternation and cooperation; these findings suggest that play may have a role in the acquisition or consolidation of these social skills. This possibility has motivated researchers to investigate further the relationship between play and social competence.

Several investigators have reported significant correlations between levels of group dramatic play and measures of peer popularity and social skills (Connolly & Doyle, 1984; Rubin & Hayvern, 1981). Children who frequently engaged in sociodramatic play were rated as more popular by both teachers and peers. These children were also rated as more socially skilled by their teachers. In addition, the high-sociodramatic-play children exhibited more positive social actions toward peers. Parallel constructive play (sitting on the floor with other children, independently playing with blocks) has also been found to correlate significantly with peer popularity, teacher ratings of social competence, and a measure of social problem solving (Rubin, 1982).

Given the high social demands of group dramatic play, the relationship between this form of play and measures of social competence is hardly surprising. A high degree of social skill may be required for children to engage in this advanced form of play, or group dramatic play may help children acquire these social abilities. (Note that because of the correlational nature of the above studies, the causal direction of the relationship cannot be determined.) The finding that parallel constructive play is also related to measures of social skill is less easy to explain. Rubin (1982) speculates that the relationship may be based on the fact that parallel constructive play closely resembles the group activities that commonly occur in preschool and elementary school classrooms. Children who frequently engage in parallel constructive play may be better able to adjust to school activities and therefore be rated as socially competent and popular by their teachers.

To investigate causal relationships between play and social competence, several researchers have conducted training studies in which children were taught or

Group play provides the opportunity for children to learn important social skills like sharing.

encouraged by an adult to engage in sociodramatic play (see Chapter 2 for a description of play-tutoring procedures). Results showed that the training not only resulted in gains in group dramatic play but also led to increases in positive peer interaction and cooperation (Rosen, 1974; Smith, Dalgleish, & Herzmark, 1981; Udwin, 1983). These findings both indicate that play training enhances social development and support the position that engaging in group dramatic play promotes the acquisition of social skills. However, as we will discuss in the section on "Causes," other factors associated with the training, such as adult and/or peer interaction, also may have been responsible for the gains in social competence.

Perspective Taking

Perspective taking is the ability to see things from other people's point of view. It involves understanding what other people see (visual perspective taking), think (cognitive perspective taking), and feel (affective perspective taking or empathy). These abilities have an important role in social and moral development. For example, children are better able to solve interpersonal problems if they accurately understand one another's thoughts and feelings. Altruistic behavior such as generosity is motivated by an understanding of other people's distress and the joy they experience as a result of a generous act. In addition, perspective-taking ability has been found to be positively related to children's level of moral reasoning (Selman, 1971).

Research by Piaget and others has shown that young children have great difficulty with all forms of perspective taking. This difficulty is generally attributed to the egocentric nature of their thought. For young children, the self and non-self are not differentiated, leading them to assume that their point of view is the *only* point of view. As children mature, the self gradually "decenters" and becomes separated from the environment. This process of decentration makes it possible for children to realize that other people can have perceptions, thoughts, and feelings that are different than their own.

Sociodramatic play may have an important role in the development of children's perspective-taking abilities. While engaging in group dramatizations, children act out a variety of roles. A child might, on different occasions, take on the role of a baby, parent, grandparent, firefighter and superhero. In order to portray such characters accurately, children must be able to mentally put themselves in other people's places and experience the world from others' points of view. This act of consciously transforming their own identities into a variety of make-believe identities may hasten the decentration process, thereby promoting perspective taking and a number of other cognitive skills (Rubin, Fein, & Vandenberg, 1983).

METACOMMUNICATIONS

Observational research by Garvey (1977) and others has revealed that children use two types of verbal exchanges while engaging in group dramatic play: pretend communications and metacommunications. Pretend communications occur when the children adopt roles and make comments appropriate for those roles. During these exchanges children address each other by their pretend names (or at least attempt to do so). For example, if two children are enacting a hospital scene, one child might say, "Doctor, I'm very sick. Can you make me better?" Pretend communications are made within the play frame that the children have established. Metacommunications, on the other hand, occur when children temporarily break the play frame and make comments about the play itself. When making these comments, children resume their real-life identities and address each other by their actual names. In the above hospital scene, if the child acting as doctor made an inappropriate action or comment, the other child might say, "Suzy, doctors don't do that." Such exchanges are used to resolve conflicts over roles, rules, the make-believe identity of objects, and the course of the story line—conflicts that arise during the course of a dramatization. Rubin (1980) contends that these conflicts are responsible for much of play's positive effects on social development.

The following transcript from a study by Giffin (1984) illustrates the extent to which children engage in metacommunicative exchanges and conflicts during the course of sociodramatic play. In this episode, Heather (age 5), Andy (age 4), and Kathy (age 3½) are enacting a story about about a wedding:

"Bad Mother"

[Heather (H.), Kathy (K.), and Andy (A.) are playing in the dress-up room of a preschool]
H.   (to K.) You're crying in the wedding place. Make the crying sound.
     (K. "cries.")

Recent research has generally supported this proposed link between sociodramatic play and perspective taking. Correlational studies have reported positive relationships between levels of group dramatic play and children's perspective-taking abilities (Connolly & Doyle, 1984; Rubin & Maioni, 1975), and a number of other studies have shown that sociodramatic play training resulted in gains in children's performance on visual, cognitive, and affective perspective-taking tasks (Burns & Brainerd, 1979). However, as was the case with research on social skills, methodological limitations, including problems with assessment instruments and the confounding effects of adult and peer interaction, have prevented these studies from providing conclusive evidence that dramatic play causes growth in perspective-taking ability.

H.	What's the matter? You want to get married is why?
	(to A.) She wants to get married so she's crying. You should get married.
	Let's say you guys were already married, OK?
A.	No! I'm going to put on the song.
	(The play stove becomes a disco booth.)
H.	Andy has to put on the song and then he'll dance with you.
	(to A.) Give me the song.
K.	You have to come and dance with me Andy.
A.	No I...Dad.
H.	And he can't dance.
	And you say what's the matter with me, Andy.
	(H. "cries.")
H.	My mother yelled at me.
	Let's say you gave me a spanking, Kathy O'Neil.
K.	No, my name is Annie.
H.	Annie, let's say you gave me a spanking. And I call you Mom.
	(to A.) Daddy, I'm crying 'cause my mother gave me a spanking and she yelled at me.
A.	I'll kill her!

Notice how Heather uses metacommunications to structure the story and to prompt the other players. Andy and Kathy each use metacommunications to rebuff other players for not using their pretend names. Through such exchanges, children gain valuable experience in solving social problems, and they also learn a lot about rules and roles in the process.

SOURCE: Adapted from Giffin (1984, pp. 96–97).

Causes

The research reviewed above has shown that training in group dramatic play can result in gains in social skills and perspective taking. As noted, however, there is some controversy over which aspect or component of the play training is primarily responsible for these gains in social development. There are several possibilities:

1. The play itself—object and role transformations that occur in dramatic play may hasten the decentration process.
2. Adult instruction—the adult-child interaction that occurs during the training may directly or indirectly teach the children new skills.
3. Peer interaction—the conflicts among children that occur in sociodramatic play may cause cognitive imbalance or disequilibrium, resulting in new learning.

Peter Smith tested the first two possibilities by carefully monitoring and controlling the adult-child interaction in a large-scale training study (Smith, Dalgleish, & Herzmark, 1981). Results indicated that adult instruction may have been responsible for many of the *cognitive* gains brought about by the training, including higher scores on measures of intelligence, creativity, and perspective taking. However, the play itself appeared to be responsible for the increased positive *social* interaction resulting from the play training. Thus it is possible that the two components of play training have an impact on different areas of development: adult instruction primarily affects cognition and play itself primarily affects social competence. This hypothesis is purely speculative and needs to be confirmed by further research.

Observational research by Garvey (1977) and others has revealed that children often engage in conflicts during the course of group dramatic play. They argue over roles, rules, the story line, and the make-believe identities of objects (see the selection "Metacommunications" on pp. 102–103 for an example). These conflicts do not occur during the dramatic play itself; rather, they occur during "frame breaks," in which the children temporarily leave their make-believe roles and assume their real-life identities. Once the conflicts are resolved, the children resume their make-believe roles and the play continues.

The peer conflicts that occur during sociodramatic play are undoubtedly responsible for some of play training's impact on perspective taking and social development. Rubin explains:

> Rule understanding, the comprehension of obligations and prohibitions, and the ability to consider reciprocal role relations may be less a function of non-literal social play per se and more the outcome of peer interaction and conflict.... When children beg to differ concerning issues of importance to them, cognitive disequilibria are likely to ensue. Since such mental states are not pleasurable, conflict resolution is necessary. Often, when disequilibrium is provoked by social conflict, compromise results. Suffice it to say that compromise is accommodative and adaptive. In short, given conflict, the child comes to realize that: (1) survival in the social world, as well as (2) popularity among peers are marked by compromises and socialized thoughts. (Rubin 1980, p. 80)

During sociodramatic play, children often use "frame breaks" to settle disputes and to plan what happens next in their dramatization.

Because peer interaction and conflict are integral parts of group dramatic play, their effects are difficult if not impossible to separate from those of other aspects of play. It may be best to think of play training as a context in which make-believe role enactment, peer conflicts, and adult instruction all combine to promote children's social-cognitive development. Perhaps some day researchers may be able to untangle the separate contributions of each component of play training, but for now the fact remains that such training appears to be effective in the development of perspective taking and social competence.

ROLES OF THE ADULT

In this chapter, we have described how play is affected by the socialization practices of adults and peers and how play contributes to the socialization process as well. Parents and teachers should take this two-way relationship into account when using play to foster social development. Children should be encouraged to engage in social play through a conducive environment and by play tutoring if needed. This will indicate whether or not the children have the prerequisite social skills needed for group play.

Providing a conducive environment for group play involves several factors. First, at least one other playmate must be available. Research reviewed earlier in this chapter indicates that familiar playmates and those of the same age tend to elicit higher levels of group dramatic play than unfamiliar or different-age children. Second, there needs to be adequate space for several children to play together. When the space per child is less than 25 square feet, aggression increases and group play tends to decrease (Smith & Connolly, 1980). Third, adequate time needs to be provided. It takes a considerable amount of time to organize and plan a group dramatization or a group construction project. If play periods are too short and group play episodes are consistently nipped in the bud, children may eventually give up trying to engage in these important types of play. Finally, certain materials, such as dress-up clothes, dolls, housekeeping props, vehicles, and blocks, tend to encourage social play (see Chapter 9). Be sure to make many of these high-social-value materials available for children.

As described in Chapter 2, play tutoring can also be used to promote social play. With outside intervention, the adult can make comments and suggestions that will lead children to play together. For example, if two children are engaging in parallel constructive play—both are on the carpet playing with blocks but are not interacting with each other—an adult might suggest that the two children build a fort or some other type of structure. Inside intervention can also be used to foster group play. The parent or teacher can take on a role and, while enacting this role, try to get several children involved in social play. For example if one child is engaging in make-believe play with trucks while another is playing with a dollhouse, the adult might begin playing with the trucks and say, "Let's deliver some furniture to the house over there." This might get the two children to integrate their solitary make-believe into group play involving both trucks and the dollhouse.

If provision and adult involvement are successful and the children begin to engage in group play, the play itself should help the child acquire social skills. If, on the other hand, these steps fail to elicit social play, then it is likely that the children lack some of the social skills needed for this type of play. Careful observation of the children's unsuccessful attempts at collaborative play can reveal the identity of these missing skills. The parent or teacher can then use reinforcement, modeling, and indirect forms of instruction such as induction or distancing to help the children acquire these skills. Another attempt should then be made to get the children involved in group play.

SUMMARY

The research reviewed in this chapter indicates that the social environment—the adults and peers with whom children interact—has an important influence on play. As a result of reinforcement, modeling, and instruction, children learn many of the social skills needed to participate in group play. Once they begin to engage regularly in such play, the play itself and the social interaction that occurs during play will help promote their social development. For example, children must learn to share, take turns, cooperate, and inhibit aggression in order to get their peers to play with them and to sustain the play. Social play may also help develop the ability to view the world from other people's perspectives.

Parents and teachers should attempt to provide settings that are conducive to social play. Most children will take advantage of such settings and begin to engage in group play on their own. Others, however, will not. Special help such as play tutoring or instruction in basic social skills may be necessary in order to involve these children in group play.

REFERENCES

Bandura, A. (1977). *Social learning theory*. Englewood Cliffs, NJ: Prentice Hall.

Burns, S.M., & Brainerd, C.J. (1979). Effects of constructive and dramatic play on perspective taking in very young children. *Developmental Psychology, 15*, 512–521.

Connolly, J.A., & Doyle, A. (1984). Relation of social fantasy play to social competence in preschoolers. *Developmental Psychology, 20*, 797–806.

Copple, C., Sigel I., & Saunders, R. (1979). *Educating the young thinker: Classroom strategies for cognitive growth*. New York: Van Nostrand.

Doyle, A., Connolly, J., & Rivest, L. (1980). The effect of playmate familiarity on the social interactions of young children. *Child Development, 51*, 217–223.

Dunn, J., & Dale, N. (1984). I a daddy: 2-year-olds' collaboration in joint pretend with sibling and mother. In I. Bretherton (Ed.), *Symbolic play: The development of social understanding* (pp. 131–158). Orlando, FL: Academic Press.

Fagot, B.I. (1977). Consequences of moderate cross-gender behavior in preschool children. *Child Development, 48*, 902–907.

Garvey C. (1974). Some properties of social play. *Merrill-Palmer Quarterly, 20*, 163–180.

Garvey, C. (1977). *Play*. Cambridge, MA: Harvard University Press.

Giffin, H. (1984). The coordination of meaning in the creation of a shared make-believe reality. In I. Bretherton (Ed.), *Symbolic play: The development of social understanding* (pp. 73–100). Orlando, FL: Academic Press.

Hartup, W. (1983). Peer relations. In P.H. Mussen (Ed.), *Handbook of child psychology: Vol. 4. Socialization, personality, and social development* (4th ed., pp. 103–196). New York: Wiley.

Hay, D., Ross, H., & Goldman, B.D. (1979). Social games in infancy. In B. Sutton-Smith (Ed.), *Play and learning* (pp. 83–107). New York: Gardner.

Hoffman, M. (1983). Affective and cognitive processes in moral internalization. In E.T. Higgins, D.N. Ruble, & W.W. Hartup (Eds.), *Social cognition and social behavior: Developmental perspectives*. New York: Cambridge University Press.

Lamb, M.E. & Roopnarine, J.L. (1979). Peer influence on sex role development in preschoolers. *Child Development, 50*, 1219–1222.

McHale, S.M., & Olley, J.G. (1982). Using play to facilitate the social development of handicapped children. *Topics in Early Childhood Special Education, 2* (3), 76–86.

Miller, P., & Garvey, C. (1984). Mother-baby role play: Its origins in social support. In I. Bretherton (Ed.), *Symbolic play: The development of social understanding* (pp. 101–130). Orlando, FL: Academic Press.

Radke-Yarrow, M., Zahn-Waxler, C., & Chapman, M. (1983). Children's prosocial dispositions and behavior. In P.H. Mussen (Ed.), *Handbook of child psychology, Vol. 4: Socialization, personality, and social development* (4th ed., pp. 469–545). New York: Wiley.

Roopnarine, J.L., & Johnson, J.E. (1983). Kindergarteners' play with preschool- and school-aged children within a mixed-age classroom. *Elementary School Journal, 83*, 578–586.

Rosen, C.E. (1974). The effects of sociodramatic play on problem-solving behavior among culturally disadvantaged preschool children. *Child Development, 45*, 920–927.

Ross, H.S., & Kay, D.A. (1980). The origins of social games. In K.H. Rubin (Ed.), *Children's play* (pp. 17–31). San Francisco: Jossey-Bass.

Rubin, K.H. (1980). Fantasy play: Its role in the development of social skills and social cognition. In K.H. Rubin (Ed.), *Children's play* (pp. 69–84). San Francisco: Jossey-Bass.

Rubin, K.H. (1982). Nonsocial play in preschoolers: Necessarily evil? *Child Development, 53,* 651–657.

Rubin, K.H., Fein, G.G., & Vandenberg, B. (1983). Play. In P.H. Mussen (Ed.), *Handbook of child psychology: Vol. 4., Socialization, personality, and social development* (4th ed., pp. 693–774). New York: Wiley.

Rubin, K.H., & Hayvren, M. (1981). The social and cognitive play of preschool-aged children differing with regard to sociometric status. *Journal of Research and Development in Education, 14,* 116–122.

Rubin, K.H., & Maioni, T.L. (1975). Play preference and its relationship to egocentrism, popularity and classification skills in preschoolers. *Merrill-Palmer Quarterly, 21,* 171–179.

Selman, R.L. (1971). The relation of role-taking to the development of moral judgment in children. *Child Development, 42,* 79–92.

Singer, J.L. (1973). *The child's world of make-believe: Experimental studies of imaginative play.* New York: Academic Press.

Smilansky, S. (1968). *The effects of sociodramatic play on disadvantaged preschool children.* New York: Wiley.

Smith, P.K., & Connolly, K.J. (1980). *The ecology of preschool behavior.* Cambridge, England: Cambridge University Press.

Smith, P.K., Dalgleish, M., & Herzmark, G. (1981). A comparison of the effects of fantasy play tutoring and skills tutoring in nursery classes. *International Journal of Behavioral Development, 4,* 421–441.

Strain, P.S. (1981). Peer-mediated treatment of exceptional children's social withdrawal. *Exceptional Education Quarterly, 1,* 93–105.

Sutton-Smith, B., & Sutton-Smith, S. (1974). *How to play with your children (and when not to).* New York: Hawthorn.

Udwin, O. (1983). Imaginative play training as an intervention method with institutionalized preschool children. *British Journal of Educational Psychology, 53,* 32–39.

Gender Differences in Play

In Chapter 3 we traced from birth to six years developmental sequences in social play, object play, symbolic play, and motor play. In Chapter 4 we studied personality development and play—individual differences in play behavior and style. Now, suppose we were asked to predict how a particular child would play in a randomly selected situation, but we knew absolutely nothing about the child. If we could ask two questions to learn two facts about the child, which facts would be most helpful in predicting the child's play behavior?

Next to chronological age as an estimate of developmental level, gender is the best single predictor of how a child would react in a randomly chosen situation. Throughout life, age and gender account for more of the variability in a person's general behavior than any other pair of personal attributes.

In this chapter we will first summarize the findings of selected research studies dealing with gender differences in the four major areas of play: physical or motor play, social play, object play, and pretend play. We will extend this discussion by adding selected findings concerning sex differences in toy preferences, team or group activities, and imaginary companions. We will also discuss environmental factors influencing play for both sexes as well as recent trends in goals and values for socialization of boys and girls. As in previous chapters, we will offer suggestions to the adult practitioner interested in affecting play, viewing parents and teachers as potential agents of change for the way girls and boys play during the early years.

GENERAL PLAY FORMS

By the time children enter the preschool classroom or day care center they show extensive sex differences as well as similarities in play behavior. Both similarities and differences will be noted in the following sections dealing with general behavior in physical play, social play, object play, and pretense play. Unless specified otherwise, the studies reviewed involved middle-class children. Consideration of how boys and girls reach the point where they play differently will be saved for subsequent sections of this chapter concerning socialization influences; consideration of how culture and socioeconomic status affect sex-differentiated play will be saved for Chapter 7, "Social Class and Culture."

Physical Play

Physical or motor play is defined as gross- and fine-muscle activity or the use of body parts in play. As we discussed in Chapter 3, objects are not the focus of this form of play but outdoor or indoor play equipment, such as large mats, climbing frames, or trampolines, are often used. Natural features of the environment may also be involved. For example, children can walk along a fallen log, skip across a grassy area,

---

DO BOYS AND GIRLS REALLY PLAY SO DIFFERENTLY?

Although many research studies have led to the conclusion that boys and girls play differently along various dimensions, it is important to avoid simple generalizations or overstatements. How common it is to hear anecdotes from teachers and parents, sometimes with some concern, about a child playing in a way some may think is totally opposite from what one would expect based upon the child's gender. Take the following illustration.

On the third floor of an urban school, a rooftop served as an outdoor play area for pre-school-aged children. Because the roof's surface was hard, little if any rough-and-tumble play occurred, although a great deal of highly charged activity involving Big Wheels or other large toy vehicles was regularly observed. Also available were a climbing frame and other outdoor playground equipment. Cindy, a lively three-year-old, was one of the spunkiest of the youngsters in gross-motor activity, which many times involved "Superhero" themes. The toy vehicles became Ram Chargers or Wind Raiders as superheroes and villains raced around the area chasing one another. Cindy always looked forward to play time and was a frequent participant in such play.

Cindy also was one of the most athletic in climbing and swinging. One day, unbeknownst to her teachers, who were momentarily distracted by an altercation involving other children, Cindy pushed a slide which had become unbolted from the roof to the wall surrounding the rooftop playground and used the slide's ladder to climb to the top of the wall, on the edge of a three-story drop to the parking lot. Imagine the fright of the teacher who saw her there. Fortunately, that teacher had the good sense not to shout to Cindy or make a hurried move toward her. Instead, she quietly and calmly approached the child, slowly extended her arms, and Cindy jumped safely down to her. Cindy soon resumed her active play and the teachers, shaken, discussed safeguards against a repetition of the incident.

---

or fall and roll down the slope of a hill.

There is a general consensus in the research literature that preschool boys display more rough-and-tumble play than do girls. Rough-and-tumble play, as defined in Chapter 3, is play fighting, not real fighting. Boys tend to engage in this form of play much more often than girls do. They chase one another, wrestle, and struggle, often while pretending to be fictional characters. Moreover, boys tend to exhibit more aggression during play than girls; aggression during social conflicts has been found to be more prevalent in boys than in girls in both laboratory and field research. In a variety of studies, preschool boys have been described as less sedentary and passive and as more active and boisterous than girls. Tizard, Philps, and Plewis (1976) reported in observational study of 12 English nursery centers serving middle- and working-class families that boys engaged in more real fighting than did girls. Using a structured laboratory setting involving 90 same-sex pairs and 30 opposite-sex pairs, Jacklin and Maccoby (1978) revealed that as early as 33 months of age boy pairs were more likely to engage in tug-of-war over a toy than girl pairs or boy-girl pairs.

Furthermore, research shows that preschool boys are more vigorous and active than preschool girls in indoor and outdoor play environments. For example, Harper and Sanders (1975) for two years recorded the total amount of time and use of space by middle-class three- to five-year-old boys and girls. Boys spent more time outside than did girls (there was no difference between girls who wore dresses and those who wore jeans). It was common to see boys playing outside and in sand, on a climbing structure, on a tractor, and around an equipment shed, and girls inside, at craft tables, or in the kitchen. Although there were no sex differences in the percent of time spent farther away from school buildings, boys used 1.2 to 1.6 times as much space and entered significantly more play areas.

In sum, then, there is considerable support for the notion that preschool boys are more likely to engage in rough-and-tumble play than are preschool girls, and to engage in more real fighting during play. Boys seem also to use more space than girls and to be outside more. However, findings are less conclusive at younger ages in connection with total level of physical activity (McCall, 1974). Marked individual variation occurs at each age, making generalizations difficult (see "Do Boys and Girls Really Play So Differently?").

Social Play

Overall, sociability does not differ greatly in young boys' and girls' play. Parten (1933) found that the play scale she developed showed age-related but not gender-related differences. However, she did find that two-thirds of the play groups children chose were same-sex groupings and that preferred and favorite playmates were usually the same sex as the child. The lack of significant differences in social play categories is well-documented (Johnson & Roopnarine, 1983), although there are some reports that girls are ahead of boys in social play during the preschool years (Tizard et al., 1976).

Others who have researched the social play of preschool-aged children concur with Parten's observation that same-sex playmates are more common and more compatible than opposite-sex playmates. Serbin, Tonick, and Sternglanz (1977) reported that the instances of same-sex parallel and cooperative play were two- and four-times more frequent than the occurrence of cross-sex parallel and cooperative play, respectively. Children tend to play with same-sex play partners perhaps because of a combination of abilities, sex-role stereotypes, and compatible interests (Hartup, 1983).

A few studies have directly compared boy-boy, girl-girl, and girl-boy play interactions. In general, it appears that same-sex contacts are more active socially than opposite-sex contacts. For instance, in the previously cited study by Jacklin and Maccoby (1978), it was found that more positive and more negative social behavior was evidenced in same-sex pairs than in opposite-sex pairs. Girls also exhibited more passivity than boys in the presence of opposite-sex play partners. These children did not generally have preschool experience or know each other previously, and modes of dress were the same for boys and girls. Langlois, Gottfried, and Seay (1973), on the other hand, compared their observations of three- and five-year old children who

FIG 6-1

Mean Affiliative Activity Directed to Same-Sex Peers as a Function of Age and Sex

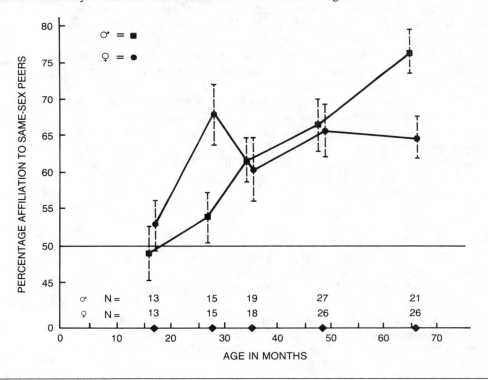

SOURCE: From LaFreniere, P., Strayer, F., & Gauthier, R. (1984)

were familiar with each other previously and who had preschool experience. The older children and three-year-old girls communicated more both verbally and nonverbally in same-sex pairs than in opposite-sex pairs and displayed more assertive behavior. However, three-year-old boys were more sociable with girls than with boys.

A recent three-year study of 98 girls and 95 boys ranging in age from one to six years and enrolled in 15 day care peer groups produced results consistent with the above findings. LaFreniere, Strayer, and Gauthier (1984) found that girls typically preferred playing with same-sex peers at an earlier age than boys did, but that at later ages during the preschool years boys' tendencies for same-sex interaction increased while those of the girls leveled off (See Figure 6–1).

Boys are less discriminant than girls at first, but then show a decided preference for same-sex playmates. In their study LaFreniere et al. found that 27-month-old girls affiliated with female peers significantly more often than with their male peers, while boys of the same age in the same groups seemed to choose play partners randomly, not on the basis of sex. As the children grew, girls showed an initial spurt in their attraction to same-sex peers that did not increase in the later preschool years, while boys showed a delayed interest that continued to increase with age (See Figure 6–1).

In conclusion, while there is little evidence suggesting significant differences in levels of social play or sociability between the sexes, there is considerable support for the notion that sex preferences in social play are different for boys and girls during the preschool years.

Object Play. Researchers have found great differences in the ways boys and girls use objects in play. Preschool-aged females show a strong propensity toward constructive play, while their male counterparts display a greater tendency for functional play (Johnson & Roopnarine, 1983). In other words, girls are more likely to use objects according to a plan that has a goal, such as completing a puzzle or coloring a page. Boys are more likely to handle toys and materials in ways that are appropriate but somewhat stereotyped and repetitious, such as pushing a small vehicle, blowing bubbles, or cranking a mechanical toy.

One possible explanation for this sex difference in tendencies toward functional or constructive play is differences in active involvement required. Research has shown that preschool girls move objects less and use them more educationally and quietly than do boys (Moore, Evertson, & Brophy, 1974). Table top activities that encourage constructive play tend to involve females predominantly (teachers as well as children) and entail sedentary behaviors, while functional play is typically associated with more active movement.

While there have been many reports of gender differences in functional and constructive play, there have been surprisingly few reports that boys and girls differ significantly in their use of objects during the early years. Researchers in play-related areas such as insightful problem solving or tool use (Vandenberg, 1981), exploration (Hutt, 1966), or object manipulation (Fenson, Kagan, Kearsley, & Zelazo, 1976) either have not analyzed their data for gender effects, possibly because of the small number of children participating in the study (Vandenberg, 1981), or have not found gender differences in object use. Hutt (1966) did, however, report that in reacting to a supertoy (see Chapter 4, pp. 76), preschool girls were more likely to be classified as nonexplorers, and preschool boys as inventive explorers; and, in a follow-up study, Hutt and Bhavnani (1972) reported that failure in boys to explore in early childhood seems to be related to a lack of curiosity and adventure and that failure in girls to explore in middle childhood is related to personality and social adjustment problems.

Finally, it is interesting that boys and girls do not appear to differ in person-versus-object orientation (Jennings, 1975) or in being patterners versus dramatists (Wolf & Grollman, 1982). Where distinct play differences surface between boys and girls are in the areas of active versus more sedentary use of objects, choice of pretend roles and themes, and general toy selections (as we will discuss later in this chapter). There are exceptions when behavior is determined by level of cognitive maturity (achievement-related behaviors with objects or greater independence from object props in pretense play) where girls may distinguish themselves because of their edge in rate of development.

Pretend Play

In general, research has shown that preschool-aged boys and girls do not differ in total amounts of pretend play or in their dispositions toward fantasy. Nevertheless, sex differences have been reported in certain aspects of pretend play.

Object Transformations. One child may use realistic or representational toys in pretend play—dolls, miniature farm animals, toy soldiers, or toy superheroes (concrete object transformations). A second child may play with substitute objects that bear little concrete similarity to the imagined object—a small cylindrical block is a lipstick, a large rectangular block is a computer (substitute object transformations). A third child may imagine a missing object and may use language and internal imagery to sustain the make-believe play episode (pretend object transformation). What is the probable gender of each child?

There is great overlap between boys and girls and tremendous variability within each sex. Research suggests that preschool girls may be ahead of preschool boys in object transformational abilities as studied in semi-controlled laboratory settings but not as observed in free-play situations or in a formal testing situation (Johnson & Roopnarine, 1983). Matthews (1977) reported that four-year-old girls were ahead of four-year-old boys in initiating fantasy play without relying on concrete props. Boys gradually became less dependent on objects in make-believe play episodes over successive trials, while girls began at a lower level than did boys and at first maintained a balance between all three types of object transformations but later on preferred substitute and pretend transformations. McLoyd (1980), in her study of low-income black preschoolers, found that girls made significantly more substitute and pretend object transformations than did boys. Fein, Johnson, Kosson, Stork, and Wasserman (1975) found that girls seemed to pretend more than boys during toddlerhood and to become less dependent on realistic concrete props at an earlier age than boys.

Lowe (1975), in a study of free-play behaviors, found that boys used stereotypically masculine items (car and trailer) more than girls did in pretend play, whereas girls did more pretending using stereotypically feminine items (dolls and brushes). Johnson, Ershler, and Bell (1980), in another free-play observation study, did not find preschool girls and boys to differ significantly in use of objects during pretend play episodes.

In summary, it is difficult to say definitely that girls are ahead of boys in object transformational skills. The extent this may be the case during the early years probably reflects girls' accelerated linguistic and cognitive development. In the second half of the preschool years (ages three to six), however, differences in modes of pretend play are probably more a matter of preference than of cognitive maturity.

Role Enactments and Play Themes. Research and anecdotal evidence suggest that during pretend play girls show a preference for home-centered interests involving dolls, dress-up cloths, and domestic items, whereas boys are more inclined to adopt more villainous and dangerous themes and plots and make more use of vehicles and guns (Sutton-Smith, 1979). In other words, while girls tend to portray family characters and to select themes based on everyday experiences, boys tend to participate in adventure themes and to enact superhero roles and seem to be more physically active in pretend play.

Matthews (1981) investigated sex role perception, portrayal, and preferences in the fantasy play of 16 four-year-olds who were observed in pairs with a playmate of the same sex. The two roles most often played were those of mother and father. Based upon how they enacted the roles during the episodes, it appeared as if boys perceived mothers as homebound and concerned with housekeeping and childcare. In the role of the wife, boys seemed to suggest that wives are inept and helpless. In the role of fathers or husbands, boys enacted leadership roles and their participation in housekeeping involved only 30% of their role play. In the girls' play, mothers were nurturant, generous, and highly managerial. But again, wives were portrayed as being helpless and incompetent. Apparently, the role of the mother is viewed in a positive light while the role of the wife is not. Girls saw the male role as being masterful and also nurturant, although they showed little desire to play the male role and spent almost 75% percent of their role play in housekeeping.

Given freedom to choose roles, preschool children usually prefer to enact roles that are stereotypical for the child's sex. Grief (1976) found that in almost all cases boys performed the roles of fathers, husbands, sons, and firemen, whereas girls usually assumed the roles of mother, daughter, wife, baby, and bride. Parten (1933) found that preschool boys acted only male roles while playing house and that boys would not enter the housekeeping corner of the nursery if dolls were present.

Boys and girls choose different kinds of activities during pretend play in part because of differences in interests, temperament, and available shared scripts. Boys soon elect to go beyond the familiar or proximal themes of house, doctor, and school and into more unfamiliar or distal themes of spacemen, superheroes, and fantastic creatures; girls appear more content to stick with the themes and roles popular with all children initially. However, although it is true that going from play content that is proximal to that which is remote from children's everyday experience is the developmental direction in general (see Chapter 3), it would be a mistake to infer that somehow boys are more advanced in this respect than girls because of their greater interest in remote or distal roles and themes in pretend play. The quality of play can never be evaluated in terms of one aspect in isolation. Organization, freedom from concrete props, use of language, and originality are all important as indicators of cognitive maturity in play, and, as we have discussed, girls often equal if not surpass the level of performance of boys in these dimensions. "Evaluating Play Scripts" highlights the subtle way boys and girls vary in their role enactments.

SEX DIFFERENCES IN OTHER PLAY-RELATED BEHAVIORS

Boys and girls can be compared not only in terms of the general play forms of physical or motor play, social play, object play, and pretend play; they also exhibit differences in the areas of toy preferences, team or group activities, and imaginary companions.

Toy Preferences. Many objects and toys are sex-typed in our society. Sex-role

EVALUATING PLAY SCRIPTS

Classification Scheme of Role Enactment Scripts of Young Children

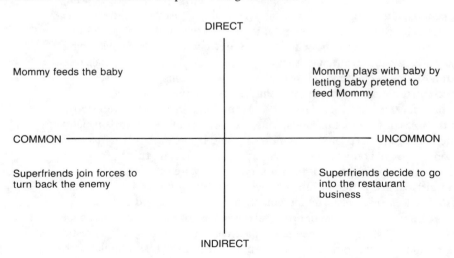

stereotyping or labeling of materials and activities is responsible in part for the fact that many young boys and girls show toy preferences that are well-engrained by the third year—preferences that appear as early as age 12 months (Sutton-Smith, 1979). The finding that some materials are more consistently preferred by either males or females has been consistently reported in the play literature for more than 50 years. Girls tend to play more frequently and longer with dolls and art materials, while boys prefer blocks and wheeled vehicles. However, as Parten (1933) noted 50 years ago (and as still appears to be the case), while girls play more with dolls, boys and girls play house about equally often when doll play is not required of the boys.

The literature also indicates that girls seem to enjoy a greater variety of play materials and activities, due to the "play asymmetry" in toy selection by boys and girls. Girls use both so-called "boy toys" and "girl toys", at least to a certain extent; boys are far more likely to shun certain so-called "girl toys." This generalization is reflected in a recent study by Liss (1981) of kindergarten children's play with traditional female, male, and non-sex-typed or neutral toys. Children were observed and rated on appropriate use of a toy, enjoyment, aggression, movement, nurturance. Boys seemed more familiar with, enjoyed, and played more appropriately with male and neutral toys, while girls played with toys in each category. Girls showed more nurturant behavior than boys, and boys were higher on noise production.

In evaluating pretense play as a process, teachers can use classification schemes such as the one proposed by Smilansky (1968) or other schemes that analyze transformation, communications, performance, and script.

Teachers need to distinguish two independent dimensions when characterizing the play scripts or themes of children to determine the sophistication level of the play. One dimension is the extent to which imaginative play reflects content close to the child's everyday existence or content removed and distant from the child's familiar, actual experiences. The second dimension is the extent to which play behavior is stereotypic and repetitive versus varied and unusual. The accompanying diagram depicts this scheme using two axes—familiarity and originality. Teachers can plan environments with judicious use of props and interventions to promote play diversified in terms of content (adventuresome and domestic themes), and to promote a high level play in terms of process (innovative over stereotypic behaviors with materials). By being sensitive to the varied levels of play scripts used by children and to their ability, personality, and situational antecedents to play behavior level, teachers and parents can encourage the transition from more to less dependency upon realistic toys by implanting in the play environment inexpensive materials suggesting a variety of pretend actions and themes.

Blocks and wheeled toys are among boys' favorite playthings.

Team or Group Activities. During the preschool years, boys and girls appear to be similar in interest and participation in games and group activities. This is probably because games and group activities are usually led by a teacher and boys and girls are encouraged to participate in them to an equal degree. However, many teachers have reported that girls are easier to manage in group situations than boys are.

On the other hand, as children get older, marked differences appear between boys and girls in group and game participation. For instance, boys are much more likely to become involved in large-group play than are girls, who seem more comfortable within a smaller group of children (Sutton-Smith, 1979).

Imaginary Companions. Children who create make-believe playmates are most likely to be three to six years old, with more girls than boys having such companions (Partington & Grant, 1984). More than half the time, imaginary companions are about the same age and the same sex as the children who have them. They are almost always friends who are humans. Best estimates are that approximately 25 percent of children enjoy this fantasy, and children who have imaginary friends tend to be brighter and to manifest more stable and creative behavior than children who do not. However, these conclusions are tentative.

Jerome and Dorothy Singer have reported that, for boys, imaginativeness and positive affect during free play are positively linked to having an imaginary companion (which is negatively correlated with watching television cartoons). For girls, having an imaginary companion was associated with persistence during play and to fewer negative emotional outbursts of anger, fear, or sadness. Both boys and girls who had an imaginary companion were more likely to help and share with peers (Singer & Singer, 1981). In general, during the preschool years—but not during middle childhood—imaginary playmates are considered a positive sign. According

Girls show a preference for playing with dolls and domestic props.

to Partington and Grant (1984), imaginary-companion fantasy may provide an important initial link between fantasy and reality. If children during their early years have difficulty with roles and rules that frame play episodes with real children, they may gain valuable experience practicing these skills with invented playmates they can control.

In sum, then, there does appear to be solid evidence that during the preschool years distinct toy preferences emerge and consolidate. These preferences are based on gender, with girls more likely then boys to try opposite-sex-typed toys and activities. In team and group activities, on the other hand, it seems that few gender-based differences occur during the preschool years. Girls as a group appear to show a stronger propensity for imaginary companions than do boys as a group, having an imaginary playmate apparently being a positive sign for most children during the early years.

ENVIRONMENTAL INFLUENCES

Boys' and girls' contrasting patterns of play behavior and interests are based on a variety of factors in complex interaction. Although genetic or temperamental factors as well as environmental or socialization factors are involved, our discussion will deal with the latter factors, as these influences are somewhat under our control.

Parental Influences. Preschool teachers sometimes comment that the initial school experience is a great *homogenizer* of individual differences among children. *Homogenization* means that children behave more and more similarly and predictably as they get used to classroom routines and as they affect one another during the school year. However, at first there is considerable individual variation in children's reactions to the demands placed upon them by other children and teachers.

Patterns that emerge in sex-differentiated preschool play in the classroom or day care center follow the general homogenization tendency. The groundwork for these patterns, is of course, laid in the home environment; family influences are the source of both the variation among children that exists at first and the consistency in play interests and behavior that grows during the school year.

The initial shaping of gender-differentiated behavior occurs within the family system of intricate interrelationships. Parents and other individuals significant in the child's home punish gender-atypical activities and reward gender-typical ones (Maccoby & Jacklin, 1974). Social learning theorists have attested that parents treat their sons and daughters differently. They may ignore doll play by their sons while encouraging nurturant and submissive behavior and discouraging assertive behaviors in their daughters.

Home influences on gender-based play interests and behavior begin immediately after an infant enters the family. Parents have almost immediate sex-typed expectations of their children. Fathers describe newborn daughters as soft, small, and delicate; fathers of newborn sons describe their offspring as large and active (Rubin, Provenzano, & Luria, 1974). Children may not actually differ in these dimensions at birth, but parents apparently believe they do.

How these parental expectations influence the socialization of boys and girls is illustrated by the way parents dress their sons and daughters differently and provide them with different toys early in life. For example, a study by Rheingold and Cook (1975) surveyed the bedrooms of 48 boys and 48 girls, examining furnishings and toys. The boys' rooms contained more vehicles, educational and art materials, sports equipment, machines, and military toys. The girls' rooms contained more dolls, dollhouses, and domestic toys and were decorated with ruffles and floral prints. These children, between the ages of 12 and 71.6 months, all had their own rooms. Not only did the boys have more toys at every age, but they also had more classes of toys. The boys were given toys that encouraged activities away from the home; girls' toys encouraged home-centered activities.

Parental expectations are also transmitted through interaction with their children. There is some evidence that fathers make themselves more available to their sons and interact with them differently than do mothers of sons, mothers of daughters, and fathers of daughters. Lamb (1977) found that fathers engaged their sons in more vigorous and physically stimulating infant games or play routines. Mothers were more likely to engage their infants in conventional activities such as pat-a-cake and to stimulate their infants with toys and other objects. Fathers held their infants primarily to play with them, while mothers usually held their children for caretaking purposes and to restrict their exploration. These parents' actions maximize the possibility for their children to acquire same-sex behavior patterns.

During children's preschool years between ages three and five, parents continue to influence sex-typed play behavior in tandem with peers and teachers. Schan, Kahn, Diepold, and Cherry (1980) investigated the relationships of parental expectations and preschool children's verbal sex-typing to their sex-typed toy play behavior.

Children's sex-typed free-play behavior was examined along with children's sex-typing of feminine, masculine, and neutral toys and with parental expectations of their children's play. As expected, girls played longer with feminine toys than did boys. Presented with pictures of the toys and asked to indicate which toys go with which sex, the children labeled the toys according to traditional sex typing. It was found that girls assigned more toys to boys than boys did to girls. When parents were asked to indicate how much they expected their child to play with the toys, they indicated sex-typed choices. However, mothers who expected their sons to play more with masculine toys had sons who played with them less. In general, parents were not very accurate in predicting which specific toys their children would select to play with when given a choice.

As a second example, Langlois and Downs (1980) investigated the reactions of mothers, fathers, and peers to gender-typical and -atypical play of three- and five-year-old boys and girls. Children's play behaviors were also observed. It was found that there were higher frequencies of play with same-sex than cross-sex toys. Mothers were more likely to reward cross-sex toy play for their sons than for their daughters and encouraged such play more than peers did. Overall, children received a great deal of discouragement for play with cross-sex toys, particularly from their peers. Fathers rewarded both boys and girls for play with same-sex toys rather than cross-sex toys, but discouraged sons more than daughters from engaging in play with cross-sex toys. These findings lend further support to the contention that parents strongly influence the development and maintenance of sex-differentiated play activities.

Peer Influences. It should not be surprising that there are considerable and extensive sex differences in children's play by the time they are three years old. These differences are accentuated when children come under the influence of teachers and peers in a classroom or day care setting in addition to the continuing effects of parents and siblings on their behavior.

Sex differences in group play have been observed in relation to subtle forms of social behavior. Research suggests that sex-differentiated play may be determined in part by responses of peers to children's activities during free play. For example, Serbin, Connor, Burchardt, and Citron (1979) investigated the effects of peer presence on the sex-typed toy choices of three- and four-year-old boys and girls. The experiment consisted of testing the children alone, in the presence of a same-sex peer, and in the presence of an opposite-sex peer. Male and female-typed toys were presented to the children. Results indicated that the probability of play with cross-sex toys was highest for both boys and girls when they were alone and was lowest when they were with an opposite-sex peer. Girls were more likely to play with cross-sex toys than were boys.

Other researchers have found similar tendencies in preschool children. Observations have shown that boys who engage in male-typed behavior receive more positive responses from peers than do girls who engage in female-typed behavior. Peer reinforcement, particularly same-sex peer reinforcement, is also effective in changing children's behaviors to become sex-typical (Lamb, Easterbrooks, & Holden, 1980). The male peer group during the preschool years is especially potent in shaping stereotypically male behavior (Fagot, 1981). Children, especially boys, risk ostracism if they fail to conform to peer group standards for play and toy use.

Teacher Influences. As noted, there is overwhelming evidence to suggest that the early channeling of children toward traditional sex-typed activities is based on children's experiences as family members. Parents, siblings, and peers lay the foundation for the sex differences observed in the classroom or day care center. By the time they come under teachers' influence, children already seem to possess well-formed notions about sex-stereotyped behaviors sanctioned by our society. What responsibility, then, does the teacher have?

Sex-differentiated play in group settings is supported by teachers' as well as peer groups' cuing and reinforcement of children's activities during free play. Fagot (1983) has reported that teacher feedback affects children's play. Teachers in this study were found to be most positive toward neutral behaviors (neither male- nor female-typed), less positive toward female sex-typed behaviors, and least positive toward male sex-typed behaviors. But although not necessarily conscious of doing so, teachers generally left children alone as long as they played in the traditional way. For instance, teachers would not attempt to encourage girls who participated little in male-preferred activities to sample that type of play.

Research has shown that there is a tendency for teachers to spend more time with children who engage in female sex-typed activity such as arts and crafts, and doll and kitchen play. Teachers of young children are usually females; preschool-aged girls and their teachers tend to focus on the same activities. Typical male sex-typed play behavior such as vehicle or truck play tends not to attract much teacher attention or reinforcement. Girls often are seen as closer to the teacher than boys are and seek structured or constructive play activities far more than boys do (Carpenter, Stein, & Baer, 1978).

Serbin et al. (1979), in their interesting study, also explored the effects of teacher presence in the vicinity of play activity and the effects of teachers' modeling play with different categories of toys (male or female sex-typed items). The gender of the teacher was systematically varied as well in order to examine the influence of this factor on the free play of boys and girls. The results showed that both boys and girls increased their rates of play participation in response to teacher presence in sex-typed activity areas. Girls in general responded more predictably in this study than boys did, but both genders were affected. The boys were more responsive to teacher involvement in male-preferred activity areas, especially when the teacher was male. These findings suggest that teacher presence and involvement in different locations in the classroom or day care center can influence children's sex-related play patterns.

Although there is little indication in the research literature that there are reliable sex differences in how young children react to physical characteristics in the classroom environment (such as the presence of clear pathways between interest centers, accessibility of toys, the ratio of hard and soft object surfaces and the like), there are reports that teachers' modification of the spatial organization of the classroom can change children's sex-typed play behavior. For example, a number of researchers have suggested that the block areas and the housekeeping areas should be linked so that the areas can be used together; this arrangement may lead to more social interaction with opposite-sex companions. Children's play experiences would be enriched by increasing the range and type of toys available. Kinsman and Berk (1979) demonstrated that removal of a divider between the housekeeping area and the block area significantly increased play between boys and girls who had been together one year or less. The removal of the divider also encouraged children to play with toys traditionally used by the opposite sex. Older preschool children, or those who had been enrolled in the same center for two years, however, did not change their patterns of play. Instead, some of these children attempted to replace the divider! Old habits die hard, even for young children. Nevertheless, this study does suggest that teacher modification of the physical environment can influence play patterns.

In sum, then, research indicates that teacher presence in, involvement with, and modification of play interest centers can influence sex-typed behavior in play group settings. Other variables in preschool classrooms and day care centers may also influence sex-typed play. For instance, the ratio of boys to girls and the size of each group may heighten or lessen tendencies for each sex group to behave in the traditional way. Teacher behavior and classroom arrangement, furthermore, appear to stem from individual beliefs and expectations, which in turn determine educational philosophy and curriculum goals. However, there is not enough research concerning the interrelation of these variables for definitive statements to be made.

ROLES OF THE ADULT

Play patterns of girls and boys during their early years are determined by each child's reinforcement history and exposure to sex-typed labeling in the home, neighborhood, and classroom or day care center. In this chapter we have reviewed research reports and arguments that suggest the following scenario: Family members, particularly parents, are initially responsible for channeling children toward traditional sex-typed activities. These early home experiences prime children to behave in stereotypic ways upon entrance into play groups. Children enter preschool or day care with strong notions about what is appropriate behavior for their gender. These beliefs are eventually strengthened by the composite reinforcement exerted by peers and teachers in the group setting. There is also continued pressure in the home to behave in "gender-appropriate" ways as part of sex-role socialization. All these influences, in combination with hormonal factors, result in the homogenization of each sex into traditional molds. Moreover, as this process is intensified in group settings, preschools and day care centers become incubators for future patterns of play and the social and cognitive skills known to be related to play (Johnson & Roopnarine, 1983). For example, as doll play fosters conversation, nurturance, and gentleness (Liss, 1981), it imitates the traditional role of the mother; girls' fondness for using fine motor gadgetry in childhood constructive play also translates, somewhat indirectly, into traditional female tasks such as hair arrangement, sewing, or drawing. Play provides practice for future roles in the family and in the job marketplace.

What, then, is the role of the adult? Should parents and teachers support this pattern or try to change it? Answers to these questions depend on individual values. Some authorities have found trends away from traditional sex typing in children's play over the past decades (Sutton-Smith, 1979). Fueled in part by growing feminism in society, a unisex movement arose in the late 1960s and early 1970s in which early childhood educators were encouraged to put more emphasis on nonsexist activities in the classroom (Simmons, 1976). Questions can be raised about whether teachers' values correspond or compete with the value systems of families. Different ethnic groups and residents of certain geographic regions of the country, for instance, may be strongly opposed to any move away from traditional sex-role socialization. Parents may not want their children to engage in play behaviors that they do not deem appropriate for their child's sex. Some teachers who are more flexible about sex roles than parents may be overzealous in encouraging families to be open to change.

Certainly there have been great changes during the past decades in play behavior of girls (Sutton-Smith, 1979). Throughout early and middle childhood the sexes share many more forms of play and games than was the case thirty years ago. Furthermore, girls today participate more and more in organized sports as soon as they are old enough to compete in them. Finally, there are a growing number of popular books on the role of games in the lives of today's working women (*e.g.*, *Games Mother Never Taught You* by Harragan, 1977). These books vary in emphasis but all advocate that the play and games of children are critically important for learning social skills and finesse useful in later life in corporate America. Mothers are either told to help their daughters learn to beat the male-dominated system, or to try to humanize the working world. In any case, the message is clear: Sex-typed play patterns lead to important consequences in life, and parents and teachers should be cognizant of those patterns and take countermeasures if deemed appropriate. For example, if parents favor change, one recommendation would be to help girls become better team players.

This chapter will end short of advocating a strong position on altering established patterns of play to fit specific goals of sex-role socialization. We believe, as we pointed out at the end of Chapter 4, "Personality and Play," that all children should be afforded every opportunity to engage in a wide range of play behaviors. We offer two general recommendations for those interested in expanding play repertories of children. Each entails crossing over traditional gender-based divisions. One recommendation is primarily for parents, the other for teachers.

We recommend that mothers and fathers make every effort to treat sons and daughters equitably by providing them with toys and other play materials, including storage and space for play. Expenditures should be about the same for boys and for girls. Time devoted to playing with sons and daughters should also be equal, and both mothers and fathers should play with sons and with daughters. Finally, and most importantly, parents should engage their children in play that is both traditionally masculine and traditionally feminine. This means, for example, that

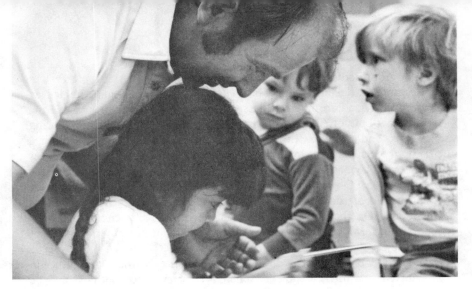

Parents and teachers can expand children's play options by encouraging and reinforcing non-sex-typed behavior.

fathers not only wrestle with their daughters and play baseball with them, but also sew with their sons and bake cookies with them. No play form or activity should be precluded on the basis of tradition. In the process, not only will parents model and reinforce novel play content and contexts, they will also show children a fresh approach to play.

We recommend that teachers attempt to display the same versatility as outlined for parents. In addition, we urge teachers to reexamine and expand play options. That means providing more opportunities for different kinds of play. Messages from encouraging research reports should be heeded; for example, Kinsman and Berk (1979) found that, while fixed patterns of sex-differentiated play were the rule, preschool children's play patterns could be changed through careful teacher intervention and environmental manipulation. We strongly recommend this kind of enterprising teacher-led experimentation. Teachers should also review and expand dramatic play options. Unfortunately, what passes for a dramatic-play interest center in some classrooms is nothing more than the customary domestic-play area—limited to the kitchen at that. If playing house must be the theme, why not at least provide props representing other rooms? Certainly such efforts will be rewarded by enriched group play, benefiting preschool girls and boys alike. And, through such efforts we may help girls and boys become the kind of men and women that will be successful models for life in the next century.

SUMMARY

Gender is an important factor in play during early childhood development. This chapter discussed gender differences in physical, social, object, and pretend play, as well as differences between boys and girls in toy preferences, team or group activity, and imaginary companions.

Research has documented that boys engage in more rough-and-tumble play than do girls, and are more aggressive during play. Less conclusive is the finding that boys often appear more active and girls more sedentary during play. Boys and girls show little if any difference in inclination toward social play or in social play development. However, there are significant differences in choice of playmates, with segregation based on gender common during the preschool years. Object play differences have been found: Girls are more likely to engage in constructive play and other table activities in preschool or day care classrooms. On the other hand, no reliable gender differences have been reported in terms of people-versus-object orientations or object-dependent versus object-independent imaginative play styles.

Generally, boys and girls do not differ significantly from one another in imaginative play interest and skill. There is some evidence that boys may be more concrete than girls in reliance on props during the third year and that girls may be more verbal, reflecting different rates of language development. More evidence exists that themes and role enactments tend to be sex-typed, with boys being more likely to exhibit fantastic or adventuresome themes involving superheroes and supervillains.

Research has supported the following conclusions: (1) Girls show an interest in a greater variety of toys and play materials than boys do; (2) girls prefer to play in smaller groups than boys do, although this is usually seen after the preschool years; and (3) girls tend to have imaginary companions more than boys do.

Environment and socialization practices greatly determine gender differences in play during the early years. Parents, peers, and teachers influence gender-based patterns. Parental expectations concerning sex-typed play are revealed in different situations provided for boys and girls in the home environment. Clothing, toys, and bedroom decorations are known to differ markedly for boys and girls. Parent-child interactive patterns exert a pervasive influence on the development and maintenance of sex differences in play from birth to six years. Peer and teacher influences transmitted through stimulus cuing and reinforcement are well-documented. Cross-gender play is most likely to occur away from a watchful peer group. Although many teachers do not encourage a wide variety of play, research has shown that their presence and involvement and their modification of play areas can alter established patterns of play.

Wanting to change traditional gender-based play patterns is a matter of an individual's value system, but an overriding consideration may be the importance of fostering a wide range of play opportunities for children during their formative years. Accordingly, parents are urged to treat their sons and daughters equitably in toy expenditures and parental time and to encourage a variety of activities through their interactions with children. Teachers are encouraged to examine how their own values and biases influence play options for children, particularly play involving role enactments, as children learn social norms.

REFERENCES

Carpenter, C.J., Stein, A.H., & Baer, D.M. (1978). *The relation of children's activity preference to sex-type behavior.* Paper presented at the 12th Annual Convention of the Association for Advancement in Behavior Theories, Chicago.

Fagot, B.I. (1981). Continuity and change in play styles as a function of sex of child. *International Journal of Behavioral Development, 4,* 37–43.

Fagot, B.I. (1983). Play styles in early childhood: Social consequences. In M. Liss (Ed.), *Social and cognitive skills: Sex roles and children's play.* New York: Academic Press.

Fein, G., Johnson, D., Kosson, N., Stork, L., & Wasserman, L. (1975). Stereotypes and preferences in the toy choices of 20-month boys and girls. *Developmental Psychology, 11,* 527–528.

Fenson, L., Kagan, J., Kearsley, R.B., & Zelazo, P.R. (1976). The developmental progression of manipulative play in the first two years. *Child Development, 47,* 232–236.

Grief, E.B. (1976). Sex role playing in preschool children. In J. Bruner, A. Jolly, & K. Sylva (Eds.), *Play: Its role in development and evolution.* New York: Basic Books.

Harper, L.V., & Sanders, K. (1975). Preschool children's use of space: Sex differences in outdoor play. *Developmental Psychology, 11,* 119.

Harragan, B.L. (1977). *Games mother never taught you.* New York: Rawson Associates.

Hartup, W.W. (1983). The peer system. In E.M. Hetherington (Ed.), P.H. Mussen (Series Ed.), *Handbook of child psychology: Vol. 4. Socialization, personality, and social development.* New York: Wiley.

Hutt, C. (1966). Exploration and play in children. *Symposium of the Zoological Society of London, 18,* 61–81.

Hutt, C., & Bhavnani, R. (1972). Predictions from play. In J.S. Bruner, LA. Jolly, & K. Sylvia (Eds.), *Play: Its role in development and evolution.* New York: Basic Books.

Jacklin, C., & Maccoby, E. (1978). Social behavior at thirty-three months in same-sex dyads. *Child Development, 49,* 557–569.

Jennings, K.D. (1975). People versus object orientation, social behavior, and intellectual abilities in preschool children. *Developmental Psychology, 112,* 511–519.

Johnson, J.E., Ershler, J., & Bell, C. (1980). Play behavior in a discovery-based and a formal education preschool program. *Child Development, 51,* 271–274.

Johnson, J.E., & Roopnarine, J.L. (1983). The preschool classroom and sex differences in children's play. In M. Liss (Ed.), *Social and cognitive skills: Sex roles and children's play.* New York: Academic Press.

Kinsman, C.A., & Berk, L.E. (1979). Joining the block and housekeeping areas: Changes in play and social behavior. *Young Children,* November, 66–75.

LaFreniere, P., Strayer, F., & Gauthier, R. (1984). The emergence of same-sex affiliative preferences among preschool peers: A developmental ethological perspective. *Child Development, 55,* 1958–1965.

Lamb, M.E. (1977). The development of parental preferences in the first two years of life. *Sex Roles, 3,* 495–497.

Lamb, M.E., Easterbrooks, A., & Holden, G. (1980). Reinforcement and punishment among preschoolers: Characteristics, effects, and correlates. *Child Development, 51,* 1230–1236.

Langlois, J., & Downs, C. (1980). Mother, father, and peers as socialization agents of sex-typed play behaviors in young children. *Child Development, 51,* 1217–1247.

Langlois, J.H., Gottfried, N.W., & Seay, B. (1973). The influence of sex of peers on the social behavior of preschool children. *Developmental Psychology, 8,* 93–98.

Liss, M.B. (1981). Patterns of toy play: An analysis of sex differences. *Sex Roles, 7,* 1143–1150.

Lowe, M. (1975). Trends in the development of representational play in infants from one to three years— an observation study. *Journal of Child Psychology and Psychiatry, 16,* 33–47.

Maccoby, E.E., & Jacklin, C.N. (1974). *The psychology of sex differences.* Stanford, CA: Stanford University Press.

Matthews, W.S. (1977). Modes of transformation in the initiation of fantasy play. *Developmental Psychology, 13,* 212–216.

Matthews, W.S. (1981). Sex-role perception, portrayal, and preferences in the fantasy play of young children. *Sex Roles,* 1(10), 979–987.

McCall, R.B. (1974). Exploratory manipulation and play in the human infant. *Monographs of the Society for Research in Child Development, 39* (Serial No. 155).

McLoyd, V.C. (1980). Verbally expressed modes of transformation in the fantasy play of black preschool children. *Child Development, 51,* 1133–1139.

Moore, N.V., Evertson, C.M., & Brophy, J.E. (1974). Solitary play: Some functional reconsiderations. *Developmental Psychology, 10,* 830–834.

Parten, M.B. (1933). Social play among preschool children. *Journal of Abnormal and Social Psychology, 28,* 136–147.

Partington, J.T. & Grant, C. (1984). Imaginary companions. In P. Smith (Ed.), *Play in animals and humans* (pp. 217–240). New York: Harper & Row.

Rheingold, H., & Cook, K. (1975). The contents of boy's and girl's rooms as an index of parents' behavior. *Child Development, 46,* 920–927.

Rubin, I., Provenzano, F., & Luria, Z. (1974). The eyes of the beholder: Parents' views of sex of newborns. *American Journal of Orthopsychiatry, 44,* 512–519.

Schan, C.G., Kahn, L., Diepold, J.H., & Cherry, F. (1980). The relationships of parental expectations and preschool childrens' verbal sex-typing to their sex-typed toy play behavior. *Child Development, 51,* 266–270.

Serbin, L.A., Connor, J.A., Burchardt, C.J., & Citron, C.C. (1979). Effects of peer presence on sex-typing of children's play behavior. *Journal of Experimental Child Psychology, 27,* 303–309.

Serbin, L.A., Tonick, I.J., & Sternglanz, S.H. (1977). Shaping cooperative cross-sex play. *Child Development, 48,* 924–929.

Simmons, B. (1976). Teachers, beware of sex-stereotyping. *Childhood Education. 52,* 192–195.

Singer, J., & Singer, D. (1981). *Television, imagination, and aggression: A study of preschoolers.* Hillsdale, NJ: Erlbaum.

Smilansky, S. (1968). *The effects of sociodramatic play on culturally disadvantaged preschool children.* New York: Wiley.

Sutton-Smith, B. (1979). The play of girls. In C.B. Kopp & M. Kirkpatrick (Eds.), *Becoming female: Perspectives on development.* New York: Plenum.

Tizard, B., Philps, J., & Plewis, I. (1976). Play in preschool centres—(1) Play measures and their relation to age, sex and IQ. *Journal of Child Psychology and Psychiatry, 17,* 251–264.

Vandenberg, B. (1981). The role of play in the development of insightful tool-using strategies. *Merrill-Palmer Quarterly, 27,* 97–110.

Wolf, D., & Grollman, S.H. (1982). Ways of playing: Individual differences in imaginative style. In D.J. Pepler & K.H. Rubin (Eds.), *The play of children: Current theory and research.* Basel, Switzerland: Karger, A.G.

Social Class and Culture

In previous chapters we presented research evidence and theory about developmental changes and gender differences in play without making any attempt to qualify these findings in terms of children's ethnic backgrounds or social class. In this chapter we invite the reader to explore with us some of what is known about how these factors influence play and how children's play behaviors are themselves expressions of cultural contexts. We will review studies that show how cultural factors affect children's play and the rate at which play skills evolve, and also how patterns of play and the choice of play topics and themes reflect cultural and subcultural identities.

Today's parents, preschool teachers, day care specialists, hospital playroom leaders, librarian story-hour leaders, and other adults who frequently come in contact with young children can attest to the increasing variation of contemporary family types in which children are being raised. Not only do children vary in their unique personalities, they also are different from one another in social class backgrounds, ethnic backgrounds, and other important ways relating to their family structure. For example, an increasing number of children are being brought up by a single parent or in a household where both parents have full-time jobs. Indeed, adults involved with children must be prepared to grapple constructively with a considerable amount of diversity.

We believe strongly that an important first step to meet this challenge is to be aware of variation in play behavior based on cultural and subcultural factors. Of course, striving to know everything about how children play around the world would be a gargantuan undertaking. Few would be interested in a task of these proportions, and it would have uncertain yields in any practical sense. It is more important to become aware of major conceptual issues. This knowledge can be instrumental in fostering attitude changes as well as in generating practical ideas for making play provisions and for interacting with young children during play.

The purpose of this chapter is to introduce the reader to theories and research in this area. First, we will survey the literature dealing with social class factors and play. Second, we will review literature on cultural variations in play. Emphasis will be on imaginative play because a great deal of research has been focused on sociodramatic play. We will discuss controversies and will attempt to give both sides where differences of opinion exist. Most important, we will attempt to explain key issues and problems.

Finally, as is our customary practice in this text, we will conclude with a section on the role of the adult in children's play. Here we will offer practical suggestions based on the material covered in this chapter.

SOCIAL CLASS AND PLAY

Most of us are familiar with the traditional popular image of the poor child without toys but with a rich imagination to compensate for material deprivation. Stories, movies, television shows, and records have done much to transmit this stereotype from generation to generation. Perhaps we are comfortable with this notion because of our propensity to cheer for the underdog or perhaps because of our wish to allay guilt we may feel over social inequalities and injustices. Be that as it may, evidence from social science research studies suggests that we should dispense with this folk myth (just as professional consensus based on current research suggests that we discard such other popular but erroneous social stereotypes as the "gifted but odd child" and the "only and lonely and spoiled child"). Research has contradicted the romantic hypothesis that material deprivation creates rich imaginations in children.

Evidence from empirical investigations suggests that materially deprived children or children classified as coming from lower social-class backgrounds may engage in less imaginative play than middle-class children. However, research results are equivocal; some studies are tainted by methodological shortcomings.

IMAGINATIVE PLAY

In Chapter 2 we examined the work of Sara Smilansky in discussing the role of the adult as a play interventionist. Her book *The Effects of Sociodramatic Play on Disadvantaged Preschool Children* (1968) not only sparked interest in play training, but also helped to establish the belief that the play of children who come from low income families is deficient in a number of respects (McLoyd, 1982). Many researchers and practitioners have taken to heart Smilansky's words that "children from the low sociocultural strata play very little and most of them do not participate in sociodramatic play at all" (p. 4). Because of the commonly accepted connection between imaginative play and symbolic development, there has been an eagerness to link social class differences in pretend play to disparities in symbolic competence in general (either as a source or as an effect) and to devise remedial play tutoring to compensate for this supposed social class gap (Dansky, 1980; Freyberg, 1973;

Lovinger, 1974; Rosen, 1974; Saltz & Johnson, 1974; Saltz, Dixon, & Johnson, 1977).

Smilansky and other researchers influenced by her work have characterized the pretend play of economically disadvantaged children, compared to that of middle-class children, as less frequent and of lower quality. Typically, descriptions of their play include adjectives like "unimaginative," "repetitive," "simplistic," "desultory," "dependent on objects," and "concrete." We might add that these terms are not far removed from the kinds of qualifiers that have been applied to the play of mentally retarded or autistic young children, qualifiers such as "personalized," "ritualistic," "less likely to combine toys" (Weiner & Weiner, 1974).

The primitive nature of the play of children from low-income families has been graphically captured by observations about them. Smilansky reported that these children frequently fought over play materials; Rubin, Maioni, and Hornung (1976) noted that these children spent a great deal of time exploring toys that were novel to them but that were old hat to middle-class preschoolers.

One of us participated in an early play training study (Saltz & Johnson, 1974), observing lower-class preschoolers for one complete semester before starting play tutoring in the subsequent semester. The children all came from families living in a designated poverty area in a large urban setting. At first, the play of these children appeared fanciful and dramatic. For example, the children would often ride around in a toy fire engine making siren noises, then suddenly stop and take out a rope to hose down a burning building. Another frequently observed play script was carrying a doll and purse and walking around the room in dress-up clothes. The children then would stop to sit in a rocking chair to feed the baby, burp the baby, and put the baby to bed. However, it soon became apparent that most children observed in such play would enact the same sequences over and over again without changing them very much, even from one week to the next. Furthermore, in the subsequent semester, the imaginative play of those children not tutored (control group) did not increase or improve. Saltz and Johnson (1974) reported: "While 94.7 percent or 38 of [the tutored] subjects were observed in dramatic free play, only 60.5 percent or 26 of the control subjects were observed. Thus, 5.3 percent or 2 of the [tutored] subjects and 39.5 percent or 17 of the control subjects were never observed in dramatic free play" (p. 627).

This same author also had the chance to observe in the early 1970s several preschools for middle-class children. His feeling was that the playskills of the "star thespians" in the low-income training program matched nicely the imaginative play skills of middle-class preschoolers. However, the performance of these outstanding children from the poverty area would have been the norm in the middle-class preschool. That is, on the average, a middle-class preschooler randomly selected would be equal to an outstanding lower-class child in imaginative play performance as expressed in a middle-class oriented classroom.

Quantity of Imaginative Play

Numerous researchers have reported results showing that middle-class preschoolers engage in more sociodramatic play than do disadvantaged preschoolers (Fein &

Stork, 1981; Rosen, 1974; Rubin, Maioni, & Hornung, 1976; Smith & Dodsworth, 1978; and Tizard, Philps, & Plewis, 1976).

Rosen (1974) replicated Smilansky's findings that showed that advantaged exceed disadvantaged preschoolers in amount and quality of sociodramatic play. Four kindergarten classes serving black children from low-income families were compared with two classes serving black children from middle-income families in terms of sociodramatic play exhibited during free-play periods. Rosen found that all advantaged children participated in role play but that only 31 out of 58 disadvantaged children showed role-play activities. Rosen reported that the advantaged children also participated significantly more in sociodramatic play. Black children from middle-class households displayed free-play behavior more similar to that of white advantaged children than to that of black disadvantaged children. Rosen used a six-point rating scale based on Smilansky (1968) to score free play behavior (1 = manipulating an object to 6 = complex sociodramatic play).

Rubin et al. (1976) coded the free play of 24 three and four-year-old middle-class children and 16 lower-class (welfare homes) children using Parten's (1932) scales for social play (solitary, onlooker, parallel, associative, and cooperative) nested within Smilansky's categories (functional, constructive, dramatic, games-with-rules).[1] Rubin et al. reported that children from welfare homes tended to display more solitary-functional and parallel- and associative-constructive play, and middle-class children tended to engage in more cooperative-dramatic play. Middle-class children manifested three times as much cooperative-dramatic play. However, this last finding, while suggestive, approached but did not reach statistical significance.

Smith and Dodsworth (1978) and Tizard et al. (1976) compared the play of working-class and middle-class English children. Smith and Dodsworth noted whether children used make-believe objects, actions, or verbalizations. In the study by Tizard et al. (1976), children's treating either objects or themselves as other than what they were constituted evidence of pretend play. Although we cannot equate these behaviors with sociodramatic play proper, both teams of British psychologists found more pretend play in the middle-class groups, findings not inconsistent with the original Smilansky thesis.

Fein and Stork (1981) observed for a six-week period the free-play behavior of middle- and lower-class children enrolled in the same YMCA day care center. Subjects included a group of younger children (3 to 4.5 years old) and a group of older children (5 to 6.5 years old). Researchers unaware of the social class of the children observed them six times, each time lasting five minutes. Behaviors were analyzed for play quality (defined on the basis of rating scores for play verbalizations), play persistence, and pretend play components. Analyses of the data showed that in both age groups middle-class children scored higher than lower-class children on the play quality measure. Middle-class children revealed more frequent sociodramatic-like behavior than did the children from low-income families attending the same day care center.

---

[1]A modified version of the Parten/Smilansky scale is described in detail in Chapter 8.

Findings at odds with the above have been reported by Golomb (1979) and Stern, Bragdon, and Gordon (1976). In the Golomb study, 30 middle-class preschoolers were compared with 30 working-class preschoolers. Children ranged in age from 3.4 to 6.1 years and were observed during free-play periods in a nursery school, a day care center, and kindergarten classes. Play behaviors were classified into episodes and scored as motor play, exploratory play, arts and crafts, pretense play, constructive activities, conversation, sandbox or water play activities, learning activities, and games with rules. Each episode was further analyzed in terms of level of complexity, social cooperation, socialized or egocentric language, and type of symbolic play. Age differences were found in each social class, but the two social class groups did not differ from each other on the play measures. Pretense occurred about 30 percent of the time, with age trends apparent for both socioeconomic groups. Older children showed more intense involvement in pretense play. While more than one role transformation within any particular play episode was rare, object and situational transformations were fairly common.

In the Stern et al. study, 19 Afro-American and 5 Caucasian lower-class and 24 Caucasian middle-class children were observed two or three times for a total of approximately one hour per child. As was the case with all the previously cited reports except Fein and Stork, the comparison groups were studied in different segregated settings. Behaviors were coded for type of fantasy play, amount of verbalization, organization, complexity, communication, clarity of meaning as well as on other quantifiable dimensions. Percentages of occurrences of behaviors in 35 different play dimensions were computed, and comparisons were made across social classes. Arbitrarily, differences of 5 percent or less, 6 to 14 percent, and 15 percent or more were defined as "no difference," "slight difference," and "large difference," respectively. Both groups of children were virtually alike or slightly different in 26 (74 percent) categories and were very different in only nine (26 percent) categories. At age three, middle-class children scored higher in verbalization, use of accessories, and use of three or more signifiers (make-believe props). However, at age four, they were surpassed by their lower-class counterparts on the above measures. Also, among four-year-olds, the degree to which play meaning could be understood on the basis of verbalization alone was greater in middle-class children; among three-year-olds it was greater in lower-class children. Neither the Golomb nor the Stern et al. study provides evidence consistent with Smilansky's original study.

Quality of Imaginative Play

Few studies are available that document overall quality or components of sociodramatic play (that is, imitative role play, make-believe with objects, make-believe with actions and situations verbally expressed, verbal communication, persistence, and interaction) or that examine object use during pretend play as a function of social class (McLoyd, 1982).

The sociodramatic play of 169 black kindergarten children (the average age of these children was 70.7 months) from two socioeconomic-status groups was compared by Griffing (1980) on the basis of rating scores for each of the six categorical components of sociodramatic play as defined by Smilansky (1968).[2] The children attended different schools serving either low- or middle-income families. In each school two boys and two girls were chosen at random from their kindergarten classrooms to engage in sociodramatic play. Children were asked to "play house" in a dramatic playroom set up in each school for this purpose. Black children from middle-income families received consistently higher ratings on a four-point scale on each of the six sociodramatic play categories. Parenthetically, children's IQs as measured by the Goodenough-Harris Draw-A-Woman and Draw-A-Man Tests were not significantly related to play performance, while maternal education level was a significant predictor of play for boys but not for girls.

Griffing's study, evaluating different components of sociodramatic play is the the only one that reported across-the-board differences in favor of middle-class children. In this study, these children enacted longer and presumably more complex pretend episodes than did lower-class children. As we have seen, other studies also contained information pertaining to qualitative aspects of imaginative play across social class. The consensus in the findings from these studies, however, is not as clear-cut as the conclusion suggested by the Griffing results.

Golomb reported no differences between middle- and working-class children in any of the measures, including the level of complexity of pretend play and socio-dramatic play. Other studies have yielded more complicated results. Fein and Stork (1981), Smith and Dodsworth (1981), and Tizard et al. (1976) all showed more frequent and generally higher-level sociodramatic play in middle- than in lower-socioeconomic-status children; however, in these studies similarities across socioeconomic status were reported in complexity of language, original use of materials, and object, role, or scene transformation (Fein & Stork); complexity of social play and dramatic impersonations (Tizard et al.); and mean length of pretend episodes (Fein & Stork, Smith & Dodsworth). In the Stern investigation, the only large difference at both ages in favor of higher-socioeconomic-status children was their greater likelihood of enacting highly specific roles, for instance, mother as opposed to parent or human being (McLoyd, 1982). Finally, while Griffing and Smith and Dodsworth found their higher socioeconomic-status children used objects in pretend play in a more imaginative way, other studies have not shown social class differences in this behavior (Fein & Stork, 1981; Stern et al., 1976).

Developmental Deficiencies Versus Differences. Perhaps by now you have asked yourself the same questions that have bothered us and a number of other researchers concerning these studies: To what extent can it be fairly stated that young children with a low-socioeconomic status do not develop their imaginative play as fully as middle-class children? Is there a delay in the rate at which children from impoverished backgrounds perform make-believe play? Is there a critical period during which children need to exhibit symbolic play or have their

---

[2]These sociodramatic play components are described in "Sociodramatic Play Inventory: Definitions" in Chapter 8 (pp. 160–161).

Social class and cultural variations in play are considered by many to be differences rather than deficiencies.

psychological development impeded? Or are the above conclusions derived from research studies, the methodology of which is suspect? For example, all of the above studies except the one conducted by Fein and Stork observed children across socioeconomic levels playing in their own segregated settings, thus possibly confounding socioeconomic differences with situational differences. If researchers had observed lower-socioeconomic-status children at play in other locations, such as in their homes, maybe what appear to be play deficiencies would turn out to be play differences?

We will address ourselves to these and other related concerns about concepts and methods later in this chapter. We merely wish to raise this developmental deficiency-versus-difference argument before discussing cultural factors and play, since this argument will pertain there as well. Just as lower-socioeconomic-status children have been stereotyped as having underdeveloped or delayed imaginative play abilities, so too have children from nations that are less technologically and economically advanced than our own.

CULTURAL FACTORS AND PLAY

Cultural or ethnic group differences in the play abilities or preferences of young children have been documented in a number of studies, supporting our belief in the important role of environmental factors in play development (Feitelson, 1977; Finley & Layne, 1971; Murphy, 1972; Seagoe, 1971; Smilansky, 1968; Udwin & Shmukler, 1981; Whiting, 1963). Cultural and socioeconomic variables are not explanatory in themselves, however. That is because cultural status and socioeconomic status are "umbrella" variables. They relate to specific environmental factors that more im-mediately influence play behavior and development, such as the availability of play materials and adult encouragement and modeling. A basic premise of this book is that it is these specific factors, rather than umbrella variables, that affect the rate and level of play behavior and development.

Imaginative Play Deficits. There is considerable variation and overlap in play expression among children and among groups. As we have seen, one generalization that has emerged from research is that low-socioeconomic-status children are less likely to engage in imaginative or sociodramatic play. This difference is presumably caused by deficiencies in play stimulation in the child's home environment. Under-developed play skills similarly have been attributed to children growing up in Third World countries where poverty exists (Ebbeck, 1973; El Konin, 1971). Sutton-Smith (1977) has suggested that perhaps the critical determining factor of play is whether children are an economic asset and therefore forced to participate in early survival training and work, circumstances that would compete with pretend play before the fifth or sixth year or life.

Children learn or fail to learn certain kinds of play because of environmental conditions. Theorists such as Singer (1973) have claimed that physical space and privacy are prerequisites for the development of imaginative play skills. Children need objects or play props to trigger their imaginations. Adults' attitudes about play and their behavior toward children at play are critical. A number of play scholars have noted the importance of active adult encouragement and modeling of pretend play to help young children develop a propensity for make-believe. One premise is that children must be taught an "as if" stance toward reality in order to be able to engage in imaginative play (Feitelson & Ross, 1973; Singer, 1973; Smilansky, 1968). If these learning conditions are missing in a social class, ethnic or cultural group, then imaginative play may be absent or severely underdeveloped.

Cross-cultural research on play behavior has shown that fantasy and imaginative play are virtually absent in some societies (*e.g.,* among Russian and East African children—Ebbeck, 1973; El Konin, 1971; Whiting, 1963) but very rich and diversified in others (*e.g.,* among New Zealand and Okinawan children—Seagoe, 1971; Whiting, 1963). According to Feitelson (1977), there are great differences in the quality of imaginative play among children growing up in different societies and in some societies imaginative play is almost nonexistent. She cites Ammar's (1954) description of childhood in rural Egypt and Levine and Levine's (1963) description of Gusii childhood in Kenya. These children were viewed as lacking in conditions for play, and adults in these societies were shown actively trying to prevent children from playing. Children were seen as passive and quiet observers of adults' doings. In her own research on Kurdish Jews, Feitelson found that an all-pervasive attitude of adults was that little children should be seen but not heard. She inferred that this attitude was responsible for young children's extreme passivity and lack of play.

Although these cultural distinctions may be legitimate, independent effects of social class and culture on children's play have not received much research attention. Limited research has been conducted on differences in play across socioeconomic levels (Eifermann, 1971; Feitelson & Ross, 1973; Freyberg, 1973) and across cultures (Ebbeck, 1973; El Konin, 1971; Seagoe, 1971; Whiting, 1963). Even less is known about social class variation in play in countries outside the United States.

Udwin and Shmukler (1981) examining low- and middle-class children in Israel and South Africa reported significant social-class but not cultural differences in imaginative play. These authors noted that the apparent deficits in imaginative play among lower-class children were not created by a lack of experiences or stimulation, but by the failure of lower-class parents to help their children with the integration of diverse stimuli that confronted them in the course of everyday life. Other investigators who have observed the play of children in different countries apparently have not included two or more countries and two or more socioeconomic levels in each country in their research designs. Based on the Udwin and Shmukler study, and through integration of other scattered evidence from reports such as those by Eifermann (1971) and Smilansky (1968) among others, we would expect social-class factors to weigh more heavily than cultural factors in contributing to the frequency and quality of children's play. The content of play would differ by culture, but only to the extent that cultural sharing and borrowing had not occurred. The level of play within each culture would vary as a function of socioeconomic level.

Imaginative Play Differences. An opposing position has been advanced by others, primarily ethnographers, folklorists, and anthropologists, who have argued that all young children can engage in make-believe play regardless of their cultural and social-class membership (Schwartzman, 1978; Sutton-Smith & Heath, 1981). According to this position, the reason play deficiencies have been attributed to certain groups of children is because of ethnocentric or class bias in researchers who display their ignorance by failing to recognize imaginative play in children who come from different cultural or socioeconomic backgrounds.

Schwartzman (1978) in her comprehensive book *Transformations: The Anthropology of Children's Play* provides ample ethnographic data about the play of children from non-Western, less technologically and economically advanced societies. She notes that ethnographic studies that have reported a paucity of play among children in rural Egypt and Kenya and among the Kurdish Jews in Israel (Ammar, 1954; Feitelson, 1959; Levine & Levine, 1963) did not have as their primary focus children's play, let alone types of play. She warns that the absence of evidence from these studies is not evidence of absence. According to Margaret Mead (1975), "Students should be warned that one can never rely on a negative statement that any toy, any game, any song is absent just because it is neither witnessed nor recalled by adults" (p. 161). Indeed, recent ethnographic accounts suggest that children around the world participate in a wide variety of play forms, play which is often combined with work (*e.g.*, Bloch & Walsh, 1983).

Earlier, Sutton-Smith (1972) developed the thesis that differences in imaginative play between Western and traditional societies may well relate to what he calls differences between "ascriptive" and "achievement" game cultures. Children who belong to an ascriptive culture engage in play that is imitative but not trans-formational and that relies on the use of realistic toy representations rather than improvised ones or none at all. In other words, children in ascriptive game cultures imitate the behavior of their elders; they replicate but do not transform. In contrast, the imaginative play of young children in achievement cultures is replete with make-believe transformations that are more flexible and diversified (subject-object, object-object, and self-other transformations).

More recently, Sutton-Smith and his colleagues have turned their attention to describing differences in imaginative play style related to cultural factors. Ethnographic work by Sutton-Smith and Heath (1981) analyzed two styles of imaginative behavior, which they call oral and literate. The oral style of imagination is usually of a rhetorical type that is embedded in verbal communication between the central performer and the group. In cultures in which the literate style predominates, imagination is often used in solitary situations and stresses detachment from the mundane world and the conjuring up of things not present. Sutton-Smith and Heath suggest that what appear to be developmental deficiencies in imagination may be differences in imagination style.

Sutton-Smith and Heath went on to show that these cultural styles can be detected in the stories told by children as young as two years of age. They compared a sample of stories told by working-class black children in the Piedmont Carolinas with a sample of stories told by middle-class white children in New York. Stories told by

---

THE ANTHROPOLOGICAL ASSOCIATION FOR THE STUDY OF PLAY

The extent that the phenomenon of play as expressed by children and adults around the world is taken seriously in academia is demonstrated by the emergence of such professional societies as The Anthropological Association for the Study of Play (TAASP). TAASP is a multidisciplinary, multinational organization that seeks to promote research, scholarship, and understanding of play and culture. The role of play in development and learning is also a focus of inquiry.

TAASP was conceived in 1974 at the University of Western Ontario where 25 persons explored the possibility of structuring an organization devoted to promoting the study of humans at play from a multidisciplinary perspective. A steering committee was established and six working committees took charge of creating the new group. The first annual meeting of TAASP was held in April 1975 in Detroit, Michigan, and its first newsletter was published in the summer of 1974. Today hundreds of professionals from many disciplines are active members of TAASP—people in psychology, education, anthropology, sociology, and physical education.

The extent that play is seen in children around the world is documented in the many articles and chapters published by TAASP in its newsletter and books (published first by Leisure Press and then beginning in 1986 by Human Kinetics Publishers). A wealth of information is available. Among titles of studies are: "An Examination of Afro-American Speech Play in Integrated Schools," "Play in the Desert and Play in the Town in Bedouin Arab Children," and "Playgrounds and Play Equipment, 1885–1925." For further information write to: The Association for the Anthropological Study of Play, P.O. Box 10, Middle Tennessee State University, Murfreeboro, TN 37132, USA.

---

the working-class Afro-American children tended to be relatively personal and to be taken for the most part from real-life experiences. White middle-income children, on the other hand, tended to tell stories in the third person which were fantasy-like in content. Of the New York stories, 95 percent were in the third person, but only 30 percent of the stories by the Afro-American children were. In each collection, however, clear evidence of imagination, albeit of different types, was seen. Piedmont children were more likely to show their talents in a collective rather than in an individualized context. Sutton-Smith and Heath suggest that often children from cultures that are more oral than literate will appear most imaginative and playful when words are the center of the activity.

METHODOLOGICAL AND CONCEPTUAL ISSUES

We have summarized selected studies that investigated the question of whether social class and cultural factors modify the course of play development and patterns of play behavior. Of central importance has been whether children from low socioeconomic groups and traditional, non-Western societies have underdeveloped skills in imaginative or sociodramatic play. As we have noted, this area of the play literature is still a matter of considerable controversy. The debate revolves around whether there are developmental deficiencies in these social-class and cultural groups or whether studies in this area have been biased by shortcomings in research methods. If the latter is true, differences among groups cannot be interpreted as discrepancies. In this section we will discuss the key methodological and conceptual questions that have arisen in research on social class and cultural factors in play.

McLoyd (1982) criticized research purporting to demonstrate social class differences in sociodramatic play on a number of grounds. Conclusions from research are only as good as the methods used to generate the data on which the conclusions are based, and the methods used in social science research typically are far from foolproof. This is very evident in some of the research studies attacked by McLoyd. First of all, McLoyd rightfully noted several technical weaknesses in many of the studies she reviewed that dealt with social-class comparisons in imaginative play. Technical problems included: (1) inadequate definition or measurement of the social-class variable, (2) lack of statistical tests in some of these studies, and (3) lack of systematic control of classroom and school variables.

Of the studies reviewed in this chapter, only Griffing (1980) used standardized indices of social class; most of the studies based social class on parents' occupation and/or educational level (Fein & Stork, 1981; Rubin et al., 1976; Smith & Dodsworth, 1978; Tizard et al., 1976; Stern et al., 1976). Use of non-standardized measures of social class makes it difficult if not impossible to determine the exact nature of the sample. Moreover, researchers have confounded race and social class (Rosen, 1974) and culture and social class (Smilansky, 1968), making it impossible in their studies to separate the influence of social class on imaginative play from the influence of the confounding variable. Given the rise in variations in contemporary family forms and the changes in the composition of social-class groups, it is important that researchers and practitioners alike pay attention to detailed demographic facts about the groups of children they study or serve. For example, there is a need to make greater differentiation among social class groups within the lower-income strata, and to note the prevalence of single-parent families. Just as working-class children certainly may be expected to be more similar in their play behaviors to middle-income children than they are to children from families with unemployed parents, children from single-parent households with less real-life exposure to two parents in the home cannot be expected to enact reciprocal mother and father roles as well as children who come from two-parent households.

In addition to the failure to perform or report statistical tests of significance (Golomb, 1979; Smilansky, 1968), another technical flaw in many of these studies is the confounding of social class with classroom factors. It is unfortunate enough that observations of spontaneous play were done exclusively in preschool or day care settings; it is further disappointing that in all cases, with the notable exception of Fein and Stork (1981), these observations were done in programs serving only one socioeconomic group or another. Thus, differences among children may reflect classroom effects rather than social-class differences. The importance of classroom variables, such as the nature of the curriculum, will be covered in Chapter 12.

As for the criticism that free-play observations were made only in schools or day care centers, the problem is whether such settings are fair locations to witness the imaginative and creative play of youngsters who are not from white middle-class backgrounds. Again, the failure to see rich imaginative play in these settings designed for middle-class children does not imply that other children are not capable of rich imaginative play in other less biased settings. The importance of setting variables is highlighted by Tizard and others' (1976) finding that low-socioeconomic-status preschoolers, unlike middle-class children of the same age, engaged in more symbolic play outdoors than indoors.

Contrasts in values and social behaviors between children's home settings and school or day care settings may make children generally less comfortable in expressing spontaneously high levels of playfulness and imagination. Second, the activity centers and thematic play materials found in middle-class-oriented schools or day care centers may be less familiar to lower-class children than they are to middle-class children. If young children are not familiar with objects, they tend to explore them initially; if children suspect their behavior will lead to adverse consequences, they tend to be inhibited and reluctant to externalize their fantasies— fantasies they do have. One mother, wishing to emphasize her point, retorted when told by a teacher that her young son did not engage in sociodramatic play at school, "If you knew my son's fantasies, it would blow your mind." For a variety of reasons, then, the classroom or day care center may not be the best place to judge the play abilities of other than middle-class preschoolers.

Several thoughtful recommendations have been made to help researchers more accurately calibrate the imaginative play abilities of low-socioeconomic-status children and children from different cultural backgrounds. McLoyd (1982) has suggested examining the spontaneous play of young children in a broader context

Research on social class and cultural differences in play needs to be conducted in home and neighborhood settings as well as in schools.

including, if not in home and neighborhood settings, then in special playrooms, perhaps two-room mobile laboratories, that can be set up at school but away from the regular classroom. Children could be made familiar with the setting and helped to view it as a safe place where they play and have fun as they please without wariness about a teacher's or a strange researcher's presence. For example, McLoyd, Morrison, and Toler (1979) found that under such conditions pairs and trios of preschoolers exhibited much richer sociodramatic play in their adult role enactments than did preschoolers aware of the presence of an adult. McLoyd recommends that coding systems be devised and employed to capture some of the play and communication patterns of lower-class or ethnically diverse children ignored in previous research. She notes that among Afro-American children, especially from low-income families, verbal communication is laced with affect and expression. Involvement or depth of role play, shown by components such as change of voice to represent changes in feelings or psychological states, needs to be codified to evaluate adequately the quality of sociodramatic play in these children.

Other play scholars who have made excellent suggestions in this vein are Fein and Stork (1981) who are also concerned that we build a more adequate descriptive data base to assess the spontaneous play abilities of different groups of children. Fein and Stork in their study, as we noted, did find a statistically significant difference in a composite score for play quality in favor of middle- over low-socioeconomic-status children enrolled in a heterogeneous day care center. They further reported that additional analyses indicated that for any specific play score assessing aspects of pretense which were age-sensitive (showing a statistically significant difference between older and younger children), lower-socioeconomic-status children were not significantly different from middle-class peers.

Fein and Stork went on to build a case for distinguishing between children's "typical" and "best" display of pretend behavior. Typical play behavior is defined as the type of play that occurs most frequently compared to other types of play that are of interest to the researcher or practitioner observing a group of children. Best play performance is the highest level of play, in terms of a specified coding scheme, that a given child displays. If children from different socioeconomic or cultural groups show substantial discrepancies between typical and best play in a given situation, then we would have to infer that certain environmental or motivational factors were operating. Perhaps only in a very few areas of the classroom or day care center is a targeted high-level behavior like sociodramatic play likely to occur with low-socioeconomic-status children. In contrast, more advantaged children may feel comfortable exhibiting such play in a variety of contexts. We could conclude that lower-socioeconomic-status children have fewer opportunities to display the high-level behavior that they are quite capable of performing. Group differences in high-level make-believe play are differences in play performance, not differences in play competence. Social class or cultural differences, then, are seen as motivational differences and are not necessarily indicators of cognitive maturity.

ROLES OF THE ADULT

Most adults who frequently deal with young children, be they teachers, parents, or other child-care or service specialists, are coming into contact with an increasingly heterogeneous generation of young people in today's world. What responsibilities do we have as we face this challenge?

We mentioned at the beginning of this chapter that we strongly believe that being informed of research studies and key issues is an important initial step to understanding cultural, subcultural and social-class influences on children's play behavior. We hope that this chapter has given the flavor of this area of the play literature which, as we have seen, is fraught with complexity, ambiguity, and controversy, particularly as it pertains to the developmental deficiencies-versus-play differences debate (Feitelson, 1977, vs. Schwartzman, 1978). We now wish to discuss some insights and realizations based on this literature and their implications for practical applications. We believe that adults concerned about children, play, and development have an obligation in two areas: attitude and behavior.

Attitudinal Recommendations. Adults have a responsibility to cultivate a positive attitude toward group differences of whatever type. They may be cultural, socioeconomic, or family structure differences. In a pluralistic society such as ours, we must foster positive attitudes in our children by showing not only tolerance and acceptance but also respect for and enjoyment of group differences. All of us are unique individuals as well as members of a social or cultural group. To center on the group at the expense of the individual or vice versa in perceiving or relating to others belies a certain primitive mode of social reasoning. Most of us fortunately recognize and appreciate individual as well as group variations.

As we have seen in this chapter, it is unwise to make broad generalizations about the relations among culture, social class, and play. Repeatedly, the history of research in the educational, psychological, and social sciences has shown that generalizations based upon differences in lower socioeconomic status, cultural tradition, and family structure give way to more refined conclusions after more detailed studies are done. Use of such dichotomies as lower- versus middle-socioeconomic status usually leads to recognition of the need for more differentiated categories and to the realization that we are dealing with many factors involved in a process. Practitioners must remember this historical trend in the social sciences and not allow researchers to perpetuate stereotypes and misconceptions through preliminary studies of complex topics. As McLoyd (1982) notes, these stereotypes or "pejorative notions...persist long after qualifying, if not outright contradictory, evidence has been proffered" (p. 26). Labeling children as deficient in language use, academic skills, or imaginative play skills based on limited information, even as the prelude to remediation, often does more harm than good. And, if apparent deficiencies do appear in certain individual areas as expressed in a specific range of situations, the sensible person will remember that the problem pertains only to the present. For all we know, a 180-degree turn for the better may occur the next day. Good teachers are known to fail a pupil, but any teacher of worth would never condemn the child's future as hopeless. Rather, the teacher respects the great potential of all children.

Behavioral Recommendations. In addition to maintaining a positive attitude toward children and play, there are a number of practical things we can do to enhance children's development and enjoyment of play.

Fein and Stork (1981) have advocated that teachers who believe that pretend play in the classroom will aid children's development should plan encouragement sessions for those youngsters who seem reluctant to participate in sociodramatic play sessions. They point out that, given the recent suggestion that play performance can be improved fairly easily and swiftly by systematic effort on the part of adults who are friendly and encouraging (Freyberg, 1973), the long, intensive play training used by some researchers (Rosen, 1974; Saltz & Johnson, 1974) may not be necessary. This practical suggestion is consistent with the interpretation of social class or cultural differences in play as motivational or performance differences and not as deficiencies in cognitive functioning or symbolic competence. According to this view, many children may be quite capable of high-level imaginative play but may require adult prompting and perhaps some encouragement to overcome initial shyness. We have also found that some children may need a second chance for performing expressive behaviors in front of others. The first time around, a child may not sing, dance, or perform dramatic play as well as he or she could have, but given time perhaps to think about it, the same child seems to relish the additional opportunity to demonstrate expressive behavior. This is shown by marked improvement in performance when a similar expressive play situation comes up again in the classroom.

Before expecting high-level play, teachers are encouraged to make sure that children have sufficient time to become familiar with materials and routines in the day care center or preschool classroom. For children whose primary language is not English, or for any child who comes from a home environment that is in marked contrast with the school environment, such familiarity is particularly important.

The knowledgeable teacher realizes that generalizations about play behavior do not always hold for individual children.

Children also may benefit by opportunities to play in a more covert or secret fashion (they will find ways to do that anyway) away from adult surveillance.

As McLoyd (1982) has indicated, the knowledgeable teacher will recognize that generalizations about play do not always hold. For example, there is not necessarily an antithetical relationship between high-level imaginative play and physical or outdoor activity. In fact, Tizard et al. (1976) found that low-socioeconomic-status preschoolers exhibited more make-believe play outdoors than indoors. Children from different social-class or cultural backgrounds perhaps take advantage of contexts for fantasy play in ways difficult for middle-class observers to recognize. We must be sensitive to such possible individual or group differences and not underestimate the potential for unusual contexts to lead to high-level imaginative or creative play in children from diverse backgrounds.

Form and content of children's play are influenced by cultural and social-class factors and furthermore express children's interpretation of or commentary on the social environments in which they grow up. As play advocates interested in having all children play to their fullest potential, we must always remain cognizant of the content of each child's own real-life experiences and provide play opportunities in line with children's backgrounds. The typical day care or preschool environment is designed for middle-class children; we should be ready to add to or to modify that environment to accommodate the diverse backgrounds of other children.

This need for adaptation is exemplified by an anecdote of Curry (1971) involving a group of Navajo children. Apparently these children were not familiar with all the props available for dramatic play in the housekeeping corner of their middle-class-oriented preschool center. Teachers found that these children did not engage in sociodramatic play. Many of the children came from homes where there was no running water and the cooking was done over an open fire. These children did not use the domestic corner as it was usually set up for free play. One day, but not by teacher design, the toys were left against the wall after cleaning. The Navajo children then vigorously engaged in sociodramatic play. The props were in the position where they were used to seeing them in their circular hogan homes! Teachers, then, can stimulate imaginative play by modifying the classroom to approximate children's home experiences. Involving paraprofessionals and parents can help teachers tune into these differences.

SUMMARY

This chapter has taken us on a rather ambitious exploration of how cultural and social class variables affect play behavior and development. In our review of the literature, we found that a prevailing theme is the controversy involving developmental deficiencies versus differences. How is the evidence or the lack of evidence of imaginative play in certain groups to be interpreted? Researchers conducting earlier training and comparative studies apparently had taken the position that certain social and cultural groups of children may suffer from underdeveloped imaginative play skills leading to or caused by deficiencies in symbolic competence. In particular, lower-class children and children from non-Western or Third World societies were characterized in this way. However, as we have seen, few researchers have systematically examined a combination of social-class and culture factors in the same study. When socioeconomic and cultural differences were compared, lower socioeconomic status seemed to dominate as the determining factor in apparent developmental delays in imaginative play skill.

Other researchers have adopted the alternative view that differences in play behavior among social classes or cultures are not attributable to fixed background factors but to ephemeral influences. That is, differences observed are differences in performance or in motivation that are transient and based on situation. If lower-class preschoolers and children from non-Western societies have not been observed to engage in rich fantasy play, it is only because we have not used the right methods or techniques to discern that play. Researchers such as Fein and McLoyd have recommended that we observe play behaviors in diverse contexts and that we distinguish between typical play performance and best play performance in evaluating the play of children from diverse social class or cultural backgrounds.

We ended this chapter by recommending that we continue to respect, appreciate and enjoy pluralism in our society, and that we consider each child unique. We also made several practical suggestions to increase our sensitivity to children's diverse home backgrounds and assure continuity between home and school environments. Specific modifications of classroom policies and environments are needed to stimulate imaginative play in certain children.

REFERENCES

Ammar, H. (1954). *Growing up in an Egyptian village*. London: Routledge & Kegan Paul.

Bloch, M.N., & Walsh, D.J. (1983, April). *Young children's activities at home: Age and sex differences in activity, location, and social context*. Paper presented at the annual meeting of the Society for Research in Child Development, Detroit, MI.

Curry, N.E. (1971). Consideration of current basic issues on play. In N. Curry and S. Arnaud (Eds.), *Play: The child strives toward self-realization*. Washington, DC, National Association for the Education of Young Children.

Dansky, J. (1980). Cognitive consequences of sociodramatic play and exploration training for economically disadvantaged preschoolers. *Journal of Child Psychology and Psychiatry, 20*, 47–58.

Ebbeck, F.N. (1973). Learning from play in other cultures. In J.L. Forst (Ed.), *Revisiting early childhood education*. New York: Holt, Rinehart & Winston.

Eiferman, R.P. (1971). Social play in childhood. In R.E. Herron & B. Sutton-Smith (Eds.), *Child's play*. New York: Wiley.

El Konin, D. (1971). Symbolics and its functions in the play of children. In R.E. Herron & B. Sutton-Smith (Eds.), *Child's play*. New York: Wiley.

Fein G., & Stork, L. (1981). Sociodramatic play: Social class effects in integrated preschool classrooms. *Journal of Applied Developmental Psychology. 2*, 267–279.

Feitelson, D. (1959). Aspects of the social life of Kurdish Jews. *Jewish Journal of Sociology, 1*, 201–216.

Feitelson, D. (1977). Cross-cultural studies of representational play. In B. Tizard & D. Harvey (Eds.), *Biology of play* (pp. 6–14). Philadelphia: Lippincott.

Feitelson, D. & Ross, G.S. (1973). The neglected factor—play. *Human Development, 16*, 202–223.

Finley, G.E., & Layne, O. (1971). Play behavior in young children: A cross-cultural study. *The Journal of Genetic Psychology, 119*, 202–210.

Freyberg, J.T. (1973). Increasing the imaginative play of urban disadvantaged kindergarten children through systematic training. In J.L. Singer (Ed.), *The child's world of make-believe* (pp. 129–154). New York: Academic Press.

Golomb, (1979). Pretense play—a cognitive perspective. In N. Smith & M. Franklin (Eds.), *Symbolic functioning in childhood*. New York: Wiley.

Griffing, P. (1980). The relationship between socioeconomic status and sociodramatic play among black kindergarten children. *Genetic Psychological Monographs, 101*, 3–34.

Levine, R., & Levine, A. (1963). *Nyansongo: A Gusii community in Kenya*. In B. Whithing (Ed.), *Six cultures: Studies of child rearing* (pp. 19–202). New York: Wiley.

Lovinger, S.L. (1974). Sociodramatic play and language development in preschool children. *Psychology in the Schools, 11*, 312–320.

McLoyd, V. (1982). Social class differences in sociodramatic play: A critical review. *Developmental Review, 2*, 1–30.

McLoyd, V., Morrison, B., & Toler, B. (1979). *The effects of adult presence vs. absence on children's pretend play*. Paper presented at Hampton-Michigan Research Exchange, Hampton Institute, Hampton, VA.

Mead, M. (1975). Children's play style: Potentialities and limitations of its use as a cultural indicator. *Anthropoligical Quarterly, 48*, 157–181.

Murphy, L.B. (1972). Infant's play and cognitive development. In M.W. Piers (Ed.), *Play and development*. New York: W.W. Norton.

Parten, M. (1932). Social participation among preschool children. *Journal of Abnormal and Social Psychology, 27*, 243–269.

Rosen, C.E. (1974). The effects of sociodramatic play on problem-solving behavior among culturally disadvantaged preschool children. *Child Development, 45,* 920–927.

Rubin, K.H., Maioni, T.L., & Hornung, M. (1976). Free play behavior in middle and lower class preschoolers: Parten and Piaget revisited. *Child Development, 47,* 414.

Saltz, E., & Johnson, J.E. (1974). Training for thematic-fantasy play in culturally disadvantaged children: Preliminary results. *Journal of Educational Psychology, 66,* 623–630.

Saltz, E., Dixon, D., & Johnson, J.E. (1977). Training disadvantaged preschoolers in various fantasy activities: Effects on cognitive functioning and impulse control. *Child Development, 48,* 367–380.

Schwartzman, H. (1978). *Transformations: The anthropology of children's play.* New York: Plenum Press.

Segoe, M.V. (1971). A comparison of children's play in six modern cultures. *Journal of School Psychology, 9,* 61–72.

Singer, J.L. (1973). *The child's world of make-believe.* New York: Academic Press.

Smilansky, S. (1968). *The effects of sociodramatic play on disadvantaged preschool children.* New York: Wiley.

Smith, P.K., & Dodsworth, C. (1978). Social class differences in the fantasy play of preschool children. *Journal of Genetic Psychology, 133,* 183–190.

Stern, V., Bragdon, N., & Gordon, A. (1976). *Cognitive aspects of young children's symbolic play.* Unpublished paper. Bank Street College of Education, New York.

Sutton-Smith, B. (1972). *The folkgames of children.* Austin: The University of Texas Press.

Sutton-Smith, B. (1977). Towards an anthropology of play. In P. Stevens (Ed.), *Studies in the anthropology of play.* West Point, NY: Leisure Press.

Sutton-Smith, B., & Heath, S.B. (1981). Paradigms of pretense. *Quarterly Newsletter of the Laboratory of Comparative Human Cognition, 3,* 41–45.

Tizard, B., Philps, J., & Plewis, I. (1976). Play in pre-school centers. II: Effects on play of the child's social class and of the educational orientation of the center. *Journal of Child Psychology and Psychiatry, 17,* 265–274.

Whiting, B.B. (1963). *Six cultures—studies of childrearing.* New York: Wiley.

Udwin, O., & Shmukler, D. (1981). The influence of socio-cultural economic and home background factors on children's ability to engage in imaginative play. *Developmental Psychology, 17,* 66–72.

Weiner, E.A., & Weiner, B.J. (1974). Differentiation of retarded and normal children through toy-play analysis. *Multivariate Behavioral Research, 9,* 245–252.

8 Observing Play

Observation is the key to understanding children's play behavior. By watching children play, we can learn much about their current play interests: the types of play they like to engage in, the toys and play equipment they prefer to use, the spaces in which they choose to play, and the themes they enjoy enacting during dramatic play. We can also discover children's levels of play development and the strengths and limitations that they exhibit while engaging in different forms of play.

As we emphasized in Chapter 2, observation of children's free-play behaviors is the starting point for adult facilitation of play. Observation serves as a crucial link between provision and involvement (see Figure 2–1). It can reveal when additional time, materials, space or preparatory experiences need to be provided to extend and enrich ongoing play episodes, and it can also indicate when adult involvement in play is appropriate and which type of involvement will be most beneficial. The information gained about children's current play activities allows parents and teachers to satisfy children's interests and needs through provision and adult involvement.

Unfortunately, not all types of observation can serve these valuable functions. Parents and teachers frequently watch children at play, but their observation is often casual and unfocused, resulting in only a vague understanding of the children's play skills and interests. This chapter presents several scales that will enable teachers and parents to observe children's play behavior more systematically. These observation scales specify exactly which play behaviors to look for and provide a way to record the occurrence of these behaviors. We will describe these scales in detail, give instructions for their use, and offer examples of how the information which they yield can be used to facilitate play. In addition, we will outline general procedures for making valid play observations, including suggestions for the use of a new technological aid, videotape equipment.

PLAY OBSERVATION SCALES

Numerous observation scales have emerged as by-products of research on the development of play (see Chapter 3). Many of these instruments are complex and complicated, impractical for applications other than basic research. The 30-category "target child" system utilized by Sylva, Roy, and Painter (1980) in their study of British and U.S. preschools is an example of such a scale. It provides a wealth of data about children's play behavior, but most teachers and parents do not have the time to learn such an elaborate coding system. Other scales, such as ones used to study the development of symbolic representation and action schemes (Rosenblatt, 1977; Fenson & Ramsay, 1980) are designed primarily for use with infants and toddlers and are therefore of limited value to preschool teachers.

We have chosen to focus on three scales that are appropriate for use by early childhood educators and parents: (a) the Parten/Piaget scale, which gives a broad view of the social and cognitive level of children's play; (b) Howes' Peer Play Scale, which gives a fine-grained analysis of social play; and (c) Smilansky's Sociodramatic Play Inventory, which provides a detailed look at group-dramatic play. These scales are all relatively easy to use, and they provide valuable information to parents and teachers who wish to enrich preschoolers' play.

The Parten/Piaget Scale

As we detailed in Chapter 3, children's play develops simultaneously along several dimensions. As children mature, their play tends to become more social. In addition, they begin to engage in more cognitively advanced forms of play, such as constructive play, make-believe, and games with rules. Early play researchers tended to focus on one dimension at a time: social or cognitive. In the mid-1970s, Rubin and his associates combined Parten's (1932) social participation scale with Smilansky's (1968) adaption of Piaget's (1962) cognitive play categories, allowing the two dimensions of play development to be assessed simultaneously (Rubin, Maioni, & Hornung, 1976).

TABLE 8-1

Social-Cognitive Components of Play: Twelve Categories[1]

	Solitary	Parallel	Group
Functional	solitary-functional	parallel-functional	group-functional
Constructive	solitary-constructive	parallel-constructive	group-constructive
Dramatic	solitary-dramatic	parallel-dramatic	group-dramatic
Games	solitary-games	parallel-games	group-games

SOURCE: Adapted from Rubin, Watson, and Jambor (1978)

[1]There are also two nonplay categories: unoccupied and onlooking.

Rubin quickly modified the scale by combining several of Parten's social play categories—associative and cooperative—into one category, group play (Rubin,

PARTEN/PIAGET CATEGORIES: DEFINITIONS

Cognitive Levels

1. **Functional play**—repetitive muscle movements with or without objects. Examples include: (a) running and jumping, (b) gathering and dumping, (c) manipulating objects or materials, and (d) informal games (parading).
2. **Constructive play**—using objects (blocks, Legos, Tinkertoys) or materials (sand, Play-doh, paint) to make something.
3. **Dramatic play**—role playing and/or make-believe transformations. Examples include:
   (a) Role playing: pretending to be a parent, baby, firefighter, shark, superhero, or monster.
   (b) Make-believe transformations: pretending to drive a car (arm movements) or give an injection with a pencil (object use).
   Use of miniature versions of real objects (toy cars, toy iron) is not scored as dramatic play unless there is evidence of role taking and/or make-believe transformations.
4. **Games with rules**—recognition and acceptance of and conformity with *preestablished* rules. Examples include: tag, Mother May I, marbles, checkers, and kickball.

Social Levels

1. **Solitary play**—playing alone with materials different from those of children within speaking distance; no conversation with others.
2. **Parallel play**—playing with toys or engaging in activities similar to those of other children who are in close proximity; however, there is no attempt to play with the other children.
3. **Group play**—playing with other children; roles may or may not be assigned.

Unoccupied/Onlooking/Transition:

Unoccupied behavior, onlooking behavior, moving from one activity to another.

Nonplay Activities:

Activities which must conform to a preestablished pattern, as in academic activities, teacher-assigned tasks. Activities involving coloring books, worksheets, computers, and educational toys (shoelace boards) are often best considered nonplay in nature.

SOURCE: Based on Rubin et al. (1978)

Watson, & Jambor, 1978). The resulting scale, which we shall refer to as the Parten/Piaget scale, consists of twelve play categories (see Table 8–1 on p. 149) plus types of nonplay behavior classified as unoccupied and onlooking.

The Parten/Piaget scale has enabled researchers to obtain data that would have been lost if either the social or cognitive dimension of play development had been assessed in isolation. For example, it was generally accepted for many years that solitary play decreases with age and is indicative of immaturity (Parten, 1932). However, recent research using the two-dimensional Parten/Piaget scale has revealed that, as children grow older, there is a shift from solitary-functional to solitary-constructive and solitary-dramatic play (Moore, Evertson, & Brophy, 1974; Rubin et al., 1978; Smith, 1978). Thus, only one form of solitary play—solitary-functional—is actually associated with immaturity.

Teachers and parents will find that the Parten/Piaget scale is a useful instrument for assessing children's overall level of play development. It has the additional advantage of being relatively easy to understand. The first step is to become familiar with the definitions of the various play and nonplay categories. These categories specify what to look for while observing play. See "Parten/Piaget Categories: Definitions" for our interpretation and modification of this scale. Note that an additional category—nonplay activities—has been added. Our experience has shown that many children choose activities such as reading (or looking at) a book or feeding fish in an aquarium during free-play periods. The new category enables these types of behavior to be recorded.

Next, a recording sheet is needed to make a permanent record of the play that is observed. We suggest using a two-dimensional grid such as the one illustrated in Figure 8–1. This form has a separate box for each of the 12 play categories, allowing the occurrence of each form of solitary, parallel, and group play to be recorded, as well as the two categories of nonplay behavior. A separate form should be used for each child observed. "Coding Play with the Parten/Piaget Scale" illustrates how a variety of different types of play behaviors are recorded on this form.

Finally, a sampling procedure must be selected so that observations can be made systematically. We have found that the multiple-scan sampling procedure developed by Roper and Hinde (1978) works very well with the Parten/Piaget scale when used with observation periods of 15 seconds. This allows enough time for the observer to figure out what type of play is occurring but is also brief enough so that it is unlikely that the type of play will change during one observation period.

The sampling system works as follows. First, shuffle the recording sheets to establish a random order for the observations. You will start your observations with the child whose sheet is on top of the pile. Observe this child for 15 seconds. Then

FIGURE 8-1

Parten/Piaget Recording Sheet

Name: _____   Observation Dates: _____

COGNITIVE LEVEL

		Functional	Constructive	Dramatic	Games with Rules
SOCIAL LEVEL	Solitary				
	Parallel				
	Group				

	UNOCCUPIED/ONLOOKING/TRANSITION	ACTIVITIES
Nonplay		

SOURCE: Adapted from Sponseller and Lowry (1974)

place a tally mark in the box corresponding to the category of play that was observed. For example, if the child was making a block structure with several other children, a mark would be placed in the group-constructive box. After coding the first child's play, place that recording sheet on the bottom of the pile and shift your attention to the child whose recording sheet is now on top of the pile. The second child is then observed for 15 seconds, the play coded, the recording sheet placed on the bottom, and so on. In this manner, children are observed in revolving order, each for 15 seconds. After all of the children have been observed one time, begin the second round of observations. Approximately three observations can be made per minute (allowing 5 seconds between each observation for recording). At this rate, each child in a group of twelve children would be observed once every 4 minutes, or five times during a 20-minute play period.

After 20 to 30 observations have been obtained on a particular child, the recording sheet will begin to reveal the child's play patterns. We recommend that parents and teachers focus their attention on two aspects of the Parten/Piaget recording sheet, taking the child's age into consideration.

First, is the social level of the child's play appropriate for his or her age? It would not be unusual for a two- or three-year-old's recording sheet to have a number of tallies in the parallel play row, the solitary-functional box, or the unoccupied/on-looking/transition box. On the other hand, such a pattern for four- and five-year-old children would be indicative of socially immature play, raising the possibility that intervention might be needed to help them learn the skills necessary for engaging in group play. In such instances, we recommend that Howes' Peer Play Scale, described in the next section, be used to take a more detailed look at the child's social play skills.

Second, does the child regularly engage in cognitively mature forms of play? One would expect four- and five-year-olds to engage in a considerable amount of constructive and dramatic play. If the Parten/Piaget record sheet reveals that most of an older preschooler's tallies fall in the functional play column, this would indicate that intervention in the form of provision (see Chapters 9 and 10) or adult involvement (see Chapter 2), may be needed to encourage constructive and dramatic play. Also, pay particular attention to the group-dramatic play category. If four- or five-year-olds rarely engage in this developmentally significant form of play, play-training procedures such as those described in Chapter 2 may be beneficial. Smilansky's Sociodramatic Play Inventory (described below) should be used to learn more about the child's specific strengths and weaknesses in group-dramatic play before such training is attempted.

CODING PLAY WITH THE PARTEN/PIAGET SCALE

The following examples illustrate how different types of play behavior are coded with the Parten/Piaget scale:

1. Two children are in the housekeeping corner. Each is pretending to cook and prepare a make-believe meal. The children are aware of each other's activities, but they do not interact. (parallel-dramatic)
2. Several children are chasing each other around the room. (group-functional)
3. A child builds a block structure. No other children are close by. (solitary-constructive)
4. Several children play London Bridge. (group-game)
5. Three children are on the floor building "transformer" robots out of interlocking plastic blocks. At the moment, they are not interacting. (parallel-constructive)
6. The three children from #5 pretend that their "transformer" robots are battling with ray guns. (group-dramatic)
7. A child, playing alone, pretends to make a phone call using a toy telephone. (solitary-dramatic)
8. A child is watching several other children playing in the housekeeping corner. (onlooking)
9. Several children are in the library corner reading books. (nonplay-activity)
10. Two children are rolling toy cars across the floor. There is no indication of make-believe, and the children are not interacting. (parallel-functional)
11. Three children are enacting a hospital scene. One child has taken the role of a doctor, one is a nurse, and the other is a sick patient. (group-dramatic)
12. One child is bouncing a ball on the floor. Several other children are nearby, but they are playing with blocks and are not interacting with the "target" child. (solitary-functional)
13. A child is wandering about, not doing anything in particular. (unoccupied)
14. Several children are working together to build a highway out of blocks. (group-constructive)
15. Two children are feeding hamsters at a science interest center. (nonplay-activity)

Howes' Peer Play Scale

Howes (1980) has developed an observation scale that examines children's social play behaviors in more detail than the Parten/Piaget scale. This instrument, the Peer Play Scale, has two categories of parallel play: Level 1, Simple Parallel Play, and Level 2, Parallel Pay with Mutual Regard. In addition, there are three group-play categories: Level 3, Simple Social Play; Level 4, Complementary/Reciprocal Play with Mutual Awareness; and Level 5, Complementary/Reciprocal Social Play.

The figure below illustrates where these examples would be marked on the Parten/Piaget recording sheet. In actual practice, tally marks would be used rather than numbered descriptions of the activities.

	Functional	Constructive	Dramatic	Games with rules
Solitary	(12) ball bouncing	(3) block building	(7) telephone call	
Parallel	(10) car rolling	(5) building robots	(1) meal preparation	
Group	(2) chasing	(14) road building	(6) battling robots (11) hospital	(4) London Bridge

	UNOCCUPIED/ONLOOKING/TRANSITION	ACTIVITIES
Nonplay	(8) watching "house" play (13) wandering around	(9) reading book (15) feeding hamsters

HOWES' PEER PLAY SCALE: DEFINITIONS

Level 1—Simple Parallel Play:

Children, in close proximity to one another, are involved in similar activities but do not engage in eye contact or any social behavior. For example, several children might be sitting near one another playing with blocks, totally absorbed in their own play. It is as though they were not aware of one another's existence.

Level 2—Parallel Play with Mutual Regard:

Children are involved in similar activities and engage in eye contact. For example, children who are playing with blocks would occasionally look at one another and at other block constructions. The children, though not socially interacting, are aware of others' presence and activities. Children at this stage often imitate each other's play. One child might, for example, copy another child's block construction.

Level 3—Simple Social Play:

Children direct social behaviors to one another. Typical behaviors include vocalizing, offering objects, smiling, touching, taking toys, and aggression. The children's play activities, however, are not coordinated. For example, children playing with blocks might make comments on each others' constructions (*e.g.,* "That's pretty."). Or, on the negative side, one child might take another child's block, and the other child respond with a verbal reprimand or aggression.

Level 4—Complementary/Reciprocal Play with Mutual Awareness:

Children engage in activities in which their actions reverse other children's actions, demonstrating awareness of each other's roles. For example, one of the children playing blocks may offer a block to another child, who receives it and then offers another block back. Or the two children might build a joint structure, taking turns adding blocks. At this level, however, no conversation or other social exchange takes place between the children.

Level 5—Complementary/Reciprocal Social Play:

Children engage in complementary and reciprocal activities, as in Level 4, and in social exchanges, as in Level 3. For example, children building the joint block structure might converse back and forth. ("Don't put that block there. It's too small.") Or several children might plan and then act out a make-believe story (*i.e.,* group-dramatic play).

SOURCE: Based on Howes (1980)

See "Howes' Peer Play Scale: Definitions" for our descriptions of these five levels.

Howes' scale focuses on two dimensions of peer play: (a) the complexity of the social interactions among children, and (b) the degree to which their activities are organized and integrated. At Levels 1 and 2, both children's social behavior and activities are undifferentiated and noncomplementary. At the intermediary levels, the children engage in social exchanges without complementary activities (Level 3) or complementary activities without social exchanges (Level 4). Only at Level 5 do children engage in both social interaction and complementary activities. "Coding Play with the Peer Play Scale" gives examples of how to record different play behaviors using this system.

We have developed a recording sheet for use with the Peer Play Scale (Figure 8–2). Parten's solitary-play category and several nonplay categories have been added so that every behavior observed during free play can be classified. We have also included a column to record instances in which a child interacts with the teacher during play. A final column has been appended in which to note play areas and play

FIGURE 8–2

Peer Play Scale: Recording Sheet

Child's Name: _____   Dates Observed: _____

Time	Solitary Play	Simple Parallel Play Level 1	Parallel Play with Regard Level 2	Simple Social Play Level 3	Same Activity with Regard Level 4	Same Activity with Social Bid Level 5	Nonplay Activities	Onlooking/ Unoccupied/ Transition	Teacher Involved (Y = Yes)	Area in or Objects Used
1										
2										
3										
4										
5										
6										
7										
8										
9										
10										
11										
12										
13										
14										
15										
Total										

materials that are being used by the child. As with the Parten/Piaget scale, a separate recording sheet is needed for each child.

The same 15-second sampling procedure that was recommended for the Parten/Piaget scale can be used with the Peer Play recording sheet. Start by observing the first child for 15 seconds. This first observation will be recorded in the Time 1 row. Place a tally mark in the appropriate column to indicate the social level of the play: solitary, levels 1–5, nonplay activity, or onlooking/unoccupied/transition. If the child was interacting with a teacher, place a "Y" in the Teacher Involved column. Finally, note the area in which the child was playing and any materials that the child

CODING PLAY WITH THE PEER PLAY SCALE

What You See

1. Two children, close to each other, are riding big trucks around the center of a room. At one point, their paths separate. The "target" child looks around the room until he finds the other child. Then he goes back to driving his truck.

2. Two children in the block area are building a house together. They direct each other as to which blocks to use and where to place them.

3. In the dramatic-play area, a boy is sitting in a chair while another child is pretending to give him a haircut. There is no conversation.

4. Two girls are working on puzzles next to each other. One child says, "I can't do it." The other responds, "Just keep trying all the pieces."

How You Code

This would be coded as Level 2, Parallel Play with Mutual Regard, because the child being observed showed an awareness of the other child. If the "target" child had not looked at the other child, it would have been Level 1, Simple Parallel Play.

This would be coded as Level 5, Complementary/Reciprocal Social Play, because the children are playing with each other and are carrying on a conversation. If they were not talking, it would be Level 4, Complementary/Reciprocal Play with Mutual Regard.

This would be coded as Level 4 because the children are playing together and showing an awareness of each other's role but are not conversing or directing social bids to each other. It would become Level 5 if they talked to each other or if one child offered a mirror to the other (a social bid.)

This would be coded as Level 3, Simple Social Play. The two children have directed social bids to each other, but they are working on separate puzzles (as opposed to working complementarily on one puzzle). If the second girl had left her puzzle to work with the first girl, it would be coded Level 5 (conversation continues) or Level 4 (no further conversation).

SOURCE: Zipser, 1982

was playing with. Then observe the next child for 15 seconds, coding play in the Time 1 row, and proceed as before. After all the children have been observed once, observe the first child again, coding the play in the Time 2 row. Approximately two observations can be made per minute because it takes about 15 seconds between observations to record all the information on the sheet.

Once a number of observations of a child have been made, the recording sheet can be examined for patterns in social play behavior. Column totals for the various social play categories will give a detailed picture of the child's level of social play. If the child primarily engages in parallel play, it is interesting to note whether the child is (Level 2) or is not (Level 1) aware of nearby children. If the child does engage in some group play, does this play typically involve social interaction (Level 3), complementary activities (Level 4), or both (Level 5)? This information can determine which aspects of peer play specific children need help with: social awareness, social communication, or the ability to coordinate activities with other children.

It is also helpful to look across the record sheet rows for patterns. One might find that a child exhibits higher levels of social play when: (a) the teacher is (or is not) involved, (b) the child is in a particular area of the classroom, or (c) the child is playing with particular play materials. This information can be very useful in attempting to enhance children's play. For example, if a child is observed engaging only occasionally in social play, and most of these instances occur in the housekeeping corner, the teacher might encourage the child to spend more time in that area. Or if it is discovered that a child exhibits social play only in the few instances in which a teacher is present, then direct adult involvement in play, such as the play-tutoring procedures described in Chapter 2, might be an effective way to improve the social level of the child's play. Specific procedures for encouraging social skills and social play behaviors are described in Chapter 5, "Play and Social Development."

Smilansky's Sociodramatic Play Inventory

Group dramatic play, also referred to as sociodramatic play, takes place when two or more children adopt roles and act out a story (superheroes versus villains) or real-life situation (a family going shopping). Although deceptively simple on the surface, this type of play places heavy cognitive, linguistic, and social demands on children. Among skills needed are symbolic representation, perspective taking, precise use of language, cooperation, and sharing (see Chapter 1). As a result, group-dramatic play is generally regarded as one of the most—if not the most—developmentally important forms of play.

The Parten/Piaget scale will indicate how frequently children engage in group-dramatic play. If the recording sheet for a child age four or older contains few tally marks in the group-dramatic box, then intervention in the form of provision and/or adult involvement may be appropriate. First, however, more information should be gathered about the child's grasp of the skills needed for engaging in this complex form of play.

Smilansky (1968), as part of her play-training study, has developed an instrument that is ideal for this purpose. The Sociodramatic Play Inventory consists of five components or attainments that characterize high-quality group-dramatic play: (a) role playing, (b) make-believe transformations, (c) social interaction, (d) verbal communication, and (e) persistence (see "Sociodramatic Play Inventory: Definitions"). The system can reveal which of these components are present in a child's play and which are missing. Intervention can then focus on the missing elements.

The Sociodramatic Play Inventory (SPI) recording sheet is a checklist: children's names are listed in rows and the five play components are listed in columns. Note that this format allows one form to be used to observe a number of different children. We have modified Smilansky's scale slightly by adding separate columns for each of

---

SOCIODRAMATIC PLAY INVENTORY: DEFINITIONS

Role-Playing:

Children adopt roles (family member, firefighter, Count Dracula) and communicate these roles through verbal declarations ("I'm the mommy") and role-appropriate behavior (taking care of a pretend baby).

Make-Believe Transformations:

Symbols are used to stand for objects, actions, and situations.

1. Objects are used as substitutes for other objects (pretending that a block of wood is a drinking cup) or verbal declarations are used to create imaginary objects (staring at one's empty hand and declaring, "My glass is empty!").
2. Abbreviated actions are used as substitutes for real actions (pretending to be hammering by moving one's hand up and down) or verbal statements are used to create an imaginary action ("I'm hammering the nails in").
3. Imaginary situations are created through verbal declarations ("Let's pretend that we're on a jet plane").

Social Interaction:

At least two children are directly interacting with each other in connection with the play episode. (In terms of the Peer Play Scale, this requires at least Level 4 play, Complementary/Reciprocal Play with Mutual Awareness.)

Verbal Communication:

Children engage in verbal exchanges related to the play episode. These exchanges

---

the three types of make-believe transformations (object, action, and situation) and for the two major types of verbal communication (metacommunication and pretend communication). The resulting sheet, illustrated in Figure 8–3, allows a more detailed look at children's sociodramatic play skills than was possible with the original scale.

The multiple-scan sampling technique recommended for use with the Parten/ Piaget and Peer Play scales is not very appropriate for the SPI. The reason is that longer periods of observation are needed in order to make a decision about the presence or absence of some of the sociodramatic play components. Persistence, for example, can be determined only after a period of observation lasting at least 5 or 10 minutes. An observation procedure similar to that used by Smilansky (1968) in her play-training study should be used with the SPI. That is, a small number of children

---

may take two forms:

1. Metacommunication statements are used to structure and organize the play episode. Children use these comments to:
   (a) designate the make-believe identities of objects ("Let's pretend the rope is a snake").
   (b) assign roles ("I'll be the Daddy, and you be the baby").
   (c) plan story lines ("First, we'll go to the market, and then we'll go to the toy store").
   (d) rebuke players who act in an inappropriate manner ("Mommies don't talk like that!" or "That's not a hose, silly—it's a snake").
2. Pretend communication statements are appropriate for the role the child has adopted. A child enacting the role of a teacher might announce to other players, "You've been naughty children. You will all have to go see the principal."

Persistence:

Children engage in sustained play episodes. Age should be a factor in determining the length of time required for crediting a child with persistence. Based on research by Sylva et al. (1980) and Smilansky (1968), we recommend that preschoolers be expected to sustain at least 5-minute episodes and that kindergartners be expected to keep their episodes going for at least 10 minutes. Play-period duration is another factor which needs to be taken into consideration. If play periods are very brief (10 to 15 minutes), the above time requirements will need to be reduced.

SOURCE: Based on Smilansky (1968)

FIGURE 8-3

Sociodramatic Play Inventory: Recording Sheet

| Name | Role Play | Make-Believe | | | Interaction | Verbal Communication | | Persistence |
		Objects	Actions	Situation		Metacommunication	Pretend	

SOURCE: Adapted from Smilansky (1968)

are observed for a long period, and then a decision is made as to which of the five elements are present in each child's play.

We recommend the following procedures when using this system:

1. Select two or three children to be the focus of your observations. These should be children who exhibited low frequencies of group-dramatic play when observed with the Parten/Piaget scale.
2. Focus your attention on these children for the entire play period, shifting back and forth among them. Watch one child for about a minute, then shift to the next child.
3. At the end of the play period, place a check in the appropriate column of the SPI recording sheet for each sociodramatic play element observed in each

child's play. If an element (*e.g.*, social interaction) occurred only briefly during the play period, place a "?" in the corresponding column to indicate that this behavior is beginning to emerge but is still not fully developed.

4. If a child appears to be missing one or more of the play components, observe the child again on another day. It is premature to conclude on the basis of only one observation that a child does not possess a particular play behavior.

After the children have been observed on several occasions, the recording sheet can be consulted to determine which elements are present and which are absent in each child's play. A child who shows the full gamut of play components would be judged competent in sociodramatic play, and the role of the adult would be minimal. On the other hand, a child who appears to be missing one or more of the components needs intervention so that these behaviors can be incorporated into play. For example, if a child does not engage in role playing, play-tutoring procedures such as those described in Chapter 2 can be used to encourage this behavior. Sets of materials that encourage role playing, such as prop boxes, can also be provided (see Chapter 9). Strategies for promoting the five sociodramatic play components are presented throughout this book (see Table 8–2 for a list of suggestions and corresponding chapters).

Be sure to take children's age into consideration when interpreting the SPI recording sheet. While group dramatic play begins to appear by two years of age, most children do not engage in fully elaborated sociodramatic play until age three or beyond (Rubin, Fein, & Vandenberg, 1983). Teachers and parents should not worry if two- and three-year-olds do not exhibit all five sociodramatic elements in their play. Also, as we explained in Chapter 7, there is some evidence that children from low-socioeconomic-status backgrounds tend to engage in more make-believe play

TABLE 8–2

Strategies for Promoting Sociodramatic Play Behaviors: Chapter Locations

Element	Provision	Involvement	Chapter
Role Playing	Prop Boxes	Play Tutoring	2, 9, & 12
Make-Believe Transformations	Toys—appropriate level of realism	Play Tutoring	2, 9, & 12
Social Interaction	Toys—high social value	Play Tutoring Parent-Child Games Instruction: Induction Distancing	2, 5, & 9
Verbal Communication	Preparatory Experiences	Play Tutoring Parent-Child Games	2, 5, & 12
Persistence	Partitioned Play Areas	Parallel Playing Co-playing Play Tutoring	2 & 10

Constructive play occurs when materials, such as unit blocks, are used to build something. Once completed, the constructions are often used as props in dramatic play.

outdoors than indoors (Tizard, Philps, & Plewis, 1976). Therefore, be sure to observe children's play across a variety of situations in both indoor and outdoor settings before concluding that they are missing any sociodramatic play skills.

GENERAL GUIDELINES FOR OBSERVING PLAY

In this chapter we have focused on three observation scales, each of which provides different information about children's play behavior. Choice of scale should be based upon purpose. If the goal is to obtain an overall view of children's play patterns, the Parten/Piaget scale is ideal. It is a good screening device that will indicate when the other, more specific observation scales are needed. If a child's Parten/Piaget record sheet indicates an overall low level of social play, then the Peer Play Scale will provide more detailed information about this aspect of the child's play. If a four- or five-year-old's group-dramatic play box contains few tallies, then the Sociodramatic Play Inventory can be used to identify which specific group-dramatic play skills the child needs.

In using any of the above scales, several guidelines should be kept in mind to obtain a valid picture of children's play behavior:

1. Try to make the observations in a setting that will allow children to display the full extent of their play abilities.
   (a) Be sure that ample materials conducive to constructive play (blocks, Tinkertoys, Legos) and dramatic play (dolls, housekeeping props, costumes, theme-related prop boxes) are available. Absence of these important types of play may be caused by lack of materials rather than lack of play skills. The relationship between play and play materials is examined in detail in Chapter 9.

(b) Be sure to observe children from disadvantaged backgrounds in both indoor and outdoor settings. Research indicates that these children often engage in more dramatic play outdoors than indoors (see Chapter 7).

2. Delay observations until children have had a chance to get to know each other. Research has shown that children exhibit higher social and cognitive levels of play with familiar peers (Doyle, Connolly, & Rivest, 1980). Observations made at the beginning of the school year can underestimate children's true play abilities. Naturally, this advice also applies to observing children who have recently transferred into a classroom.

3. Observe children's play behavior over time to ensure that it is representative of their typical play behaviors. It is unwise to base decisions about play on a single day's observation. Children may happen to be paired with playmates with whom they do not get along, or with play materials that do not match their interests. Illness, problems at home, and other temporary conditions may also influence play on a particular day. Always try to spread observations over as long a period as possible to minimize the effects of any transient factors. Two or three observations spread over at least a week would be a bare minimum.

VIDEOTAPE RECORDINGS

Videotape equipment is becoming increasingly available in homes and schools. This equipment can be used in several ways to assist the observation of children's play.

First, video equipment provides a solution to a major problem associated with play observation: How can a busy parent or teacher find the time to make systematic observations of play? A video camera aimed at important play areas (housekeeping corner, block area) records ongoing play without requiring any attention or effort on the part of the adult. The tapes can be replayed when time permits. Videotape recordings can be used to analyze behavior with respect to any of the three systems described in this chapter. One problem associated with unmonitored videotaping is that only the children who choose to play in target areas will be taped. This can be solved by manually taping the children who do not play in these areas.

Second, video recordings provide a much more detailed record of play behavior than is possible with firsthand observation. In addition to showing the type of play, the tapes will reveal (a) the materials that are played with, (b) the interaction between the target child and other children and adults, (c) the language used, and (d) the nonverbal gestures of children and adults.

Third, teachers and parents can use videotapes to improve their observation skills. Several teachers, for example, might view a tape of a play episode and score it with one of the above systems. They could then compare how they each coded the different play behaviors. In this manner, the teachers' inter-rater reliability or consistency would be greatly enhanced.

Finally, teachers can use videotapes to evaluate and improve their play involvement skills. In a study by Wood, McMahon, and Cranstoun (1980), preschool teachers taped their interactions with children during free-play periods with small audiocassette recorders. The recordings were then transcribed (see examples in Chapter 2) and examined by the teachers. As a result, many of the teachers changed their play involvement strategies. Teachers who tended to be too directive and domineering became less so, and those who focused most of their attention on management activities began to participate more in their students' play. This kind of self-evaluation could be accomplished more efficiently with video equipment. Video recordings would provide a much more detailed record of teachers' activities and children's reactions to those activities. In addition, videotapes, unlike audiotapes, do not need to be transcribed.

SUMMARY

In this chapter we described three useful observation systems: (a) the Parten/Piaget scale, which provides a general view of the social and cognitive level of children's play; (b) Howes' Peer Play Scale, which gives a detailed analysis of the social level of children's play; and (c) Smilansky's Sociodramatic Play Inventory, which provides a close look at the components which constitute high-quality group-dramatic play. Guidelines were presented for the use of each of the scales.

The authors of this book have all taught undergraduate and graduate early childhood education courses dealing with play. As part of the course requirements, we have had our students—mostly teachers in training or practicing preschool and kindergarten teachers—use observation systems like the ones described above to code children's free play behaviors. Our students' reaction to these systems has been overwhelmingly positive. Many of our students have commented that they had, in their previous casual observations, never realized how complex children's play was nor what a rich a source of information it could be. Others reported that they discovered, much to their surprise, that some children rarely interacted with others while playing or seldom engaged in make-believe play. Once such problems are discovered, it is not difficult to plan ways to enrich the children's play (see Chapters 2, 5, 9, and 10 for suggestions). However, without systematic observation, adults may not notice that children are displaying immature play patterns; thus, nothing will be done to help these children reap the full benefits of play activity. We hope that you will try the three systems described in this chapter. You will learn a lot about children in the process, and you will be better able to enrich their play experiences.

REFERENCES

Doyle, A., Connolly, J., & Rivest, L. (1980). The effect of playmate familiarity on the social interactions of young children. *Child Development, 51*, 217–223.

Fenson, L., & Ramsay, D.S. (1980). Decentration and integration of the child's play in the second year. *Child Development, 51*, 171–178.

Howes, C. (1980). Peer play scale as an index of complexity of peer interaction. *Developmental Psychology, 16*, 371–372.

Moore, N.V., Evertson, C.M., & Brophy, J.E. (1974). Solitary play: Some functional reconsiderations. *Developmental Psychology, 10*, 830–834.

Parten, M.B. (1932). Social participation among preschool children. *Journal of Abnormal and Social Psychology, 27*, 243–269.

Piaget, J. (1962). *Play, dreams and imitation in childhood.* New York: Norton.

Roper, R., & Hinde, R.A. (1978). Social behavior in a play group: Consistency and complexity. *Child Development, 49*, 570–579.

Rosenblatt, D. (1977). Developmental trends in infant play. In B. Tizard & D. Harvey (Eds.), *Biology of play* (pp. 33–44). London: Heinemann.

Rubin, K.H., Fein, G. G., & Vandenberg, B. (1983). Play. In P. H. Mussen (Ed.), *Handbook of child psychology: Vol. 4. Socialization, personality, and social development* (4th ed., pp. 693–774). New York: Wiley.

Rubin, K.H., Maioni, T.L., & Hornung, M. (1976). Free play behaviors in middle and lower-class preschoolers: Parten and Piaget revisited. *Child Development, 47*, 414–419.

Rubin, K.H., Watson, K.S., & Jambor, T.W. (1978). Free-play behaviors in preschool and kindergarten children. *Child Development, 49*, 534–536.

Smilansky, S. (1968). *The effects of sociodramatic play on disadvantaged preschool children.* New York: Wiley.

Smith, P.K. (1978). A longitudinal study of social participation in preschool children: Solitary and parallel play reexamined. *Developmental Psychology, 14*, 512–516.

Sponseller, D., & Lowry, M. (1974). Designing a play environment for toddlers. In D. Sponseller (Ed.), *Play as a learning medium.* Washington, DC: National Association for the Education of Young Children.

Sylva, K., Roy, C., & Painter, M. (1980). *Childwatching at playgroup & nursery school.* Ypsilanti, MI: High/Scope Press.

Tizard, B., Philps, J., & Plewis, I. (1976). Play in pre-school centres—II. Effects on play of the child's social class and of the educational orientation of the centre. *Journal of Child Psychology and Psychiatry, 17*, 265–274.

Wood, D., McMahon, L., & Cranstoun, Y. (1980). *Working with under fives.* Ypsilanti, MI: High/Scope.

Zipser, A.E. (1982). *Preschool interactive play maturity as a function of classroom type and sibling status.* Unpublished Master's thesis. University of Wisconsin.

9

Toys and Play Materials

W hen we think of play, toys inevitably come to mind. This is because all forms of play are closely linked with objects and materials. In functional play, children pound, push, roll, bounce, and otherwise manipulate a variety of objects. Constructive play involves using materials to build things. In dramatic play, objects become props to support make-believe stories. Many games involve materials such as cards, dice, or balls. One study of British preschools found that 97 percent of children's free-play activity involved some kind of material (Tizard, Philps, & Plewis, 1976).

Parents and educators recognize the toy-play relationship and spend millions of dollars each year keeping children well supplied with play materials. Mergen (1982) reports that as many as 5,000 new items are introduced every year by more than 1,200 U.S. and foreign toy manufacturers. The president of the Toy Manufacturers of America recently estimated that American parents had 150,000 different toys and playthings from which to choose (Mergen, 1982).

This chapter will begin with a brief discussion of the interaction between children and playthings. Different types of play materials will be described under four categories: instructional materials, real materials, constructional materials, and toys. Then, research on the effects of playthings on the social and cognitive level of children's play will be reviewed, with the issue of toy realism examined. The role of the adult in children's toy play will then be discussed. Finally, we will make suggestions for resolving conflicts over play materials.

INTERPLAY BETWEEN CHILDREN AND PLAY MATERIALS

One important aspect of the interplay between children and play materials is the direct physical experience with the world that occurs in the process of play. When very young children engage in repetitive functional play with objects, they act on the objects and observe the results of their actions. In Piaget's terms, the child assimilates the object (a rubber ball) to action schemes that he or she already possesses (rolling) but must also change or accommodate those actions to fit the characteristics of the object. In our example, the child's movements are adjusted to the size and weight of the ball. As a result, intellectual growth and adaption take place.

As children reach preschool age, their play shifts from functional to constructive and dramatic. In the process, the role of play materials changes. Children begin to use objects to stand for other things, gaining valuable experience with symbolic representation. While still cognizant of the physical properties of the materials with which they play, children are increasingly able to ignore those properties and use the materials in any way they choose. For example, three-year-olds will tend to use miniature cups, saucers, and silverware as props in mealtime dramatizations, while four- and five-year-olds are apt to use these same objects as "spaceships" in a Star Wars theme. As children grow older, play materials become increasingly subject to the requirements of the play.

Play materials also act as a stimulus or resource for play. Certain types of materials tend to elicit specific forms of play. Materials such as blocks, Tinkertoys, and Legos inspire constructive play, whereas dolls, dress-up clothes, and housekeeping props encourage make-believe. Materials can also affect the social quality of play; some encourage solitary play, others group play. Play materials can therefore indirectly affect children's growth by stimulating types of play important for development. Later in this chapter we will examine research on how materials influence play patterns, and we will suggest how this information can be used to encourage desirable forms of play.

TYPES OF PLAY MATERIALS

Systems for identifying, describing, classifying, or grouping play materials are needed because of the tremendous number of play objects available. Classifying playthings—describing and understanding them—helps us use them more effectively with young children.

There are many classification systems for playthings. Toy manufacturers use children's chronological ages to describe and group play materials. In this system, there are toys for two-year-olds (stacking toys), others for three-year-olds (table blocks), still others for those who are four (construction sets), etc. Some manufacturers list recommended age ranges for their play materials. A major problem with this system is that it ignores individual differences in rate of development, though age ranges offer a partial solution. Chronological age is a rather inexact criterion for selecting materials.

Another system classifies materials by the type of play they are supposed to represent (Matterson, 1965). For example, wash basins and plastic floating toys would be classified as "water play" materials, and dolls and dress-up clothes as "housekeeping" materials. Classifying play items by probable use, however, ignores the fact that children often choose to use play materials in ways different than adults intend. For example, a child might incorporate pieces of dress-up clothes into a block construction.

A third system focuses on the motor patterns children use while playing with objects (Community Playthings, 1981; Krown, 1971). This system groups play materials into at least two categories: small-motor and large-motor toys. Another category is often created for blocks, even though some blocks can fit the other two categories. The rationale for the small-motor category is that materials of this type give practice to small muscles and improve fine-movement skills. Play materials such as stacking toys and pegboards are grouped in this category. Play materials that fall into the large-motor category are those that encourage large-muscle use and whole-body movement and coordination. Examples of materials in this category are wheel toys, such as scooters, and bounding and jumping toys.

This motor classification system presents several problems. First, motor patterns are intertwined, and as children play with small-motor toys such as puzzles, they frequently need to use their large muscles (*e.g.*, to lift and position the puzzle). Second, there are important play materials that cannot be described or classified by this system, such as dress-up clothes and props for dramatic play.

Another, more comprehensive system for describing and classifying play materials focuses on the general purpose or function of the material as identified by commercial manufacturers (Hartley, Frank, & Goldenson, 1952; Yawkey & Trostle, 1982). This system does not imply that children will use the materials in the specific way identified by the manufacturers. Instead, the system suggests general ways in which materials can be grouped and used. In addition, the system attempts to balance kinds of play materials to maximize growth through play.

This system classifies materials into four main categories: instructional materials, real objects, constructional materials, and toys.

Instructional Materials

Instructional materials are manufactured by commercial toy companies to promote learning and development. Since they are designed to teach specific skills and concepts, they are more didactic, structured, and outcome-oriented than other types of play materials. All areas of the curriculum, including reading, mathematics, science, and social studies, use skills taught by these materials. Examples of skills and concepts embedded in these materials include:

- understanding part-whole relations
- self-help skills such as tying shoelaces
- recognizing colors and learning their names
- arranging items by size
- understanding one-to-one correspondence

Formboard puzzles can promote eye-hand coordination and give children experience with the concepts of one-to-one correspondence and part-to-whole relationships.

Materials in this category include puzzles, stacking toys, nesting objects, and pegboards.

Puzzles. Puzzles are usually designed to promote eye-hand coordination and provide practice matching shapes and sizes, developing one-to-one correspondence, and ultimately constructing a whole from its parts. Yawkey and Trostle (1982) noted that the most common type of puzzle for very young children is the formboard with removable inserts. Formboard puzzles are easily manipulated by toddlers because of the small number (from four to six pieces) and large size of the inserts. Knobs are often attached to the inserts to assist manipulation.

Jigsaw puzzles are designed for older children. Because the pieces of a jigsaw are smaller than those used in formboards and there are many more of them, jigsaws require more advanced small-motor skills and a higher level of conceptual development. Of course, jigsaws do vary in difficulty. Those intended for beginners may have as few as three to eight pieces and contain very simple pictures.

Stacking Toys. These toys are designed to give children practice arranging objects by size, from smallest to largest, or by color. Stacking toys help to teach children the concept of seriation and promote hand-eye coordination as well.

Stringing Toys. There are many kinds of stringing sets, including wood, plastic, and metal. Stringing sets usually consist of a waxed cord and small pieces with their centers drilled out. Children put the cord through the centers of each of the pieces, providing practice in eye-hand coordination and in sequencing.

Nesting Materials. These materials are designed to develop sequencing skills and an understanding of size relationships. The child's task is to order the pieces by size, one inside the other, in succession. Yawkey and Trostle (1982) felt that nesting toys provide a version of the game Peek-a-Boo: The child sees an object, inserts it in a larger one, and then watches it disappear from view. Nesting toys come with four or more pieces and in numerous shapes (eggs, dolls, kangaroos).

Pegboard Sets. This popular instructional material promotes recognition of shapes (*e.g.*, square versus circle) as well as eye-hand coordination. Children insert pegs into holes in the pegboard to copy patterns or to make designs of their own.

Other examples of instructional materials include sorting games (arranging objects by one dimension or more), templates (drawing around the outlines of objects), locking games (opening and closing various items), button boards (matching button to buttonhole), shoelace boards (lacing and tying), zippering boards (opening and closing), and computer games.

Real Materials

Real materials are objects that have specific, nonplay uses in the adult world. These materials make excellent playthings because they tend to be versatile and self-motivating (that is, adults use them and children want to be like adults). Examples of playthings in the real material category include sand, mud, water, clay (and child forms such as Play-doh), food, wood, woodworking tools, and adult (dress-up) clothing.

Sand, Water, and Mud. These materials have no defined form and are shaped by the containers in which they are placed. They are inexpensive and extremely versatile. Using containers as funnels, tubes, and molds, children learn how sand and water react. Although somewhat messy, sand and water can be used easily indoors in commercially manufactured tables. Sand can, of course, also be contained in both indoor and outdoor sandboxes.

Coarse sand, commonly called "builder's sand," is preferable to fine sand for indoor play. Fine sand—the kind found on beaches—is more expensive, has a tendency to cling to children's clothing, and is more difficult to clean up.

Mud is another versatile natural play material. It can be smooth or gritty, runny or dry, and it is easy to mold. Of course, it is also quite messy. For practical suggestions on how to use mud in preschool settings, see Hill (1977).

Clay and Play-doh. Clay is another natural material that is ideally suited for play. It can be rolled, torn, mashed, or used with many other items such as popsicle sticks and cookie cutters. Plastic modeling clay and Play-doh can be used with or substituted for real clay.

Food. Foods are natural play materials regardless of their state—raw, cooked, ground, or frozen. Children can experience the different properties of food by using many of their senses. Selected foods can also be made by children, with adult guidance. Some of the foods easily made through play activities are peanut butter, gelatin, applesauce, cookies, and popcorn.

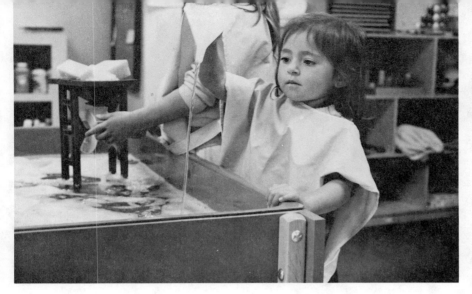

Play with water, sand, and other natural materials provides many opportunities for learning.

Wood and Woodworking Tools. Wood in varied shapes and sizes usually can be obtained without cost from local lumberyards. White pine, rather than plywood or any of the hardwoods, is best-suited for play because it is soft, pliable, lightweight, and relatively splinter-free.

Among tools that can be used with wood are:

- hammers and nails
- screw drivers and screws
- workbench and vise
- saws
- nuts, bolts, and wrenches

To protect them against injury, children using woodworking tools must be closely supervised.

Constructional Materials

Constructional play materials are designed to be used by children in numerous ways. Unlike instructional materials, which have rather specific uses, constructional materials offer many possible outcomes. Legos, for example, can be built, torn down, and rebuilt hundreds of times in hundreds of different ways. In addition, children can consider the building process complete at any point in the construction. Puzzles, on the other hand, are not complete until the last piece is inserted to finish the picture or design.

Blocks. Blocks come in many different shapes, sizes, colors, and materials (wood, cardboard, plastic). It is traditional to categorize blocks as being either small building blocks or large hollow blocks. Small building blocks are further divided into unit blocks and table blocks. Unit blocks come in a standard unit, and all other sizes and

Large hollow blocks encourage both construction activity and dramatic play.

shapes in the set are multiples of the unit. Although the standard unit varies among manufacturers, the size of 1 3/8 × 2 3/4 × 5 1/2 inches is used by most toy companies. This standardization permits mixing of blocks from different manufacturers without destroying the size relationships or the building quality of the blocks. The blocks are usually made of kiln-dried maple or birch; the edges beveled and the surfaces sanded to reduce splintering. These features make unit blocks durable but also expensive. Figure 9–1 illustrates the different shapes and sizes in a typical set of unit blocks. Readers wishing to learn more about unit blocks should read *The Block Book* by Hirsch (1974).

Table blocks, the other type of small building blocks, are smaller and less expensive than unit blocks. These blocks vary considerably in size, shape, and materials from manufacturer to manufacturer. Several companies add other wooden objects such as

HOW TO STORE SMALL AND LARGE BLOCKS IN CENTERS AND CLASSROOMS

Storing small and large building blocks in centers and classrooms becomes routine for experienced caregivers and teachers. Here are some suggestions:

1. Make ample room for storage in containers or stack them on open shelves at a height children can reach.
2. Make space available for storage of blocks near the block-building area. The child's interest diminishes as the distance to reach blocks increases.
3. Stack the blocks lengthwise on the shelves. If they are stacked with the ends out, all the blocks look alike, and it is difficult to determine size or shape without removing them from the shelves.
4. Paint block shapes on shelf bottoms so that children know where to return blocks.

toy houses to their table block sets to encourage dramatic play. For suggestions on storing unit and table blocks, see "How to Store Small and Large Blocks in Centers and Classrooms."

The second major subgroup of blocks consists of large wooden, cardboard, and plastic blocks. Children must use both hands to carry these large wooden blocks, but they are hollow to reduce weight. These blocks come in six shapes: unit, half unit, double unit, half double unit, diagonal, and plank. The unit size varies with toy companies. They are usually made from pine or maple or a combination of the two woods. The edges are beveled, the sides sanded, and the surfaces waterproofed.

Large cardboard and plastic blocks are less expensive and less durable than their wooden counterparts. They are nevertheless quite strong. The cardboard blocks, for example, are constructed with an inner core which enables them to support as much

FIGURE 9-1

Nineteen Types of and Names for Unit Blocks

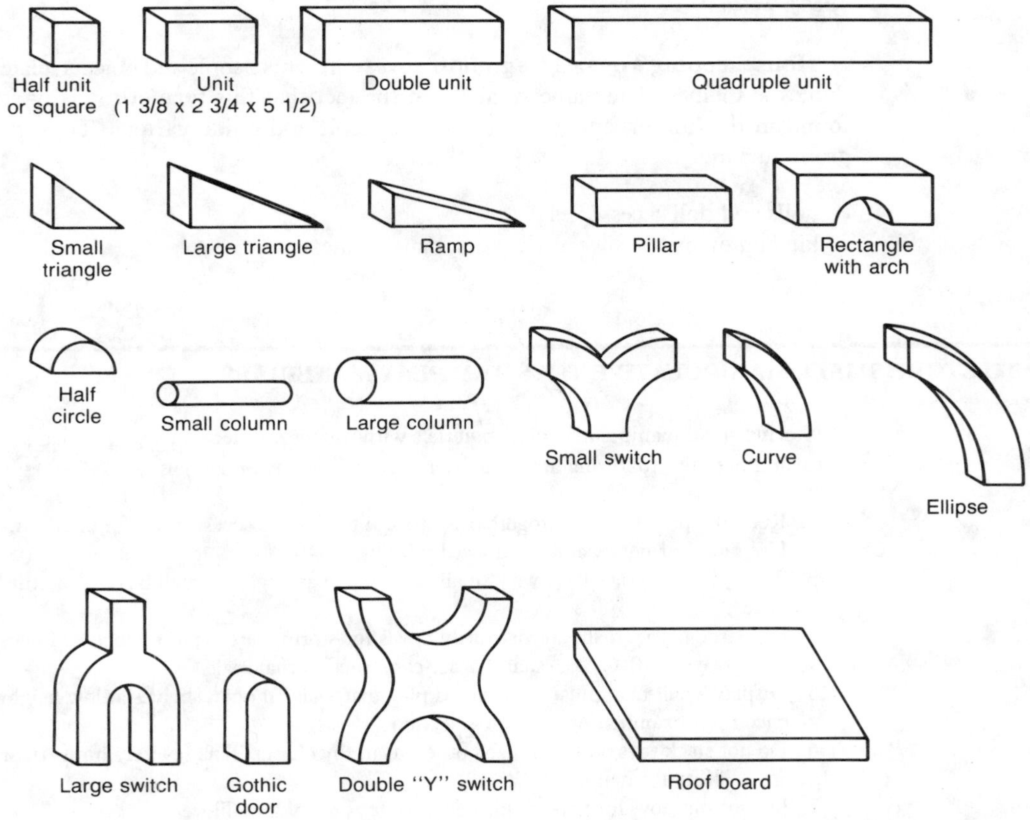

Half unit or square — Unit (1 3/8 x 2 3/4 x 5 1/2) — Double unit — Quadruple unit

Small triangle — Large triangle — Ramp — Pillar — Rectangle with arch

Half circle — Small column — Large column — Small switch — Curve — Ellipse

Large switch — Gothic door — Double "Y" switch — Roof board

as 200 pounds. The outsides of the blocks are usually colorfully decorated. One manufacturer has brick designs painted in red and blue; several other companies use solid colors on each side. The sizes of these blocks vary among manufacturers.

Building Sets. These sets have many pieces. As is characteristic of all constructional materials, the pieces can be put together in many different ways. They are excellent playthings for almost any age because they are so flexible and versatile. Examples include Tinkertoys, Lincoln Logs, dominoes, Legos, and A-B-C blocks.

Toys

Toys are miniature replicas of objects in the child's physical and social environment. Some toys are facsimiles of real objects such as houses, cars, and animals; others are replicas of fantasy objects such as spaceships, superheroes (He-Man), and super-villains (Darth Vader). Because these play materials are miniatures, children can easily manipulate them and use them anywhere. Most toys fit into one of three subgroups: housekeeping, transportation, and animate (Yawkey & Toro-Lopez, 1985).

Housekeeping Toys. This group of toys represents people and objects related to domestic themes. The name stems from the fact that this type of toy is typically found in the housekeeping corner of preschools and kindergartens. Toys in this group include:

- dolls and doll accessories
- kitchen utensils—silverware, pots, pans, dishes

HOW TO STORE SMALL MANIPULATIVE TOYS AND PLAY MATERIALS

Storing small manipulative play materials with numerous pieces creates problems of space and use. The following are suggestions for storing such materials.

1. Keep the pieces of a toy together in storage to provide accessibility for children.
2. Use racks for jigsaw and formboard puzzles.
3. Place play materials with very small pieces such as pegs, in small baskets or sturdy boxes.
4. Use large plastic dishpans or sturdy boxes for storing larger pieces such as Legos, Tinkertoys, A-B-C blocks, and other construction materials.
5. Display small manipulative toys and play materials on open shelves at low heights to encourage examination and self-selection.
6. Do not stack toys on top of each other, as in toy chests. This severely limits their accessibility for children.
7. Do not mix toys for young children with toys for older children.

- miniature tables, stoves, and refrigerators
- irons, ironing boards, and brooms
- baby carriages and cradles

Transportation Toys. Transportation toys include miniature trains, cars, trucks, wagons, and ships. They appeal to both younger and older children and come with many accessories, such as garages.

Animate Toys. This group of toys represents animals, people, and creatures of all types. Usually animate toys are made of plastic and are ideal for both solitary and group make-believe play. Replicas of television, movie, and cartoon characters are are extremely popular with children of all ages. We offer relevant suggestions in "How to Store Small Manipulative Toys and Play Materials." For sources of additional information about toys, see "Associations Serving the Toy and Hobby Industries."

EFFECTS OF PLAY MATERIALS ON PLAY BEHAVIOR

Early childhood educators have long been aware that children's play is affected by available play materials. That realization has sparked a number of research studies, beginning in the early 1930s. Research falls into two categories: (a) studies on the effects of different types of toys on social and cognitive play levels; and (b) effects of toy realism and structure on dramatic play. The results of these studies have important implications about which types of play materials to provide to children.

Play Levels

Early researchers investigated the effects of different kinds of play materials on the social quality of preschoolers' play (Parten, 1933; Van Alstyne, 1932). They found that certain materials appeared to elicit group play whereas others tended to encourage solitary or parallel activity. These early findings have been replicated by recent researchers (Hendrickson, Strain, Tremblay, & Shores, 1981; Rubin, 1977). Taken together, the results of this research indicate that housekeeping props, dress-up clothes, dolls, cars, and other vehicles are associated with high levels of group play. Art construction materials (scissors, paints, crayons), instructional materials (beads, puzzles), and clay tend to be used in solitary and parallel play. Children's play with blocks appears to be equally divided between the social and nonsocial categories.

Researchers have also found that certain materials tend to encourage different cognitive levels of play (Rubin, 1977). The same materials that promote group play (housekeeping props, dress-up clothes, dolls, and vehicles) also tend to be associated with dramatic play. Paints, crayons, and scissors are usually used in constructive play, while Play-doh, clay, and sand and water tend to be used in functional play.

Blocks are associated with both constructive and dramatic play (Rubin & Seibel, 1979).

The social and cognitive forms of play stimulated by these different play materials are summarized in Table 9-1. Adults wishing to encourage a particular form of play can do so by providing ample supplies of the materials with a "+" in the play form column. Sometimes play tutoring in the form of modeling or verbal prompting may be needed to get children to play with these materials in the desired way (Chapter 2).

ASSOCIATIONS SERVING THE TOY AND HOBBY INDUSTRIES

The following associations offer further information about toys and other play materials. Drop each a postcard requesting that your name be placed on their mailing lists for free toy catalogues, materials, and other information about the toy industry.

Bicycle Manufactures Association
1055 Thomas Jefferson St., N.W.
Washington, DC 20007

Electronic Industries Association
Consumer Electronics Group
2001 Eye Street, N.W.
Washington, DC 20006

Hobby Industry Association of
  Northern California
4547 Mission Street
San Francisco, CA 94112

Juvenile Products Manufacturers
  Association
66 East Main Street
Moorestown, NJ 08057

Mid-Atlantic Craft and Hobby
  Industry Association
P.O. Box 43
Fairless Hills, PA 19030

Midwest Toy and Hobby Association
100 East Ogden Avenue
Westmont, IL 60559

National Association of Doll
  Manufacturers, Inc.
605 Third Avenue
New York, NY 10022

National Ornaments and Electric
  Lights (NOEL) Christmas Association
15 East 26th Street
New York, NY 10010

British Toy and Hobby Manufacturers
  Association Limited
80 Camberwell Road
London, England SES OEG

Licensing Industries Association
75 Rockefeller Plaza
New York, NY 10019

Hobby Industries of America
319 East 54th Street
P.O. Box 348
Elmwood Park, NJ 07407

Licensed Merchandisers' Association
200 Park Avenue, Suite 303 East
New York, NY 10166

Mid-American Craft-Hobby
  Association, Inc.
P.O. Box 2188
Zanesville, OH 43701

Miniatures Industry Association of
  America
1113 15th St., N.W., Suite 1000
Washington, DC 20005

New England Toy Representation
  Association
200 University Avenue
Westwood, MA 02090

Rocky Mountain Toy Representatives
4526 West Northview Avenue
Glendale, AZ 85301

TABLE 9-1

Types of Play Encouraged By Selected Play Materials

	Social Level		Cognitive Level		
	Nonsocial[1]	Group	Functional	Constructive	Dramatic
Housekeeping toys		+			+
Dolls		+			+
Dress-up clothes		+			+
Vehicles		+			+
Blocks	+	+		+	+
Puzzles	+			+	
Beads	+		+		
Art construction (scissors, paints)	+			+	
Clay, Play-doh	+		+		
Sand and water	+		+		

[1]Nonsocial = solitary and parallel play.

Toy Realism and Structure

Realism and structure are related features of toys. Realism refers to the degree to which a toy resembles its real-life counterpart. Barbie dolls, with their detailed features and life-like accessories, are more realistic than rag dolls. Structure refers to the extent to which toys have specific uses. High-realism toys are considered to be highly structured and to have very specific uses. For example, a realistic replica of a police car lends itself to only one use, being a police car. The less realistic Community Playthings cars, which look like blocks of wood with wheels attached, are much less structured and can easily represent any kind of a vehicle. Figure 9-2 illustrates how play materials form a continuum from completely unstructured materials like mud, sand, and water to highly structured instructional materials like shoe-lacing boards, which can be used in only one, adult-specified way.

FIGURE 9-2

The Structure of Play Materials

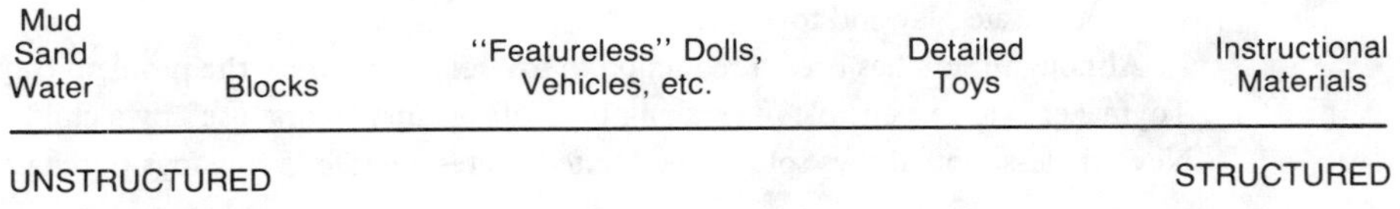

Mud Sand Water	Blocks	"Featureless" Dolls, Vehicles, etc.	Detailed Toys	Instructional Materials
UNSTRUCTURED				STRUCTURED

A number of researchers have investigated the effects of toy realism and structure on children's dramatic play (Jeffree & McConkey, 1976; Johnson, 1983; McLoyd, 1983; Olszewski & Fuson, 1982; Pulaski, 1973). In general, findings suggest that realistic, highly structured props encourage make-believe in younger (two- and three-year-old) preschoolers but not in older children. Very young children, due to a lack of representational skills, appear to need realistic replicas of theme-related objects to get started in dramatic play. As they get older, children's representational skills grow to the point where realistic toys are no longer required for make-believe. Results of Pulaski's (1973) study indicate that realistic toys may actually interfere

TOY SAFETY

What kinds of dangers are inherent in playthings? There are three categories. First, accidents are caused by *mechanical* features of toys. Sharp points, edges, and small parts can cause cuts, bruises, choking, suffocation, or strangulation. *Thermal* features of toys can cause burns, as can *electrical* features of toys. Many other accidents are caused not by features inherent in playthings, but by how toys are used. Most accidents occur when an adult or child falls on, trips over, or is hit by a toy. The second most common accident occurs when children fall off a riding toy. Most serious injuries occur in one- to three-year-olds.

There has been a steady decline in the number of toy-related accidents treated in hospital emergency rooms over the past decade, according to the U.S. Consumer Product Safety Commission. For example, from 1981 to 1983, such accidents declined from 130,000 to 118,000 annually. What has caused this decline?

First, *manufacturers* have become increasingly sensitive to producing safe products, and have grown less reluctant to withdraw unsafe playthings from the consumer market. In part, they seem to be responding to the increase in class-action and individual lawsuits during the 1970s. Second, there has been considerable *government* supervision in recent years. Toymakers must design and manufacture their products to meet government regulations. The Federal Hazardous Substances Act (1973) and the Consumer Product Safety Act (1978) have set safety regulations for toys and other children's articles. For example, toys with small parts must be clearly labeled as dangerous for children under age three, and toys with heating features (toy ovens) must be labeled as unsafe for children under age eight. Third, there has been *consumer* action. Parents and educators have become increasingly aware of the need to protect children from unsafe toys and unsafe use of toys. Careful toy selection and proper supervision of children at play is the most effective way to protect children from toy-related injuries. We need to be always on the alert for unsafe play and toys.

Although there has been a reduction in toy-related injuries, the problem continues. Toymakers are responsible for making toys safe against "worst use" by a child. Nevertheless, not all toys sold in the United States are safe. Some toys purchased in with the imaginativeness of kindergarten and primary-grade students' pretend play.

These findings suggest that preschools serving very young children should have large supplies of realistic toys available to stimulate dramatic play. Kindergartens and preschools serving primarily older students should be well stocked with less realistic toys but also have some realistic props for children who want them. Pulaski (1973) found that some kindergarten and primary-grade children who were classified as having a "low fantasy" predisposition seemed to enjoy make-believe play much more when realistic props were available. For a more detailed review of play material research, see Christie and Johnsen (1987).

---

convenience stores or by mail, hand-me-downs, or toys bought at garage or yard sales may not be safe. If we encounter a dangerous toy, or discover that a toy is unsafe in any way, we should call the Toll Free Hotline: 800-638-CPSC or 800-638-2772 (800-638-8270 in Alaska and Hawaii, 800-492-8104 in Maryland) to report this.

In a recent release from the New York Times News Service, Anne-Marie Schiro summarized guidelines for toy safety developed by the Consumer Product Safety Commission and the Toy Manufacturers of America. Following these guidelines will help reduce the risk of toy-related injuries:

1. Select toys that are suited to children's abilities and that hold their interest.
2. Be sure to read labels and instructions and share this information with children.
3. Throw away plastic wrappings so that they do not pose a safety hazard.
4. Do not purchase toys with long strings or cords for very young children. Such toys may cause strangulation. Also avoid toys with parts that can be swallowed.
5. Check toys periodically for wear and damage. If a toy cannot be repaired, it should be replaced or discarded.
6. Supervise children's play to make sure that toys are being used properly.
7. Store toys intended for older children in locked enclosures or on high shelves so that young children do not have access to them.
8. To prevent falls, teach children to put their toys away on shelves or in containers. Storage chests, if they must be used, should have removable lids or safety latches to keep the lid securely open.
9. Electric toys should be kept away from very young children.
10. Choose toys with the following features:
    a) Nontoxic paint
    b) Flame-retardant fabrics
    c) U.L. approved seal (if electric)

More information on toy safety may be obtained by writing to the Toy Manufacturers of America, 200 Fifth Avenue, New York, NY 10010.

ROLES OF THE ADULT

With so many different types of play materials available, parents and teachers have an important responsibility in selecting and purchasing play materials. Adults should attempt to provide play materials that are well-made, safe, and suited to children's abilities and play interests. "Toy Safety" (pp. 180–181) contains guidelines from the Consumer Product Safety Commission and the Toy Manufacturers of America.

In addition to selecting toys, adults must also make other decisions about play materials. Parents and teachers need to decide when to put toys out for children to play with and when to store the materials. They also can draw children's attention to materials that are not being used and can even make toys the focus for informal teaching. In the following sections, we contrast the roles of adults as they relate to children's use of toys in free-play periods with those in teaching situations.

Free Play

In free play, children follow their own inclinations and needs as they initiate and direct their own activities with toys and other play materials. As we explained in Chapters 2 and 8, the adult's main roles at this time are as provider and observer. Adults need to provide adequate time, space, and materials for play (see Figure 2–1, p. 28). Once that is done, the adult can step back and observe the ongoing free play. If all children are engaging in high-quality, creative play activities, nothing more needs to be done. If, on the other hand, observation reveals that some children are not playing at all, or only exhibit low social and cognitive levels of play, or are bogged down in repetitive play episodes, the adult might want to intervene.

One of the easiest and least obtrusive ways to influence children's play behavior is to manipulate the availability of materials in a play setting. For example, if children are not engaging in mature forms of play, the parent or teacher can provide materials that encourage desired types of play (see Table 9–1). As an example, one of the authors recently conducted an observational study of children's play patterns in several preschool and kindergarten classrooms. It quickly became apparent that the children in one of the kindergartens were not engaging in much dramatic play. Rather, they spent most of their time in rough-and-tumble and constructive play. Occasionally, the children used their block constructions in make-believe "transformer" robot play, but these episodes were brief and violent in content. A look around the classroom revealed that very few materials that encouraged dramatic play were available. So, after the research study ended, the author went back to the kindergarten and asked the teacher to add a number of materials to encourage dramatic play: dolls, doll clothes, play dishes, a doll house, toy vehicles, and dress-up clothes. He noted an immediate, statistically significant shift from functional and constructive play to dramatic play. In addition, the dramatic themes that were enacted involved less violence and aggression. This basic shift in play patterns persisted long after the novelty of the new props had worn off.

If observation reveals that children have become bogged down in repetitious play episodes, adults can sometimes introduce new materials to extend and enrich the play. For example, if children are tired of playing family members, the adult might provide prop boxes, each containing objects related to different themes. Prop suggestions for a variety of themes, including post office, grocery store, police officer, space exploration, firefighter, and baker, can be found in Chapter 12 (Table 12-1, pp. 241–248). Only one prop box should be used at a time. When children tire of the theme, put the box away and bring out a new one. The prop box can be introduced again later in the year, and the children will respond to it as if it were brand-new.

Parents and teachers should also look for signs that children no longer require realistic toys for make-believe play. That change will be indicated when children begin using detailed, realistic props in ways that they are not intended to be used. For example, a child might use a toy telephone to iron clothes or a toy car as a make-believe hamburger. These signs show that it is time to begin gradually shifting to a larger percentage of low-structure props to enhance the creativity of the child's play.

Guided Play

At times, parents and teachers may wish to guide children's play with toys to help them learn a particular concept or skill. This type of guidance can be an excellent way to integrate play with other parts of the school curriculum. For example, play with unit blocks can be an occasion for introducing children to a number of mathematical and scientific concepts.

- identification of different block shapes (rectangle, triangle, square)
- the concept of equality and inequality (finding blocks that are the same size and different size)
- classification (grouping large blocks in one pile and small blocks in another)
- seriation (ordering blocks by size)
- one-to-one correspondence (matching every half-unit block with a small triangle)
- properties of wood
- the concepts of balance and stability (experimenting with different block configurations)

To achieve learning goals, toys and play materials can be used in three different ways (Peters, Neisworth, & Yawkey, 1985). For example, suppose a teacher wanted to use block play to teach the concept of seriation. First, the teacher could plan for *free discovery*. During a free-play period, the teacher would make blocks and a variety of other play material available. The children would be free to select the materials and to choose how to use them. Some children might choose to play with the blocks and could discover the principle of seriation as a result of their block-play experiences. Second, the teacher could use *prompted discovery* in which only play materials selected by the teacher are made available to the children. In this instance the teacher would put out only the unit blocks and would encourage the children to use them in different ways. Third, the teacher can use *directed discovery*, directly guiding the children to focus on relevant attributes of the blocks by asking questions or posing problems for the children to solve. The teacher might ask, "How could you arrange the blocks by size?" or suggest, "Try to make some stairs with the blocks." Directed discovery can either be planned in advance or take place during free play when the teacher senses a "teachable moment." The latter, of course, requires careful observation of children's free-play behavior.

Directed discovery is employed in the "spokesman-for-reality" role described in Chapter 2. It should be used sparingly with children who are just beginning to use make-believe in their play. However, with older preschoolers and kindergartners who are skilled dramatists, directed discovery can be an effective procedure for linking play with academic learning.

RESOLVING CONFLICTS OVER PLAY MATERIALS

Because children's social skills are limited, competition and conflicts will inevitably arise over play materials. When parents and teachers understand the reasons or problems underlying conflicts over playthings, the conflicts can be resolved more easily. Some common problems include:

1. *Inadequate supply.* If the number of children wanting to use a particular type of play material (*e.g.*, tricycles) exceeds the supply of that material, conflict will arise. The most obvious solution is to obtain a larger supply of the material, but that, of course, is not always possible. Another solution is to have the children use the material on a rotating schedule. Adults can also suggest alternative activities in order to divert children's attention from the plaything being fought over.
2. *Conflicting activities in the same location.* If several children are attempting to build elaborate block structures in the same general area in which other children are racing toy trucks, it will be only a matter of time before a "truck driver" knocks down one of the other children's block structures. These types of conflicts can be prevented by restricting the use of certain play materials to specific areas of the classroom. For example, vehicle play might be permitted only in a large, open area of the room, and block building restricted to a protected corner. Room arrangements and use of space will be discussed in more detail in Chapter 10, "Physical Environment and Play."
3. *Inaccessible materials.* Sometimes lack of access to materials causes children to compete for the few playthings that are available. Review the storage suggestions in this chapter. Having play materials in sight, within reaching distance, and in order (which is kept by the children) will make more materials available for play, reducing the potential for conflict.
4. *Material in disrepair.* Aside from posing a safety hazard, play equipment that is damaged and not working can contribute to conflict by reducing children's play options. If most of a center's wheeled vehicles are in a state of disrepair, the children will be forced to compete for the few vehicles that do work. Ex-

perienced early-childhood specialists make it a rule to check toys and other play materials regularly to make sure they are in good working order. Equipment can be kept in good condition for longer periods if children are involved in developing and implementing rules for its use.

SUMMARY

Toys and other playthings are an important aspect of children's world of play. Research has shown that the types of materials available have a considerable influence on children's play behavior. Parents and teachers can use this research data to help provide children with materials that will encourage high social and cognitive levels of play.

Research has also revealed an interesting interaction between children's age and the realism of dramatic play props. Very young children need realistic toys to get started in make-believe play. As they grow older and their representational skills improve, most children no longer require realistic replicas for make-believe. Many older preschoolers and kindergartners appear to play more imaginatively with abstract props than with realistic toys. Adults should keep this developmental trend in mind when providing materials to stimulate dramatic play.

Toys also provide many learning opportunities for children. Much of this toy-induced learning occurs spontaneously in free play. However, adults can help the learning process by using directed discovery to draw children's attention to certain properties and relationships of the materials with which they are playing. If not overdone, guided discovery is an ideal way to integrate play with academic learning.

REFERENCES

Christie, J.F., & Johnsen, E.P. (1987). Preschool play. In J. Block & N. King (Eds.), *School play* (pp. 201–247). New York: Garland.

Community Playthings. (1981). *Criteria for selecting play equipment for early childhood education: A reference book*. Rifton, NY: Community Playthings, Inc.

Hartley, R., Frank, L., & Goldenson, R. (1952). *Understanding children's play*. New York: Teachers College Press.

Hendrickson, J.M., Strain, P.S., Tremblay, A., & Shores, R.E. (1981). Relationship between toy and material use and the occurrence of social interactive behaviors by normally developing preschool children. *Psychology in the Schools, 18,* 500–504.

Hill, D.M. (1977). *Mud, sand, and water*. Washington, DC: National Association for the Education of Young Children.

Hirsch, E.S. (Ed.). (1974). *The block book*. Washington, DC: National Association for the Education of Young Children.

Jeffree, D.M., & McConkey, R. (1976). An observation scheme for recording children's imaginative doll play. *Journal of Child Psychology and Psychiatry, 17,* 189–197.

Johnson, J.E. (1983). Context effects on preschool children's symbolic behavior. *Journal of Genetic Psychology, 143,* 259–268.

Krown, S. (1971). *Threes and fours go to school.* Englewood Cliffs, NJ: Prentice-Hall.

Matterson, E.M. (1965). *Play and playthings for the preschool child.* New York: Penguin.

McLoyd, V.C. (1983). The effects of the structure of play objects on the pretend play of low-income preschool children. *Child Development, 54,* 626–635.

Mergen, B. (1982). *Play and playthings: A reference guide.* Westport, CT: Greenwood Press.

Olszewski, P., & Fuson, K.C. (1982). Verbally expressed fantasy play of preschoolers as a function of toy structure. *Developmental Psychology, 18,* 57–61.

Parten, M.B. (1933). Social play among preschool children. *Journal of Abnormal and Social Psychology, 28,* 136–147.

Peters, D.L., Neisworth, J.T., & Yawkey, T.D. (1985). *Early childhood education: From theory to practice.* Monterey, CA: Brooks-Cole.

Pulaski, M.A. (1973). Toys and imaginative play. In J.L. Singer (Ed.), *The child's world of make-believe: Experimental studies of imaginative play* (pp. 74–103). New York: Academic Press.

Rubin, K.H. (1977). The social and cognitive value of preschool toys and activities. *Canadian Journal of Behavioral Science, 9,* 382–385.

Rubin, K.H., & Seibel, C.G. (1979, April). *The effects of ecological setting on the cognitive and social play behaviors of preschoolers.* Paper presented at the meeting of the American Educational Research Association, San Francisco.

Tizard, B., Philps, J., & Plewis, I. (1976). Play in pre-school centres—I. Play measures and their relation to age, sex, and I.Q. *Journal of Child Psychology and Psychiatry, 17,* 251–264.

Van Alstyne, D. (1932). *Play behavior and choice of play materials of pre-school children.* Chicago: University of Chicago Press.

Yawkey, T.D., & Toro-Lopez, J.A. (1985). Examining descriptive and empirically based typologies of toys for handicapped and nonhandicapped children. *Topics in Early Childhood Special Education, 5*(3), 47–58.

Yawkey, T.D., & Trostle, S.L. (1982). *Learning is child's play.* Provo, UT: Brigham Young University Press.

Physical Environment and Play

A major thread running through this book is that children's play behavior is affected by the setting or context in which it occurs. In Chapter 5, we examined the impact of the social environment—the interpersonal transactions between children and adults—on play patterns. The physical environment is the setting or stage upon which these social transactions occur (Wachs, 1985). The physical environment of play consists of inanimate features of settings such as the space in which play occurs, the materials that are present in that space, and how the space and materials are arranged. As we shall see, the physical environment can have a substantial effect on children's play behaviors. Awareness of these influences can help parents and teachers structure play settings to promote higher social and cognitive forms of play.

This chapter will begin with an examination of differences between indoor and outdoor play. Next, we will discuss how specific features of indoor and outdoor play environments affect children's play patterns. Indoor features include spatial density, arrangement of space, amount of equipment, and activity centers. The outdoor section will focus on playgrounds, reviewing research on different types of playgrounds and playground design features linked with high levels of play. Neighborhood play settings will also be discussed. In each section we will attempt to identify means by which adults can provide optimal settings for play.

COMPARING INDOOR AND OUTDOOR PLAY

Research indicates that children tend to engage in different cognitive forms of play in indoor and outdoor settings. Predictably, large-motor play—running, climbing, jumping—is more common outdoors than indoors (Roper & Hinde, 1978; Smith & Connolly, 1972). Outdoor play areas are usually larger than indoor settings, permitting more room for large-motor play to occur. Outdoor play spaces also have more equipment such as climbing frames, slides, and swings that encourage large-motor activity. Constructive play, on the other hand, occurs more often in indoor settings because of the abundant supply of construction materials found in most preschool and kindergarten classrooms (Henniger, 1985). Such construction materials are rarely found on traditional school playgrounds.

It is less clear whether the social level of play differs between the two locations. Henniger (1985) reported that preschoolers engaged in more parallel play outdoors than indoors. Two other studies, however, failed to find any differences in social play levels between the two settings (Smith & Connolly, 1972; Tizard et al., 1976). Obviously, more research is needed before conclusions can be drawn.

Investigators have found that preschool boys when at school prefer playing outdoors more than do girls (Harper & Sanders, 1975; Sanders & Harper, 1976). As was reported in Chapter 7, a preference for outdoor play has been found among low socioeconomic-status children (Tizard, et al., 1976). Other evidence suggests that indoor and outdoor school settings have different effects on play depending on children's sex and social class. For example, preschool boys have been found to engage in more make-believe play outdoors, whereas girls exhibit more pretend play in indoor housekeeping centers (Sanders & Harper, 1976). Tizard et al. (1976) reported that lower-class preschoolers, unlike their middle-class counterparts, engaged in more dramatic play and in longer play episodes in outdoor settings than in classrooms.

Taken together, these findings highlight the importance of providing ample amounts of both indoor and outdoor play. Outdoor play allows children to engage in the large-motor activities needed for proper physical development. In addition, outdoor play appears to encourage make-believe in middle-class boys and in children of both genders from low-income families. Indoor classroom settings, on the other hand, tend to stimulate dramatic play in middle-class girls. Constructive play is more common among both sexes in indoor settings. For children to have a balanced "diet" of play activities, both indoor and outdoor play are necessary.

INDOOR SETTINGS

A considerable amount of children's play—both at home and at school—occurs indoors. It is important therefore to know how specific features of indoor play environments affect play behavior. This section will review research relating to four aspects of indoor settings: spatial density, arrangement of space, amount of equipment, and activity centers.

Spatial Density

Spatial density refers to the amount of space per child in a play setting and is an index of crowding. Lower numbers (20 square feet per child) indicate crowded settings;

higher numbers (70 square feet per child) indicate less crowded conditions. Experiments with animals have established that social behavior tends to break down in very crowded conditions, raising the possibility that spatial density may have an effect on the social quality of children's play.

Early studies on the effects of spatial density on preschoolers' play showed conflicting findings: increased crowding was reported to cause more aggression according to some researchers (Hutt & Vaizey, 1966) and less aggression according to others (*e.g.*, Loo, 1972). Results concerning positive social interaction have been equally mixed. Several studies have found that, as crowding increases, the level of social play decreases (*e.g.*, Loo, 1972), while others have reported no change (*e.g.*, McGrew, 1972). One study conducted in Dutch preschools actually found more positive social interaction (group play) in crowded settings than in less crowded ones (Fagot, 1977).

Smith and Connolly (1980) have pointed out several problems that may account for these conflicting results. In some of the investigations, the amount of space and number of children were varied while the amount of equipment remained constant, suggesting that differences in the amount of equipment per child may have affected the children's play. A second problem involves the definition of aggression. Some investigators distinguished between rough-and-tumble play and true aggression, while others lumped the two behaviors together.

To get a true picture of the effects of crowding, Smith and Connolly (1980) conducted an extensive study in which space, number of children, and amount of equipment were systematically varied. Spatial densities of 15, 25, 50, and 75 square feet per child were examined. (These figures refer to space usable for play. Space occupied by furniture or containing other obstructions was not counted.) Results showed that less space per child reduced the amount of gross-motor activity (running, chasing, and rough-and-tumble) during play. In other words, as crowding increased, large-motor play decreased. Less space per child (increased crowding) had little effect on the children's social behavior until spatial density reached 25 square feet per child. When the density was changed from 25 to 15 square feet per child, there was a marked increase in aggression and a significant reduction in group play.

Smith and Connolly's findings indicate that spatial density can influence children's play behavior and imply that teachers should monitor this variable. "Measuring Spatial Density" contains instructions for determining the spatial density of classrooms. If calculations reveal that less than 25 square feet of usable space is available per child, steps should be taken to reduce crowding. Possible solutions include: (a) rearranging furniture so that more space is usable for play; (b) reducing the number of students in the room, perhaps by distributing them among several rooms; or (c) restricting future enrollments if additional space is not available.

The finding that reducing the space available per child also reduces gross-motor play has several implications. If teachers are concerned that too much chasing and rough-and-tumble play occur in a classroom, perhaps there is too much space. Adding more furniture or rearranging existing furniture to break up large open areas might help alleviate this problem. Teachers wishing to increase gross-motor play should, of course, do the opposite. One other way to promote large-motor play in

Spatial density refers to the amount of space available per child in a play setting. It can be easily determined by use of the following formula:

$$\text{Spatial density} = \frac{\text{room area} - \text{unusable space}}{\text{number of children}}$$

First, determine the total *room area* by measuring the length and width of room and multiplying these two numbers together. Second, use the same procedure to determine the area (in square feet) of each piece of furniture and each space which cannot be used for play (narrow areas between furniture, areas reserved for adults, and "quiet" areas in which play is not allowed). Add all the unusable areas together to determine the total *unusable space*. Third, subtract the total *unusable space* from the *room area* to determine the total amount of space usable for play. Fourth, divide this last figure by the *number of children* in the class.

The following example, in which 12 children are in a classroom measuring 15×20 feet, will illustrate how these calculations are made:

		Sq. Ft.
Room Area:	15×20 feet	300
Unusable Area:	Table 1: 5×3 feet	15
	Table 2: 5×3 feet	15
	Table 3: 2×4 feet	8
	Area between Tables 1 & 2: 1×5 feet	5
	Bookcase: 1×9 feet	9
	Total Unusable Area:	52

$$\text{Spatial density} = \frac{300 - 52 \text{ sq. ft.}}{12}$$

$$= \frac{248 \text{ sq. ft.}}{12}$$

$$= 21 \text{ sq. ft. per child}$$

Smith and Connolly (1980) found that reducing the amount of space per child from 75 square feet to 25 square feet had little effect other than reducing the amount of large-motor play. However, reducing the space per child from 25 square feet to 15 square feet resulted in a large increase in aggressive behavior and a decrease in group play, both negative consequences. In the above example, only 21 square feet of play space is available for each child. The setting is therefore too crowded. Consult the text for suggestions on remedying this situation.

small areas is to provide climbing equipment. Smith and Connolly (1980) found that when less space was available, children engaged in increasing amounts of vigorous play on a climbing frame and slide. Directions for building a space-efficient climbing structure and slide can be found in Wardle (1980). The structure, while designed for toddlers, can easily be scaled up for use with older children.

Arrangement of Space

The amount of space in a play setting is not the only spatial feature related to play. How space is arranged can also have an effect on children's play patterns. In this section we will highlight some of the more important findings from research on spatial arrangements. For a more complete review, see Phyfe-Perkins (1980).

Several studies have dealt with the issue of open versus partitioned space. Results of two of these investigations suggest that small, partitioned areas result in higher quality play than large, open areas. Sheehan and Day (1975) found that dividing a large day care center into smaller areas with partitions reduced the incidence of rowdy behavior and increased the amount of cooperative interaction during free play. Field (1980) compared the play of preschoolers in classrooms with differing spatial arrangements and teacher-child ratios. She found that the highest social and cognitive levels of play occurred in the classroom with small partitioned areas and that the lowest level of play occurred in large open areas. Differences in teacher-child ratios, however, made it impossible to determine if the variations in play patterns were caused solely by spatial arrangements.

Rooms should also be arranged so that young children can easily see where play-things are located. If furniture is arranged in such a way that preschoolers' view of play equipment is blocked by shelves or partitions of any sort, then the children may not realize that certain activities are possible in the classroom. Pollowy (1974) found that increasing the ease with which children could see materials resulted in a greater use of available equipment by children.

Kinsman and Berk (1979) found that opening up a classroom by removing a barrier between the housekeeping center and the block area had beneficial effects on preschool and kindergarten students' play. Removing the barrier resulted in more boy-girl play, particularly in the housekeeping area. Play that integrated materials from the two areas also increased (blocks were used as props in the housekeeping center) but only among the older children.

Apparently, the issue of open versus partitioned space is a complex one. Research evidence suggests that partitioning a large, open room into smaller areas can have beneficial effects. Such arrangements tend to discourage large-motor activity (running, chasing, and rough-and-tumble play) and encourage dramatic and constructive play. One should be careful, however, about where partitions or barriers are placed. Openings should be left between complementary areas, such as the block and housekeeping centers, so that activities can cross over and become integrated with each other. Teachers should also make sure that partitions do not block children's view of available play equipment.

A case study by Walling (1977) sheds light on other important aspects of spatial arrangement. Teaching a group of three- and four-year-old preschoolers, Walling was disturbed by the amount of aggressive behavior and rough-and-tumble play occurring during free-play periods. She also was concerned that the children rarely used the housekeeping corner or engaged in dramatic play. She began to suspect that her room arrangement (see Figure 10–1) might be contributing to the low quality of the children's play. On close inspection, she discovered several problems:

1. There was too much open space in the middle of the room, which may have contributed to the large amount of chasing and rough-and-tumble play.
2. The different play areas—block, book, art, and housekeeping—were not well-defined. For example, the housekeeping area was in an open corner of the room. As a result, it did not seem very "house-like," and the housekeeping equipment got strewn all over the room.
3. Some of the adjacent areas were in direct conflict with each other. For example, the block (noisy) and book (quiet) areas were next to each other.
4. There was no clear pathway through the room. To get from the entrance of the room to the other side, children had to go near the block area (often knocking down other children's block structures) and through a line of tables used for art projects. This led to many confrontations between children.

Walling rearranged her room and eliminated many of these problems. She repositioned the tables and added several partitions to break up the large open spaces and create a clear pathway through the classroom. The partitions also served to physically define the housekeeping and other play areas. Several areas were relocated so that they would be in better relationship with one another. For example, the block area was moved away from the books and closer to the housekeeping corner. The resulting arrangement is illustrated in Figure 10–2.

After a week of becoming adjusted to the new arrangement, the children began to show changes in their play. Use of the housekeeping center and block area increased substantially. Rowdy and aggressive behavior decreased significantly. Walling found that she could spend less time settling disputes and disciplining children and more time interacting positively with children as they played.

While just a case study, Walling's findings do suggest several guidelines for indoor room arrangements. These include:

1. Break up large open spaces with partitions and furniture if you wish to discourage running and rough-and-tumble play.
2. Separate conflicting areas, such as noisy (*e.g.*, music) and quiet (*e.g.*, reading) areas, and place complementary areas (*e.g.*, blocks and housekeeping center) close to each other.
3. Be sure there is a clear pathway through the classroom.
4. Use partitions and furniture to clearly delineate different play areas.

Remember that if an opening is left between the block and housekeeping areas,

FIGURE 10-1

Walling's Original Room Arrangement

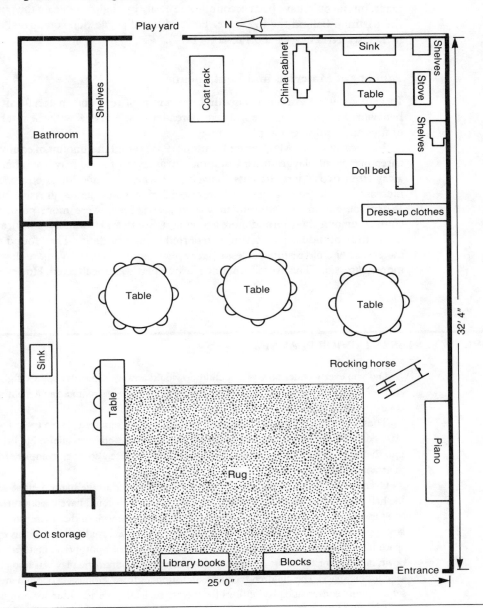

SOURCE: Kritchevsky and Prescott (1977, p. 50)

children will be encouraged to integrate their play between the two centers (Kinsman & Berk, 1979). That was not a feature of Walling's classroom rearrangement, but it could have been accomplished easily by slightly altering the position of the partition behind the toy stove. For additional suggestions on spatial arrangements, see Kritchevsky and Prescott (1977).

Amount of Materials and Equipment

In Chapter 9 we examined how different kinds of toys and materials affect play behavior. In this section, we will take a broader view and deal with the total amount of toys and equipment in play settings.

In an early study, Marguerite Johnson (1935) varied the amount of equipment on three preschool playgrounds. Equipment was added to one playground and taken away from two others. Results showed that when the amount of equipment was increased, children engaged in fewer social games and less aggressive behavior. When the amount of equipment was reduced, there were more positive social contacts among children and more aggression. Smith and Connolly (1980), as part of their study of indoor play settings, reported similar findings. They found that less materials per child resulted in less solitary play, more parallel play, more sharing, and more aggression. The overall amount of group play was not affected. However, as the

---

CHILDREN'S TASTES IN INDOOR PLAY SPACES

Did you ever wonder how young children would arrange their play spaces if given a chance? An intriguing demonstration of a truly child-centered room arrangement was conducted by Pfluger and Zola (1974).

These researchers had all the equipment and furniture removed from a typical preschool classroom and put into an adjacent hallway. The children were then allowed to bring back into the room anything they wished to play with. They were also given complete freedom in arranging these materials.

Over several weeks, most of the equipment was returned to the room. Left standing in the hall were the tables and chairs and a piano, all of which could have been returned with adult assistance. Many of the items were placed against the wall so that there would be a large open space in the middle of the room. The children enjoyed free use of this open space but not just for gross motor activities. They often took appropriate materials and sat down on the floor for an art or construction project. Sociodramatic play was also often seen in this space. The children took toys and supplies from various curriculum areas and set up complex dramatic play settings for themes such as space adventure or hospital.

This study provides a glimpse of what the world may be like for children and how their views often differ from the those of the adults on whom they depend. Would you ever try this experiment yourself? What are some of your misgivings?

FIGURE 10–2

Walling's Revised Room Arrangement

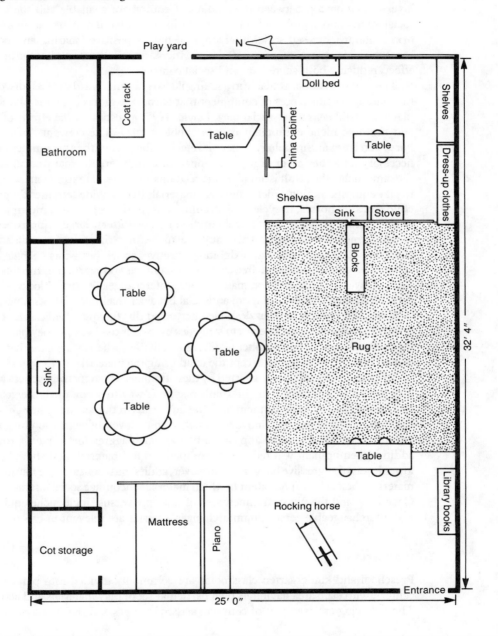

amount of material per child decreased, the size of play groups increased.

These findings indicate that, in both indoor and outdoor settings, there is an inverse relationship between the amount of equipment available and the level of social interaction in children's play. Decreasing the amount of materials in a setting brings about increased social interaction of both a positive (sharing and positive contacts) and negative (aggression) nature. Increasing the materials has the opposite effect, reducing both aggression and social contact.

The type of material available in a setting is also relevant. Wardle (1983) discovered that adding specific pieces of equipment that encourage group dramatic play (*e.g.*, a playhouse) did *not* reduce social play. Doyle (1977) investigated the effects of single and multiple niche equipment on preschoolers' play. The concept "niche" was borrowed from anthropology, where it refers to the part of the environment that is necessary for a species' or organism's survival. If there are too many occupants for the same niche, the result is antagonistic relations and possible extinction. As applied to play equipment, single niche items are materials that provide activities for just one child (rocking horses, tricycles, toy brooms, and short jump ropes); multiple niche items provide activities for several children (teeter-totters, large jump ropes, and jungle gyms). Doyle found that multiple niche materials were associated with children's getting along and exhibiting positive social behaviors. Single niche equipment, on the other hand, frequently led to conflicts and aggression. In a follow-up study, Doyle (1978) found that materials with interchangeable parts (blocks, Lincoln logs, Tinkertoys) resulted in more antisocial behavior than materials with parts that were not interchangeable (puzzles). He interpreted this finding as indicating that the former materials lend themselves to struggles over their use because they have utility for children engaged in a number of different activities, whereas the latter have parts that no one else would want except the child using the material.

Several applications are suggested by these findings. If parents or teachers wish to increase social interaction in children's play, one way to accomplish the goal is to reduce the amount of equipment and play materials in the setting. They should be cautious, however, not to remove too much, or high levels of aggression may result. On the other hand, if there appears to be too much aggression in play, providing additional equipment will reduce the competition for materials and should lead to lower levels of aggressive behavior. Moreover, adults must consider the nature of the materials themselves. The extent to which materials encourage social interaction (see Chapter 9) and the physical dimensions of multiple versus single niche equipment and interchangeable versus noninterchangeable parts are relevant in this respect.

Play Areas

Preschool and kindergarten classrooms are commonly divided into play areas or centers, with each area having its own particular set of play materials and activities. The following are examples of common classroom areas and their materials:

1. Art area—paints, easels, brushes, scissors, glue, wallpaper books, small pieces of wood and styrofoam, paper, felt pens, crayons, clay, and Play-doh.

2. Block area—unit blocks, large hollow blocks, and small replicas (vehicles, people, and animals).
3. Floor play area—large vehicles, bean bags, balls, Tinkertoys, and empty boxes.
4. Housekeeping area—replicas of kitchen furniture and appliances, small table and chairs, dishes and eating utensils, used adult furniture, dress-up clothes, dolls, doll beds, and baby strollers.
5. Music area—phonograph, cassette player, rhythm instruments, and autoharp.
6. Book area—books and rug.
7. Table-toy area—Legos, puzzles, games, pegboards, dominoes.
8. Science area—animals in cages, aquarium, objects to sort and feel (shells, seeds, stones), magnifying glass, seeds to grow, ant farm, water table, and sand box.
9. Woodworking area—tools, nails, screws, wood, workbench, and vise.

Several research studies have compared children's play patterns in different play areas. Shure (1963), for example, found that preschoolers exhibited different social levels of play in different areas. Solitary play predominated in the game (table toy) area, whereas group play predominated in the block and housekeeping areas. Parallel play was exhibited most often in the art and book areas. Results of a series of studies by Pellegrini (1984) indicate that preschoolers' language varies when they play in different areas. Children were found to use more imaginative, explicit, and cohesive language in the housekeeping center than in block, art, or water and sand areas.

In general, these findings point out the importance of the housekeeping and block areas. Both of these areas tend to encourage high levels of social play. Housekeeping areas have the additional advantage of stimulating more mature, complex language. The other types of play areas are, of course, also valuable because of the various types of activity—art, music, reading, construction, large motor exercise, sensory exploration—that they encourage.

One additional type of play area worthy of mention is the theme corner. Theme corners are settings that suggest specific themes for dramatic play (such as a grocery store, office, bakery, restaurant, ice cream parlor, or doctor's office). These centers have theme-related props and furniture; for example, a store center might have a table with a cash register, shelves, empty product boxes and cans, and shopping bags. Woodard (1984) tells how early childhood education students at her university set up a number of theme corners in the university's laboratory preschool. Some were extremely inventive. Entryways were made from refrigerator cartons to attract children's interest and to separate the centers from the rest of the room. The "veterinarian's office" included a waiting room with a table for a receptionist and chairs for patients, an examination room, and a kennel with cardboard cages with stuffed animals in them. The "ice cream shop" had yarn pom-pom balls that could be used as scoops of ice cream. One theme center was introduced at a time and left for several weeks. Each was located near the permanent housekeeping center so that children could integrate their domestic play themes with those of the theme corner. Woodard found that the children, particularly the boys, began engaging in more sociodramatic play when the theme corners were introduced. Such centers would make excellent additions to any preschool or kindergarten classroom.

OUTDOOR SETTINGS

Children spend a considerable amount of time playing outdoors. The exact amount of outdoor play depends on a number of factors including geographical location, season of the year, time of day, and weather (Naylor, 1985). Children play in organized areas known as playgrounds as well as in nonstructured outdoor settings.

Before the beginning of this century, most outdoor play occurred in unplanned neighborhood or rural settings. However, between 1880 and 1920, there was a concerted effort to establish a network of playgrounds, special areas devoted to an array of organized play experiences. This movement was motivated during the Industrial Revolution by concern over the growing numbers of immigrant children who had no place to play except in city streets (Mergen, 1982). Proponents believed that these children would be much better off playing in organized settings. The resulting playgrounds with their swings, jungle gyms, slides, and other immovable equipment are still with us today in most towns and cities. Fortunately, there have been exciting new developments in the playground field, leading to better, more stimulating play environments.

First, different kinds of playgrounds will be described. Then, specific features of playgrounds which lead to higher levels of play will be examined. Not all outdoor play occurs in organized areas, so children's play in undesignated neighborhood settings will also be discussed.

Playground Types

Until recently, only one type of playground was available in this country—the traditional steel and asphalt variety. Growing awareness of deficiencies in these traditional playgrounds, coupled with the influence of European play environments, has led to increased playground research and to the development of new types of playgrounds. We will now examine the traditional playground and two alternatives—contemporary and adventure playgrounds—and point out each design's strengths and weaknesses.

Traditional Playgrounds.
Traditional playgrounds consist of large, open areas covered with packed dirt, grass, or most often asphalt. Equipment—isolated, widely spaced pieces of steel—typically includes monkey bars, swings, slides, seesaws, and merry-go-rounds. The site is usually surrounded by a chain-link fence. This design, which stems back to the early 1900s, is by far the most common type of playground in the United States (Frost & Klein, 1979).

The main advantage of traditional steel-and-asphalt design is that it requires very little maintenance, which perhaps explains its popularity with some city officials. Such playgrounds also provide lots of room and equipment for gross-motor exercise.

From the child's perspective, however, traditional playgrounds have many disadvantages. The static pieces of equipment, which can be used only in limited ways, make these places boring. As a result, children rarely use them, and when they do, it is only for brief periods. A study conducted in New York City found that, during peak play hours, traditional playgrounds were empty more than 88 percent of the time. The average length of stay was only 21 minutes (Hayward, Rothenberg, & Beasley, 1974). Naylor (1985) cites a number of studies which indicate that, given a choice, children prefer playing in the street to playing on traditional playgrounds.

A second disadvantage is that traditional playgrounds encourage only large-motor play. Campbell & Frost (1985) found that more than 77 percent of the play occurring on a traditional playground was of the gross-motor variety, compared with less than 3 percent dramatic play. The social level of the play on such playgrounds also tends to be very low. Boyatzis (1985) reported that almost 60 percent of the play on traditional playground equipment was nonsocial (solitary or parallel).

Finally, there is the matter of safety. It is estimated that 150,000 playground injuries are treated by doctors and at hospitals every year, most of these occurring on traditional playgrounds (Frost & Henniger, 1981). The hard surfaces and metal equipment found on the playgrounds were major causes of these injuries. (For more information on playground safety, write to the U.S. Consumer Product Safety Commission, Washington, DC 20207, and ask for the pamphlet "Play Happy, Play Safe: Playground Equipment Guide.")

These three disadvantages—low usage, low-level play, and high injury rates—have led to growing dissatisfaction with the traditional playground and have spurred the development of contemporary and adventure playgrounds.

Contemporary Playgrounds. Contemporary playgrounds, sometimes referred to as creative or designed playgrounds, were developed to provide children with a more varied, stimulating environment for play. They are made primarily of wood with selected metal fixtures. Equipment commonly found in these playgrounds includes wooden climbing platforms, enclosures for dramatic play, ladders, tire nets, suspension bridges, pulley cables, tire swings, balance beams, tunnels, and slides. Equipment is not spread out and isolated, as it is on traditional playgrounds. Rather, it is centrally located and linked. There are ideally three types of surfaces: (a) hardtop surfaces of concrete or asphalt for tricycles, wagons, and other wheeled vehicles; (b) soft surfaces of sand or wood chips, placed under and around all of the equipment; and (c) grass for children to sit and play on (Wardle, 1984). Sandboxes, ponds, and gardens are often included, exposing children to a variety of natural materials. Figure 10–3 illustrates a contemporary playground incorporating all of these features. It should be noted that contemporary playgrounds vary considerably; many do not include all of the above features. But even with some features missing, these playgrounds still provide a much greater variety of play experiences than do their traditional counterparts.

Contemporary playgrounds can be divided into two subgroups: (a) commercial play environments, such as the modular wooden and steel structures made by Big Toys and Columbia Cascade; and (b) community-built playgrounds made from lumber and salvaged materials such as tires, railroad ties, cable spools, and pipes (Frost & Klein, 1979). The commercial structures offer the convenience of being

FIGURE 10-3

Contemporary Playground With Separate Sections for 2- to 3-Year-Olds and 4- to 5-Year-Olds

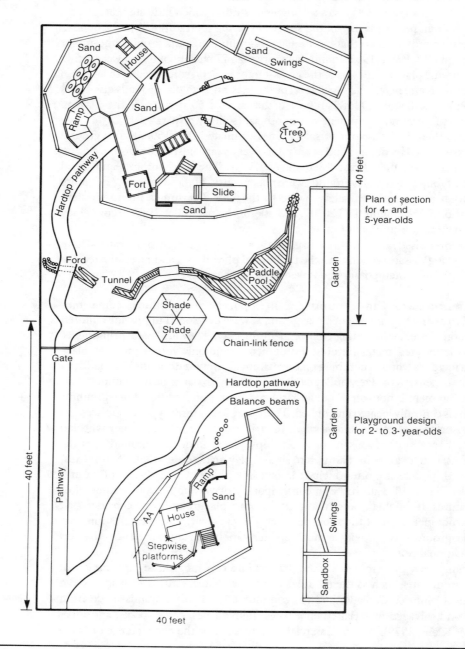

ready-made, but they are also very expensive. Community-built playgrounds are much more economical and can offer a wider variety of play experiences than the commercial models. Because they are constructed by parents and teachers for the children who will use them, these playgrounds become ventures in which the community can take pride. This sense of community pride tends to discourage vandalism, which is often a problem with playgrounds. In addition, the playground design can take into account the unique characteristics of the setting, such as available space, climatic conditions, and the play needs of the children. A major disadvantage of community playgrounds is that some insurance carriers will not cover them. The safety of this type of playground varies considerably, depending on design and construction. Instructions for building community playgrounds are available in a number of publications (Frost & Klein, 1979; Wardle, 1984).

Little research has been conducted to compare the effects of contemporary and traditional playgrounds on play patterns. Results of the few studies done indicate that children engage in more dramatic play and more group play in contemporary playgrounds, while functional play is more common in traditional ones (Campbell & Frost, 1985). In addition, children spend more time playing in contemporary playgrounds than in those of traditional design (Hayward, Rothenberg, & Beasley, 1974). These findings are hardly surprising, considering the features of the two types of playgrounds.

Adventure Playgrounds. Adventure playgrounds are play spaces that use the natural environment and an assortment of discarded materials as their equipment. They differ from the previously described types of playgrounds in several important ways. The structures, except for storage sheds and perhaps a clubhouse, are temporary. The children build, tear down, and rebuild their own play structures. More natural materials are available, such as mud, ponds, gardens, fire pits; often animals inhabit the area. There are many more loose materials for children to manipulate: lumber, crates, rope, cable reels, tires, hammers, nails, saws, and other old tools. A much wider variety of activities is permitted, including building, tearing down, making fires, cooking, digging, and mud sliding. Finally, there is always at least one adult, called a playleader, who supervises and facilitates the play.

Adventure playgrounds originated in Denmark in 1943 and became very popular in England after World War II. Bombed out city blocks provided an ideal setting for these "junk" playgrounds (Frost & Klein, 1979). This type of playground is slowly gaining a foothold in the United States. The American Adventure Playground Association was founded in 1974, and by 1982 adventure playgrounds were located in at least 25 American cities (Vance, 1982).

Advantages of adventure playgrounds include the tremendous diversity of available activities, the flexibility created by all the "loose parts" in the environment, the sense of competence and responsibility instilled in children through being able to build and shape their own environment, and the skills that are learned in the process of building structures. Not surprisingly, research has shown that children engage in a far greater variety of activities on adventure playgrounds and that this type of playground is much more popular with children than are either traditional or contemporary designs (*e.g.,* Hayward, Rothenberg, & Beasley, 1974).

Unfortunately, several disadvantages exist. First of all, adventure playgrounds are unsightly, causing some neighbors to object to their presence. This problem can sometimes be solved by building high fences around the area. Adventure playgrounds are also relatively expensive, at least in the long run. Start-up costs are not high, but playleader salaries are a continuing expense. Finally, the worst drawback concerns liability. Adventure playgrounds look very dangerous, with their open fires, ponds, loose nails, and sharp tools. Fear of injury and resulting litigation, coupled with the high cost of liability insurance, has caused many a city official to have second thoughts about establishing adventure playgrounds. It is somewhat ironic that an impressive array of evidence from the United States, England, and Europe indicates that adventure playgrounds are no more dangerous than traditional playgrounds (Vance, 1982), no doubt because of the constant supervision of playleaders. As long as adventure playgrounds are perceived as dangerous, it is going to be very difficult to establish them in this country. However, the important advantages offered by this type of play setting make such an undertaking well worth the effort.

Playground Design Features

Attempts recently have been made to identify the specific properties of playgrounds which hold children's interest and lead to a variety of types of play. While this area of research is still in its infancy, several design features appear to be associated with high levels of play. These features include linkages, flexible materials, graduated challenge, and a wide variety of experiences. All of the features are related to the amount of diversity and complexity that a playground offers. Diversity concerns the different types of experiences possible in a setting and is related to getting children started in play. Complexity refers to the number and variety of responses that objects elicit (Ellis, 1984). The more complex a piece of equipment is, the more children can do with it. Complexity determines how long objects can hold children's attention.

Linkages. One of the best ways to increase the complexity of individual pieces of playground equipment is to link them. A lot more can be done with platform, slide, and tire net when they are connected than when they stand in isolation. Linkage has the additional advantage of promoting a continuous movement from one activity to another. It also gets children together in a central location, promoting social interaction. These advantages of linkage are supported by research. Bruya (1985), for example, found that preschoolers spent more time playing on wooden platforms when the structures were linked together than when they were separate. The linked arrangement also resulted in more social contacts among the children.

Most contemporary playgrounds rate highly in linkage. In Figure 10-3, note how the structures are linked in several clusters and how the separate play areas are connected by the concrete pathway. Traditional playgrounds, on the other hand, are characterized by widely scattered, isolated pieces of equipment. Linkages are not inherent in adventure playgrounds, since the structures are built by the children themselves. However, experience has shown that children often link together the structures they build on these playgrounds (see the photos in Frost & Klein, 1979, pp. 209–214).

Flexible Materials. Flexibility refers to the extent to which materials can be manipulated, combined, and changed. The more flexible the material, the more children can do with it. Flexibility is therefore directly related to complexity and to the ability to hold children's interest.

The static, single-use pieces of equipment found on traditional playgrounds are very low in flexibility. Sand and water, found in many contemporary and adventure playgrounds, represent the other extreme. They are infinitely manipulable. Adventure playgrounds have the additional advantage of having a number of "loose parts" (pieces of wood, tires, ropes, tools, pieces of pipe) which children can use in a multitude of different ways. Adventure playgrounds are therefore the definite leader in flexible materials. Contemporary playgrounds with sand, water, and a number of loose parts also rate highly in terms of flexibility.

A study by Weilbacher (1981) sheds additional light on this issue. She examined differences in how children played when the same equipment was movable, or stationary. Although the study was set on an indoor stage, the equipment was the large-motor type commonly found on playgrounds. The nonmovable equipment was called "static" because the children could not manipulate or change the pieces of the apparatus, while movable equipment was termed "dynamic" because youngsters could disassemble the pieces and use them in many different ways throughout the play area. Analysis of videotapes revealed that children in the static environment often used the equipment in unique ways (climbing up a ladder backwards) but then eventually abandoned the equipment altogether and played social games such as "ring-around-the-rosy." In contrast, children in the dynamic environment discovered that the movable equipment suggested alternative uses in pretend play (turning the ladder over and using it as if it were a car), which led to more cooperative behavior. Weilbacher concluded that the loose parts of the dynamic environment fostered a variety of sociodramatic play episodes which were equipment dependent, whereas the social games occurring in the static environment were independent of the equipment. She noted that both types of environments provide valuable play opportunities.

Graduated Challenge. Graduated challenge involves presenting several levels of difficulty for each activity. It insures that developmentally appropriate activities are available for children of varying ages. A playground should have simple challenges for very young children, such as low things to climb, ramps and short slides with gentle inclines, small steps, and low platforms. There should also be bigger challenges for older children, such as higher platforms, rope ladders, and longer, steeper slides. Graduated challenge enables each child to find an optimal level of challenge: not too easy or too difficult.

Lack of graduated challenge is one of the major problems with traditional play-grounds. Such playgrounds usually have only one size of each type of equipment, and therefore offer only one level of challenge. This level is too difficult for some children: they either avoid playing on the equipment or risk accidents. It is too easy for others, resulting in boredom or inappropriate use (swinging crookedly, climbing up slides backwards, walking on top of monkey bars). If playground equipment does not provide a range of challenges, older children are tempted to increase the challenge level by using the equipment in an unsafe manner. This can lead to serious injury.

Most contemporary playgrounds rate highly in graduated challenge. The linked structures on these playgrounds usually provide at least two levels of challenge. In Figure 10–3, for example, note that there are actually two separate playgrounds, each with its own level of challenge. The main structure for two- and three-year-olds has low platforms, a gently inclined ramp, and short stairs, whereas the main structure for the four- and five-year-olds has much higher platforms, taller ladders, a slide, and a tire net. The latter structure also has a ramp and stairs for less experienced players. Adventure playgrounds also rate highly in graduated challenge. Children construct their own structures that can be adjusted to fit their needs and abilities.

Variety of Experiences. Variety refers to the number of different types of activities available in the playground. Diversity is needed to catch children's attention and get play started. A large number of activities insures that children will find activities that suit their momentary interests. In addition, variety enhances the learning potential of the environment. Richard Dattner explains:

> A playground should be like a small-scale replica of the world, with as many as possible of the sensory experiences to be found in the world included in it. Experiences for every sense are needed, for instance: rough and smooth objects to look at and feel; light and heavy things to pick up; water and wet materials as well as dry things...things that make sounds (running water) or that can be struck, plucked, plinked, etc.; smells of all varieties (flowers, bark, mud)...The list is inexhaustible, and the larger the number of items on it that are included, the richer and more varied the environment will be for the child. (as cited by Frost & Klein, 1979, p. 196)

Adventure playgrounds obviously offer the greatest variety of experiences, but contemporary playgrounds with running water, sandboxes, and gardens can come in a close second (see Figure 10-3). Traditional playgrounds, with their single-use equipment, offer little in the way of variety.

Promoting Different Types of Play. Playgrounds should ideally provide opportunities for all types of play. A variety of exercise equipment promotes large-motor play and develops strength, balance, and coordination (Beckwith, 1982). Loose parts and natural materials such as sand and small rocks are needed to encourage constructive play. Enclosed, house-like structures and elevated forts encourage dramatic play (Wardle, 1983). Finally, some play equipment should foster social interaction and group play. Three types of equipment are ideal for this purpose: (a) linked platforms, which allow children to congregate and watch others play; (b) equipment such as wide slides and tire swivel swings which can be used by several children at a time; and (c) equipment that *requires* more than one child to work effectively (seesaws).

Traditional playgrounds have adequate provisions only for large-motor play. Contemporary playgrounds are usually better, having structures that encourage both gross-motor exercise and dramatic play. The playground illustrated in Figure 10-3 has three enclosed structures to encourage make-believe play: a house for younger children and a house plus a fort for older ones. A variety of exercise equipment is also available, including swings, ladders, balance beams, tire nets, and monkey bars. It is important to note that playgrounds in this category vary widely; some do not provide for both types of play. Beckwith (1982) cautions, for example, that certain commercial play structures consist primarily of linked decks, with little exercise apparatus. Such structures do not provide for the exercise needs of growing children. Adventure playgrounds do an excellent job of providing for all types of

Enclosed house-like structures encourage group-dramatic play in outdoor settings.

play. Not only do they offer many opportunities for exercise and dramatic play, but the loose parts and tools encourage a great deal of constructive play activity.

Table 10–1 summarizes how each playground type rates in the design features discussed above. Adventure playgrounds are clearly superior in these criteria with contemporary playgrounds a close second. Given the difficulties associated with establishing and maintaining adventure playgrounds in this country, contemporary playgrounds are probably best for most schools and communities. These areas can be

TABLE 10-1

Design Features of Playgrounds

	Traditional	*Contemporary*[1]	*Adventure*
Linkages	−[2]	++	+
Flexible Materials	−	+	++
Graduated Challenge	−	+	+
Variety of Experiences	−	+	++
Types of Play Promoted:			
Functional Play	+	+	+
Constructive Play	−	−	++
Dramatic Play	−	++	+
Group Play	−	+	+

[1]Assumes that the contemporary playground contains all of the positive features discussed in the text (sand, a variety of exercise equipment, a dramatic play enclosure, wide slides and platforms). Without these features, some of the "pluses" would change to "minuses."

[2] − = weakness; + = strength; ++ = major strength.

made more effective by incorporating some of the key features of adventure playgrounds. For example, adding loose parts will greatly increase the complexity of the setting and provide a stimulus for constructive play. Another desirable feature is the constant presence and supervision of a playleader, needed with all types of playgrounds if they are to be truly safe. An adult should always be there to assist and encourage children in their play and to prevent equipment from being used inappropriately and unsafely.

Neighborhood Play Settings

An impressive body of evidence indicates that children spend the greatest amount of their outdoor time in undesignated play spaces, rather than on playgrounds (Moore, 1985). In urban areas, streets and sidewalks are the most frequently used play settings (Naylor, 1985), but front and back yards, vacant lots, and telephone booths are also used. These neighborhood play spaces lack the separate, defined play areas that characterize playgrounds (Moore, 1985).

Several studies have examined children's play in playgrounds and neighborhood play settings (see Moore, 1985). In general, this research found that children engaged in the greatest amounts of dramatic and constructive play on adventure playgrounds. The highest levels of motor play occurred on traditional playgrounds. Neighborhood play spaces, on the other hand, were found to encourage more social play, particularly between children of different ages and genders.

These findings prompted Moore (1985) to conjecture that all types of play settings—traditional playgrounds, adventure playgrounds, and neighborhood play spaces—have the potential to contribute to children's development. He argues that we should not only provide new and improved playgrounds but also strive to improve the whole fabric of children's play in urban, suburban, and rural environments. Special attention should be given to the "neighborhood of play" including: designated playgrounds; paved play areas for ball games and informal motor play; grassy areas for games for all ages; and a variety of play areas for infants, toddlers, preschoolers, school-age children, adults—all of these within the normal fabric of the neighborhood. He suggests making a network of play by linking together all the elements of the play environment, making paths between children's homes, parks, playgrounds, school, and other favorite play spaces, thus creating safe play opportunities all along the way.

SUMMARY

The first section of this chapter examined differences between indoor and outdoor play. Evidence indicates that both settings have advantages. Outdoor preschool settings promote more large-motor play in general and higher levels of dramatic play among boys and children from low-income families. Indoor preschool settings lead to more constructive play in general and to increased dramatic play among girls. Findings indicate that play in both locations should be encouraged.

Research shows that several features of indoor play settings have an impact on play patterns. Spatial density affects the social level of children's play, particularly when less than 25 square feet of space is available per child. Such crowded conditions should be avoided. The arrangement of space is another important variable. Partitioning large, open areas into smaller areas is usually beneficial. However, it appears that openings should be kept between complementary centers such as block and housekeeping areas. Other recommendations for room arrangement include separating conflicting activity centers, clearly delineating different play areas, and maintaining clear pathways through the classroom. Finally, the amount of equipment in a setting appears to have a inverse relationship with social interaction. Social play can be increased by reducing the overall amount of equipment in a room or playground or by adding materials that encourage social interaction. Caution is needed, however, because if the amount of equipment gets too low, aggression will increase. By manipulating spatial density, room arrangements, and amount of equipment, teachers and parents can provide more stimulating indoor play settings and can help promote high social-cognitive levels of play.

Several design features of playgrounds have been found to encourage high levels of play. These features include linkages, flexible materials, graduated challenge, a wide variety of experiences, and provisions for all types of play. Adventure playgrounds rate highest in these criteria, and contemporary playgrounds are a close second. Traditional steel and asphalt playgrounds, on the other hand, rate poorly in all these features. We hope that, as the shortcomings of the traditional design become increasingly apparent, these areas will be replaced with contemporary or adventure playgrounds.

REFERENCES

Beckwith, J. (1982). It's time for creative play. *Parks and Recreation, 17*(9), 58–62, 89.

Boyatzis, C.J. (1985, March). *The effects of traditional playground equipment on children's play interaction.* Paper presented at meeting of the Anthropological Study of Play, Washington, DC.

Bruya, L.D. (1985). The effect of play structure format differences on the play behavior of preschool children. In J.L. Frost & S. Sunderlind (Eds.), *When children play* (pp. 115–120). Wheaton, MD: Association for Childhood Education International.

Campbell, S.D., & Frost, J.L. (1985). The effects of playground type on the cognitive and social behaviors of grade two children. In J.L. Frost & S. Sunderlind (Eds.), *When children play* (pp. 81–88). Wheaton, MD: Association for Childhood Education International.

Doyle, P.H. (1977). The differential effects of multiple and single niche play activities on interpersonal relations among preschoolers. In D.F. Lancy and B.A. Tindall (Eds.), *The study of play: Problems and prospects* (pp. 199–207). West Point, NY: Leisure Press.

Doyle, P.H. (1978). The effect of preschool play activities on children's antisocial behavior. In M.A. Salter

(Ed.), *Play: Anthropological perspectives* (pp. 145–156). West Point, NY: Leisure Press.

Ellis, M.J. (1984). Play, novelty, and stimulus seeking. In T.D. Yawkey & A.D. Pellegrini (Eds.), *Child's play: Developmental and applied* (pp. 203–218). Hillsdale, NJ: Erlbaum.

Fagot, B.I. (1977). Variations in density: Effect on task and social behaviors of young children. *Developmental Psychology, 13,* 166–167.

Field, T.M. (1980). Preschool play: Effects of teacher/child ratios and organization of classroom space. *Child Study Journal, 10,* 191–205.

Frost, J.L., & Henniger, M.L. (1981). Making playgrounds safe for children and children safe for playgrounds. In R.D. Strom (Ed.), *Growing through play* (pp. 168–176). Monterey, CA: Brooks/Cole.

Frost, J.L., & Klein, B.L. (1979). *Children's play and playgrounds.* Boston: Allyn and Bacon.

Harper, L.V., & Sanders, K.M. (1975). Preschool children's use of space: Sex differences in outdoor play. *Developmental Psychology, 11,* 119.

Hayward, G., Rothenberg, M., & Beasley, R.R. (1974). Children's play and urban playground environments. *Environment and Behavior, 6,* 131–168.

Henniger, M.L. (1985). Preschool children's play behaviors in an indoor and outdoor environment. In J.L. Frost & S. Sunderlind (Eds.), *When children play* (pp. 145–150). Wheaton, MD: Association for Childhood Education International.

Hutt, C., & Vaizey, M.J. (1966). Differential effects of group density on social behaviour. *Nature, 209,* 1371–1372.

Johnson, M.W. (1935). The effect on behavior of variation in the amount of play equipment. *Child Development, 6,* 52–68.

Kinsman, C.A., & Berk, L.E. (1979). Joining the block and housekeeping areas: Changes in play and social behavior. *Young Children, 35*(1), 66–75.

Kritchevsky, S., & Prescott, E. (1977). *Planning environments for young children: Physical space* (2nd ed.). Washington, DC: National Association for the Education of Young Children.

Loo, C. (1972). The effects of spatial density on the social behavior of children. *Journal of Applied Social Psychology, 2,* 372–381.

McGrew, W.C. (1972). *An ethological study of children's behavior.* New York: Academic Press.

Mergen, B. (1982). *Play and playthings: A reference guide.* Westport, CT: Greenwood Press.

Moore, G.T. (1985). State of the art in play environment. In J.L. Frost & S. Sunderlin (Eds.), *When children play* (pp. 171–192). Wheaton, MD: Association for Childhood Education International.

Naylor, H. (1985). Outdoor play and play equipment. *Early Child Development and Care, 19,* 109–130.

Pellegrini, A.D. (1984). The effects of classroom ecology on preschoolers' functional uses of language. In A.D. Pellegrini & T.D. Yawkey (Eds.), *The development of oral and written language in social contexts* (pp. 129–141). Norwood, NJ: Ablex.

Pfluger, L.W., & Zola, J.M. (1974). A room planned by children. In G. Coates (Ed.), *Alternative learning environments.* Stroudsburg, PA: Dowden, Hutchinson, and Ross.

Phyfe-Perkins, E. (1980). Children's behavior in preschool settings—A review of research concerning the influence of the physical environment. In L.G. Katz (Ed.), *Current topics in early childhood education* (Vol. 3, pp. 91–125). Norwood, NJ: Ablex.

Pollowy, A.M. (1974). The child in the physical environment: A design problem. In G. Coates (Ed.), *Alternative learning environments.* Stroudsburg, PA: Dowden, Hutchinson, and Ross.

Roper, R., & Hinde, R.A. (1978). Social behavior in a play group: Consistency and complexity. *Child Development, 49,* 570–579.

Sanders, K.M., & Harper, L.V. (1976). Free-play fantasy behavior in preschool children: Relations among gender, age, season, and location. *Child Development, 47,* 1182–1185.

Sheehan, R., & Day, D. (1975). Is open space just empty space? *Day Care and Early Education, 3*, 10–13, 47.

Shure, M.B. (1963). Psychological ecology of a nursery school. *Child Development, 34*, 979–992.

Smith, P.K., & Connolly, K.J. (1972). Patterns of play and social interaction in preschool children. In N. Blurton-Jones (Ed.), *Ethiological studies of child behaviour* (pp. 65–95). Cambridge, England: Cambridge University Press.

Smith, P.K., & Connolly, K.J. (1980). *The ecology of preschool behavior.* Cambridge, England: Cambridge University Press.

Tizard, B., Philps, J., & Plewis, I. (1976). Play in pre-school centres—II. Effects on play of the child's social class and of the educational orientation of the centre. *Journal of Child Psychology and Psychiatry, 17*, 265–274.

Vance, B. (1982). Adventure playgrounds: The American experience. *Parks and Recreation, 17*(9), 67–70.

Wachs, T.D. (1985). Toys as an aspect of the physical environment: Constraints and nature of relationship to development. *Topics in Early Childhood Special Education, 5*(3), 31–46.

Walling, L.S. (1977). Planning an environment: A case study. In S. Kritchevsky & E. Prescott (Eds.), *Planning environments for young children: Physical space* (pp. 44–48). Washington, DC: National Association for the Education of Young Children.

Wardle, F. (1980). Building a structure to facilitate toddler play. *Day Care and Early Education, 8*, 20–24.

Wardle, F. (1983). *Effects of complexity, age, and sex on the social and cognitive level of young children's play in an outdoor setting.* Unpublished doctoral dissertation, University of Kansas.

Wardle, F. (1984). Building outdoor play environments for children two to five. *Lutheran Education, 120*(1), 23–30.

Weilbacher, R. (1981). The effects of static and dynamic play environments on children's social and motor behaviors. In A.T. Cheska (Ed.), *Play as context* (pp. 248–258). West Point, NY: Leisure Press.

Woodard, C.Y. (1984). Guidelines for facilitating sociodramatic play. *Childhood Education, 60*, 172–177.

Play and the Electronic Media

In Chapters 9 and 10 we discussed the significance of the physical environment and toys in play during children's early years. An important topic relevant to the focus of these chapters was not considered: the electronic media.

Electronic media, in comparison with *printed* media (books, newspapers, comic books, or magazines), include such categories as movies, audio- and videocassettes, records, television, radio, video and arcade games, electrical or computerized toys, and computers and their software. The importance of electronic media in children's learning and development has been recognized by parents and professionals for many years. Electronic media as a factor in the socialization and education of young children is known to operate on both formal and informal levels. For instance, teachers use multimedia instruction in classrooms, and parents and others are well aware of how much children learn from television and other forms of media outside of school. In many ways, the media can be seen not only to affect play, but are also used as vehicles or objects of play.

In the first section of this chapter we will review literature on the relationship between many types of electronic media and play behaviors. We will focus on television and its influence on play, including a report on experimental studies that have investigated television viewing's effects on specific play behaviors. We will also discuss play in relation to radio, motion pictures, video games, and electronic and programmable toys. In the second section of the chapter we will turn to play and the role of computers in early childhood development and education. As with the other chapters of this volume, we will suggest practical applications for parents and teachers, based on the theory and the research findings presented.

Technological advances will continue to have their impact on society. These advances are raising important new issues in the field of early childhood education. Parents and teachers need to know how to best convert these technological advances into advantages for children. That is not the least of our challenges. We must share a commitment to preventing "technological child abuse" through

inappropriate use of electronic media in the lives of children—in their homes, in the schools, in day care centers, and in their other early environments.

TELEVISION

General Influence

Of the several important forms of the electronic media that affect the play and development of young children, the most influential is television. Television is available in well over 95% percent of homes in the United States. It should be considered a major socializing agent in the child's life. In her book *The Plug-In Drug,* Marie Winn (1977) asserts that television can inhibit fantasy and creativity. She emphasizes that television encourages a certain kind of cognitive passivity, a "show me" or "entertain me" orientation. Time spent in front of the television set "watching the parade pass by" is time spent not doing other activities that may be more beneficial to the child, such as play or homework. As a prime suspect in "technological child abuse," television has received such nicknames as the "one-eyed monster," the "idiot box," and the "boob tube."

Support has been marshaled for these allegations. Research by Jerome and Dorothy Singer and their associates has indicated that preschool-age children who watch a great deal of television are less playful than young children who watch less television (Singer & Singer, 1979). Perhaps television promotes general passivity and dependence as Winn suggests; television viewing may also interfere with the development of the ability to create and use internal images, an important component of pretense play (Sherrod & Singer, 1977). Other researchers have reported consistent findings. For example, a laboratory study by Huston-Stein and her colleagues demonstrated that children who watched a cartoon containing high levels of action and violence engaged in less fantasy play afterward than did groups who had seen no television or a program with low amounts of action and violence (Huston-Stein, Fox, Greer, Watkins, & Whitaker, 1981).

More recent research by the Singers has investigated the relationship of play and aggressive tendencies to specific kinds of television programs. A common finding is that the percent of time spent viewing action-adventure programs relative to the total hours of television watched is negatively correlated with playfulness and that preschoolers who watch a lot of cartoons are more likely to behave aggressively (Singer & Singer, 1980). Interestingly, in this more recent work, the Singers found that playfulness is not related solely to watching television 3 to 4 versus 5 to 6 hours daily. Rather, playfulness is associated with positive emotions and cooperativeness and leadership behaviors in school and is linked with a host of other variables such as the child's social class and gender. However, their study showed that children who tended to exhibit more problem behavior and less mature social behavior at school were among the heavier television viewers at home. They frequently watched shows depicting violence but watched few programs with positive social messages such as "Mister Rogers' Neighborhood."

Use of TV to Foster Play

The bulk of research conducted on television viewing and the play of young children suggests that television is a negative influence, preempting play time and possibly impeding creativity. Some researchers, however, believe that television can be used to build play competence in children. These researchers have reasoned that, after all, there are some common elements that the medium shares with make-believe play—visual fluidity, time and space flexibility, and fantasy-reality distinctions. The content of specific programs, furthermore, may stimulate fantasy play by giving children ideas for certain play episodes.

As we discussed in Chapter 2, adults can use specific techniques to guide children's play for the better. Can such guidance counteract any negative effects derived from television? How might teachers and parents use television to promote play competence?

The early play-intervention studies that used television programs such as "Mister Rogers' Neighborhood" revealed that television, by itself, had little holding power over children in a group setting. For example, Singer and Singer (1976) reported that children found peer interaction more appealing than watching "Mister Rogers' Neighborhood." However, the Singers found that adult-mediated television viewing— *i.e.*, an adult helping children to pay attention to certain aspects of the "Mister Rogers' Neighborhood" program—increased imaginative free play. Higher play scores were seen in those children randomly assigned to an adult tutor who taught make-believe games without a TV set (Singer & Singer, 1976). Friedrich and Stein (1975) corroborated that the most reliable positive effects on preschool play occur when television is combined with having a teacher actively tutor children at play.

OTHER FORMS OF ELECTRONIC MEDIA

Radio. Teachers and parents commonly assume that radio cannot be used with young children in any positive manner. Mental effort is needed by preschoolers to transform messages transmitted aurally into visual images. From story or prose comprehension research studies, it is known that young children often have difficulty generating images. Unlike television, radio does not provide ready-made pictures.

Although not much research on the subject has been done since the advent of television, there is evidence that preschool children can comprehend and benefit from exposure to radio. In an interesting study, Greenfield (1982) presented stories to four- and five-year-old preschoolers via television and radio and compared the kinds of errors they made in retelling the stories. In general, the children made a similar number of content errors in retelling stories conveyed by both media. They did, however, use more sound effects, dialogue, and figurative or expressive language in their descriptions of the radio stories.

Young children's difficulties in understanding and remembering content transmitted over the radio may stem from their infrequent exposure to that medium. To remedy this, an innovative radio program was designed several years ago by the Wisconsin Educational Radio Network (Usitalo, 1981). The program consisted of thirty 15-minute radio adventures designed specifically for young children in home or school settings. Parents and teachers could write for an adult guidebook summarizing the stories told and containing lists of related activities adults could do with children. One story, for example, was about a grandfather's lost ring and the family's attempt to find it by retracing the places Grandpa had been that day, one of which was the airport. Related activities recommended included drawing a picture of the airport, pretending to be airplanes with different children as the central control tower, and telling stories about airplane rides.

It has been said that radio stimulates imaginativeness more than television does because it leaves visual gaps for listeners to fill in with their imaginations. However, some previous experience is required for that. To use radio (or audiocassettes or phonograph records) as a play-enhancing device, it is necessary to help young children practice using their imagination and provide them with related activities and explanatory supports in order to compensate for the limitations of an exclusively aural medium.

Movies. As do television and radio, movies can influence the play and development of children. Time spent watching movies, however, is a much smaller percent of children's daily or weekly activities.

Movies often are made especially for young children. Characters such as the Care-Bears and the Smurfs reflect a concern for fostering positive social behavior in children. Plots or storylines are usually simple and provide good material for later make-believe play. Of course, there are action-adventure movies as well. These have a powerful influence on the child's imagination and play. Superheroes and super-villains are very popular in children's role enactments. Adults should shape and redirect content from such movies to match more acceptable play patterns and cultural norms.

Watching movies or television and listening to the radio are essentially passive activities that may affect play at a later time by triggering the imagination in some way. We must recognize, however, that the acts of watching or listening are themselves forms of play. When children participate in these activities, they not only escape from reality in some sense, but also enjoy what they are doing at the time. As Mergen (1982) notes: "Roller coaster rides, car chases, aerial combat all become almost as exciting on the screen as they are in life." The enjoyment of motion in the playground or on the screen is an aspect of physical play sometimes referred to as vertigo (Caillois, 1961).

Video Games. Video games such as Rocky's Boots and Pac Man are made possible by the marriage of television and the computer. Not to be confused with video-computer-assisted instruction, video games are clearly for fun, not learning. Very popular with older children, they have found their way into the lives of younger children as well.

Video games are the first form of the electronic media that we have reviewed so far that are interactive. Television, radio, and movies are all essentially one-way communications. One of the major attractions of video games is that they allow the child to control what appears on the cathode ray tube (Greenfield, 1984). The combination of visual attractiveness and the potential for interaction is very appealing. The electricity turns children on, and with video games you can see the electricity as well!

Few adults would recommend the use of video games to foster learning in children during the preschool years. Arguments advanced by researchers such as Greenfield (1984) that the use of video games promotes hand-eye coordination and spatial skills are not backed by empirical evidence and seem dubious at best. Moreover, there is evidence that violent video games may desensitize young children to violent behavior and may make them feel more comfortable with violence, much as violent television shows do. Silvern and his associates, for example, found that the video games Space Invaders and Roadrunner raised the level of aggressive play and lowered the level of desirable behaviors in five-year-old children (Silvern, Williamson, & Countermine, 1983). Nevertheless, preschool children often say they prefer video games to academically oriented computer software (Johnson & Hoffman, 1984).

Electronic Toys. Electronic toys, such as battery-operated toys and electric trains, are rarely found in day care centers, preschool classrooms, or children's bedrooms or toy boxes. Safety reasons preclude their use by young children without careful supervision. However, there is a subcategory of electrical toys that pose fewer risks and that are becoming a more prevalent part of the early childhood environment. These are computerized toys.

Smith (1981) divides computerized toys into several categories, including toys that make music and game toys. These kinds of toys have flooded the market in recent years.

Toys that make music have preprogrammed tunes that can be brought up by pressing the right buttons or keys. Sometimes there is a delay in tone after the switch is pushed, which might be confusing to a child, but in general these musical activities

offer the child a way to discover a sense of rhythm not likely to be discovered with simple band instruments. Computer-toy versions of musical instruments sometimes lure children into musical appreciation and interest. For other children, they are just noisemakers.

Game toys that are computerized include hand-held, lap, and table toys of speed, sport, and wit. Simon Says requires the child to remember a numbered sequence of musical notes with brightly colored flashing lights. Sport games, which include baseball, football, hockey, and soccer, are hand-held versions of arcade or video games. Some of these games involve different levels of built-in difficulty that can be selected by the player. These games are usually not intended for younger children, however, and may become frustrating for them. For the skilled player, these games often become boring because the player can "win at will."

Programmable Toys. The computer age has resulted in an overwhelming number of computer toys. Unlike video games or electronic toys, which are "pre-scripted," programmable toys involve a computerized activity that must be performed by the child or adult in order for the toy to work. Toys such as Big Track, for example, are programmed by the child, who learns basic concepts of programming by directing the robot or army tank to move in certain directions for certain distances, taking a specified number of turns and steps. Programmable toys can be used in make-believe play and are considered by many educators an excellent prerequisite or alternative activity to "two-dimensional" computer use— a topic treated in the second part of this chapter.

The Roles of the Adult

As research has documented, television can have positive effects. It is important for parents and teachers, however, to monitor the television viewing of their children, particularly younger children. Unfortunately, adults generally exert little control. Many parents or teachers place no limits on what children watch on TV. Parental and teacher monitoring of television watching fosters a sense of control over television and also gives the adult the opportunity to help the child use television content in make-believe play. Discussing television shows with children, moreover, can be a valuable learning activity that often helps the child distinguish fantasy from reality. The research on the use of TV to promote play demonstrates how important it is for adults to guide young children's television viewing to make it beneficial, not harmful.

As for the other forms of the electronic media, the main point for parents and teachers to remember is that these forms, with the exception of programmable toys, are limited by the fact that the child is essentially passive, that is, not in control. Electronic media therefore need to be supplemented with active experiences so that children become creators as well as consumers of fantasy. Teaching children to use other forms of the electronic media such as cameras, audiocassettes, or video cameras, together with the use of printed media and three-dimensional materials as well, are necessary to fulfill this goal. Moreover, we can assist children in play and learning with the newest form of the electronic media—computers.

ROLE OF COMPUTERS IN EARLY CHILDHOOD DEVELOPMENT

Computers are making their way into the lives of more and more young children nowadays. It is somewhat startling to realize that not long ago computers were not present at all in homes and schools and that young children and their parents and teachers were not exposed to them. Recent surveys document the increasing prevalence of computers in the homes of young children and in early education and child care programs. For example, a Mike Wilson Survey of 58,000 licensed child care centers in June 1985 revealed that of the 490 responding centers reporting use of microcomputers, 75 percent were preschools, 18.8 percent were day care programs, 4.4 percent were Montessori schools, and 2 percent were Head Start programs. The survey further found that child care centers that served children over five years of age were seven times more likely to use microcomputers than were programs that served only children under this age (Wilson, 1985). Estimates of the number of homes with computers range from 16 to 25 percent. At least one third of the educational software purchased for those computers targets children under seven years of age (Talmis, Inc., 1984). There is every reason to believe that the growing use of computers in homes, day care centers, and schools will continue in the future.

The literature has kept abreast of this recent trend in today's society in one way—but not in another. On the one hand, a great deal has been published that can perhaps best be described as "concept papers" or "think pieces," in which the author takes a general stand on computers and young children and discusses some specific issue or topic, for example, software selection and evaluation. On the other hand, only a limited number of publications that can be called research reports or empirical studies have been available to answer important questions that have been echoed during the relatively short time computers have been around. But while researchers may be faulted for not moving fast enough when the phenomenon first emerged, research findings are now being disseminated at an accelerated pace. Furthermore, commendable attempts have been made to synthesize these results. The following research reviews are highly recommended: Brady and Hill (1984); Clements (1985); Simon (1985). Both "soft think pieces" and "hard empirical studies" will be cited in discussing three related topics: (1) developmental readiness; (2) effects or consequences; and (3) implementation.

Developmental Readiness

Teachers in general were quick to embrace computers as friends or partners in education. Early childhood educators, however, initially remained somewhat wary of mixing computers and young children. Part of this ambiguity lingers, probably because many teachers are unsettled by the newness of computers and do not know how to use them. Another reason for cautious reactions to computers in early childhood education, however, relates to traditional values and principles in the field. Valid and important concerns include: Are computers really appropriate for children under six years of age? What value do computers have for teaching young children? Will computers interfere with normal development in some way?

Such questions about the possibly harmful effects of microcomputers on young children were raised even as researchers praised this technological device as a wonderful way to stimulate children positively in hitherto unheard of ways. Papert (1980) in his book *Mindstorms: Children, Computers, and Powerful Ideas* pioneered the move to introduce children to computers as "objects to think with." Papert espoused Piagetian views on the benefits of self-directed discovery in children's learning. Cognitive development is enhanced when children are given the opportunity to use their thought processes to resolve conflicts in problem-solving situations. Specifically, Papert invented LOGO language and "turtle graphics" (made by moving a small triangular cursor, called a "turtle," on the screen) within "micro-worlds" set up on the microcomputer screen. Papert and his followers lauded the microcomputer and made some rather provocative claims. For example, they asserted that the computer's ability to make the abstract concrete on the monitor screen in response to the child's initiative would accelerate the child's cognitive development. "The child, even at preschool ages, is in control: The child programs the computer. As they teach the computer how to think, children embark on an exploration into how they themselves think. The experience can be heady: Thinking about thinking turns the child into an epistemologist, an experience not even shared by most adults" (Papert, 1980, p. 19). Some empirical studies that have shed light on Papert's hypotheses will be reviewed later in this chapter.

In considering developmental readiness, the psychological or psychomotor prerequisites for using microcomputers, Papert strongly asserts that young children need concrete, direct exercises before using LOGO. Proponents of LOGO do not intend to replace or skip real-life, concrete experiences. Before engaging in turtle geometry on the screen where the child selects the goals and then programs the computer to carry out the necessary steps, the child is first taught to "play turtle" physically, moving about in different directions in a specified number of steps, then to program a walking friend or a floor-crawling robot. Only afterward does the child give the screen cursor the various body-centered commands like "forward," "backward," "left," or "right" with some measure of distance. Furthermore, since the turtle leaves a path where it moves, pictures of various shapes, designs, or patterns can be created. Young children obviously need to know quite a bit before the computer can be programmed to make and complete a square, for instance.

Programming in LOGO is not usually successful for children under six years of age because of their inability to type commands without a great deal of adult assistance. That limitation appears to be more cognitive than psychomotor. For instance, Hungate and Heller (1984) reported that most of the four-year-olds they studied had little difficulty finding and pressing particular keys and then looking to the screen for results. Moreover, the presence of extraneous keys did not always present difficulties. But many children, after performing tasks splendidly for a while, regressed to random, playful key pressing, often alternating between working at and ignoring the task. However, Hungate and Heller found that almost all children completed at least one task.

Cognitive rather than psychomotor limitations, then, are chiefly responsible for young children's inadequate performance with computers. First, as previously indicated, many preschoolers simply do not yet know certain necessary facts such as what a square is or that 20 is bigger than 5 (Brett, 1983). It is impossible to teach children to program in LOGO if they do not possess these basic understandings, or if they do not know in which direction or how far they wish the turtle to move. Second, young children's attention span is short. Their perceptual attention is closely related to action, and they are easily distracted. Preschoolers enjoy a great deal of action— moving simply to make things happen and to obtain a concrete result. A third cognitive limitation is that preschoolers, five years of age or younger, often focus on a particular feature of a stimulus and ignore the other features entirely. This tendency to center on one aspect of a situation, together with their orientation toward concrete objects, makes it very difficult for them to follow long-term plans, especially on a symbolic level, as is involved in the use of the cursor on the screen of the monitor. Finally, to what extent are other basic cognitive processes insufficiently developed to allow for programming in LOGO? Very young children have difficulty remembering, are unable to seriate or engage in systematic reasoning, and possess limited symbolic capabilities (Brady & Hill, 1984; Johnson, 1985).

As a result of these known limitations, special considerations must go into designing and implementing computer activities for use by young children. For example, Croft and Hess (1985) endorse beginning with some simple preprogrammed packages. They make the following specific recommendations. "We suggest beginning with software similar to the Learning Company's Butterfly Home (in Juggles' Rainbow) because input is simple (the children can press any key) and the results on screen are colorful, engaging, and immediate. Introduction to pre-programming experiences like these during the early years will help children be more comfortable with computers in elementary school" (p. 317).

A second adaptation is the use of Instant LOGO or Single Keystroke or other similar programs that require less work for the child to move the turtle. In these simplified forms of LOGO, it is possible for youngsters under six years of age to make their own graphic designs by using an "instant key" input system. Instant key systems avoid the frustrations that result when the child tries to learn complicated command procedures. Youngsters press one key and are able to observe the turtle cursor move in a specified manner, leaving a tangible trace on the monitor display screen. For example, when the child types "F" (and presses the return key) the turtle makes a straight line for a given distance. Pressing the "L" key causes the turtle to turn fifteen degrees to the left, and pressing the "R" key makes the turtle turn fifteen degrees to the right. Youngsters store their programs by using the "P" key and typing a name for it. Using the "I" key brings back (invokes) the program. Such simplified versions of LOGO can be used by children ages 4½ to five years who are familiar with the computer keyboard and who have had previous experience using programming software (Croft & Hess, 1985).

Developmental Consequences

Researchers and practitioners have been concerned with two possible effects of mixing computers and young children. One concern involves social behavior; the other relates to cognitive ability and performance in academic areas.

Social Behavior. Does the use of microcomputers by preschoolers disrupt play and somehow change the course of social and cognitive development?

Fein, Campbell, and Schwartz (1983) addressed themselves to three main issues: (1) Will computers encourage solitary activities rather than those fostering social interaction and cooperation? (2) Will computer curricula overemphasize preparation for school and deemphasize play and creative expression? (3) Will computer activities promote a narrow view of young children's abilities? Two preschool classrooms were systematically observed for a period of four weeks, both when computers were present and when they were not. Computers were introduced as just another feature of classrooms that were already brimming with activities and materials. Children could draw, color, and move objects around the screen by using joysticks and keyboards, either as a solitary activity or in a group. Room was provided for both operators and observers.

The researchers found that the computers themselves produced little change in behavior. In one classroom the children seemed to become more involved in their activities, with a rise in functional play and a drop in make-believe play when the computer was present, while with the addition of computers in the second classroom children became more easily distractible, but no discernible alteration in play patterns emerged. It was found that at times children enacted complex fantasy themes using objects on the screen as the focus of their stories and displayed other behavior repre-

Studies have shown that computers do not necessarily have a negative effect on children's social play.

senting age-appropriate achievements. However, computers did not appear to be the primary determinant of the behavior of individual children.

Other researchers have emphasized that computers often have a positive impact on the social dynamics of groups of children using them. For example, Borgh and Dickson (1985) found that in a semistructured situation with a peer, preschool boys and girls alike showed little difficulty in and enjoyed using a standard keyboard to control animated action. High levels of social interaction occurred between pairs of children, similar to the finding of Hawkins, Sheingold, Gearhart, and Berger (1982), who reported that significantly more collaboration occurred among fifth graders working with computers than working on other classroom tasks.

Muller and Perlmutter (1985) conducted a study to evaluate what happens when a computer is introduced into a preschool classroom. They first examined the amount of sharing, verbal and nonverbal instruction, and initiation of interaction exhibited by four-year-olds working on an Apple II computer during a 1½-hour free-play period. They reported that the presence and use of the computer seemed to provide a focus for problem-solving interaction among the preschool children, who were often seen helping and instructing each other with little teacher intervention. Some of these children were then observed over an additional 5 weeks in a subsequent study with attractive new jigsaw puzzles present instead of computers. Children worked the puzzles while alone 55 percent of the time, while they had spent only 11 percent of their time alone at the computer. Only 7 percent of puzzle time was spent with a peer, compared to 63 percent of computer time that had been spent with a peer. Unlike computer-use interactions, no turn-taking took place with the puzzles. Muller and Perlmutter concluded that preschool-age children do not shy away from others when a computer is present in the classroom. Children do not require extensive structure or teacher intervention, either. Preschoolers enjoyed working with a peer at the computer, where they engaged in a great deal of social behavior. The researchers stated that the computer allows and may even enhance the expression of social skills by young children.

Role of Computers in Early Childhood Development **221**

In short, studies to date show that fears regarding the impact of computers on young children are unfounded. Indeed, the indication from these studies is that the effect of computers on social behavior seems much more beneficial than detrimental. Of course, a great deal more needs to be learned about how positive social interaction is best achieved and how parents and teachers can employ computers constructively with their children.

Cognitive Effects. As we discussed earlier in this chapter, Seymour Papert canonized "Saint LOGO" as an educational tool to accelerate children's attaining concrete and then formal operational reasoning. He maintained that microcomputers increase children's understanding of spatial and quantitative concepts dealing with physical reality. For example, Papert claimed that children programming a computer to draw a house would learn on their own the basic rules of geometry, which would increase problem-solving skills in general, provided the children remained in the microworld learning environment of LOGO for a sufficient time. However, there have been sharp criticisms that such claims are overstatements.

Krasnor and Mitterer (1983) concluded that on the basis of what is known about cognitive development there is no reason to expect playful learning with LOGO will promote general problem-solving skills. However, specific skills may be improved through their engagement in the structured format of LOGO. Moreover, the teacher's or parent's role is not incidental or passive as Papert's self-discovery education would have it. The teacher or the parent must first direct and teach children, who must be developmentally ready for LOGO, to appreciate fully its finer aspects. It is not surprising, therefore, that little evidence exists in support of the original claims concerning LOGO (Simon, 1985).

However, that is not to say children do not in fact learn anything from using computers. Several research studies have evaluated the effects of computer assisted instruction (CAI) on learning in preschoolers and kindergartners. There is evidence that microcomputers can assist language arts readiness as well as mathematics readiness and can help children with learning tasks. In language arts, Smith-Willis, Riley, and Smith (1982) found that microcomputers improved visual discrimination skills in a group of 50 preschoolers. Piestrup (1981) showed that CAI materials helped develop reading readiness, visual discrimination, and language skills in preschool children. In mathematics, software entailing numbers, shapes, and patterns often promotes readiness for formal arithmetic instruction. In fact, gains found in mathematical areas from using CAI with children as young as kindergarten age typically have been the most dramatic (Clements, 1985).

Benefits from various software packages—be they computer languages such as LOGO or CAI programs—derive not only because microcomputer involvement engages the child cognitively in drill and practice activities or in thinking games, but also because of the symbolic and social nature of the involvement. Dickson (1985), in an interesting paper, developed the argument that the most useful cognitive effects come from practicing skills in different symbolic systems (such as pictorial, print, sound, and number systems) involving various senses (such as the auditory, the visual, and the kinesthetic). Furthermore, these positive intellectual outcomes are augmented when the skills are displayed in a social context. His perspective is broader and more encompassing than earlier views that judged LOGO versus CAI software as competing instructional tools. His perspective enables us to appreciate how computers can enhance a fuller range of talents such as art and music as well as logic, mathematics, and language. That should help us avoid inadvertently encouraging a narrow view of learning with computers. For teachers, parents, and researchers, the danger forecast by some critics who have dwelt upon the dark side of microcomputer use in early childhood education seems less realistic (see Summer 1984 issue of *Teachers College Record*).

There is little question that by using microcomputers in various activities, young children stand to gain in a cognitive sense. Theoretically, children should gain greater awareness of symbol systems and greater facility in following directions, analyzing problems, being exact, thinking about thinking, and examining situations from the point of view of microcomputers and of other children. However, very little research has been done to document the value of computers to develop specific cognitive processes in children or to promote general problem-solving skills. As we have seen, somewhat more convincing evidence exists to support the hypothesis that children can benefit from CAI and other computer activities and exercises to consolidate lower-level skills such as improving memory for factual information, distinguishing objects, letters, numbers, and shapes on the screen or learning to read from left to right.

Three important issues must be raised in order to better evaluate the cognitive and social value of using microcomputers. First, the proverbial chicken or the egg dilemma. It is hard to know, given the importance of developmental readiness for participating in and benefiting from microcomputer activity, whether such activity really adds to young children's skills and abilities or merely provides the youngster with the opportunity to exhibit existing skills. Children's behaviors with microcomputers may simply reflect the knowledge, concepts, and social skills that children already possess. Of course, constructively using microcomputers—or being involved in any other challenging intellectual activity—cannot hurt and could help reinforce and strengthen children's intellectual and social skills. Still, that is quite different from stating that these skills are a consequence of microcomputer use.

A second issue is that researchers who have cited evidence for cognitive or social effects of microcomputer use by young children generally have not included contrasting educational treatment conditions in their research. An exception is the study by Muller and Perlmutter (1985), presented earlier in this chapter, in which they compared microcomputers with jigsaw puzzles for effects on instructional, task, and social behaviors. However, in setting up such experiments, as in all cross-media research, it is difficult to find learning or play objects that will allow for plausible comparisons. For instance, in the Muller and Perlmutter experiments, perhaps selecting jigsaw puzzles was better than selecting pots and pans but maybe not as good as if behavior at typewriters had been compared to that at microcomputers.

A third issue especially important to raise in a book about play is whether what the child is doing with the computer can rightfully be defined as play behavior. Simon (1985) notes that this is hard to determine in part because of the difficulty in defining what play is. Given our view of play as intrinsically motivated, process-oriented, possessing positive affect, and representing a change from real life (see Chapter 1), it would appear that some but not all behavior with the computer can be called play (as is the case in behavior with any other artifact or technology). Children doing computer activities that are obligatory and have external rewards, such as in CAI activities sponsored or controlled by adults, would be less likely to experience those activities as play. On the other hand, some playful elements can exist in any learning situation including ones using microcomputers. As one example, consider the child using drawing programs or LOGO. Often such activity transcends exploration and learning and becomes truly playful. As a second example, consider simulation software programs in which program learning and use are cast in hypothetical situations such as going on a whale hunt (Voyage of the Mimi) or conducting a small business (Lemonade Stand). These programs often possess the three characteristics that Malone (1984) stated are required to make a computer activity motivating, appealing, or interesting (playful?): challenge, fantasy, and curiosity. Challenge means that the program is developmentally appropriate and stimulates the child with a problem at or slightly ahead of the child's existing ability level; fantasy means the program depicts some make-believe adventure or event; curiosity means that the child is captivated by the software. Interestingly, Malone has found that programs with "internal" fantasy have more appeal than ones with "external" fantasy. Programs with "external" fantasy disassociate the activity and the goal (the fantasy is artificial and imposed externally), as in pretending to kill off monsters by solving math problems; "internal fantasy," in contrast, unites the activity with the goal, such as in the previously mentioned Lemonade Stand in which children try to reach their sales' projections through problem-solving, estimation, and the use of other thinking strategies. The former type of program is more blatantly work-disguised-as-play; the latter type of program can be more genuinely enjoyed as play.

Practical Implementation

Growing research and practical experience have led to the realization that computers are neither the threat nor the panacea they were first considered to be by professionals in the field of early childhood education. Many examples from the research literature show that parents and teachers do not need to fear that using microcomputers during the early years will be hazardous to the social and emotional well-being of young children. On the other hand, those who would advocate the use of this relatively new technology as a new magic wand in education and child development are equally off the mark.

In the next section we will define current positions on using microcomputers with young children and examine several specific teaching practices. Two main strategies have emerged for incorporating computers into the learning environments of young children.

General Approaches. Some people in the field of early childhood education feel that computers and young children do not mix well. Because the computer is a two-dimensional machine or an "impoverished tool," they say it should be disqualified as an educational device for preschoolers. According to this extreme point of view, children should not be exposed to computers during the early years. According to them, it is pointless if not dangerous to make children sit still before a computer, moving only a finger to construct a straight line. Rather, they say, children should paint with large muscle movements and eventually master the hand-eye coordination needed to draw a straight line. They conclude that children need to feel the texture of the paper and need to smell the paint!

There are more positive and realistic positions, which perhaps may be best

FIGURE 11–1

An Example of a Computer Evaluation Form

Computer Evaluation

Name _____

	I	II	III	Total

I. Computer Familiarity
  A. Identify
    1. Computer
    2. Monitor
    3. Disk Drive
    4. Printer
    5. Disk				

II. Computer Usage
  A. 1. Insert Disk
    2. Boot Disk
    3. Select Program
    4. Escape
    5. Return				

B. Keyboard Familiarity
    1. Numerals (#/min.)
    2. Letters (#/min.)				

III. LOGO
  A. Commands (Define)
    1. Forward
    2. Right/Left
    3. Clear Screen
    4. Show/Hide Turtle
    5. SETBG/DETPC				

B. Procedures
    1. Line
    2. Square
    3. Web
    4. Optional				

SOURCE: From Children's House, State College, PA

described as the "curriculum approach" and the "optional activity approach." According to the curriculum approach, the use of computers in classrooms, day care centers, or children's libraries is systematically planned. Related activities and other materials are used with the computer which together focus on a particular concept or lesson. Different areas of the curriculum are covered including language, art, science, and social studies. Moreover, earlier activities are used to prepare preschoolers for the keyboard. For example, at the Children's House Montessori School in State College, Pennsylvania, children use blocks, worksheets, puzzles, collages, and games involving movement to prepare for computers. Both software and LOGO are used. The Lamplighter School in Dallas adopts a similar strategy. Carefully sequenced activities are planned for each child. The child's progress is carefully noted on charts listing component skill areas. An example of a computer evaluation form is shown in Figure 11–1 on the preceding page.

The main difference between the curriculum approach and the optional activity approach is the emphasis in the latter on flexibility in the way children interact with computers. Rather than having a structured format, different software programs are accessible for children to use as they like. Each approach is well-represented in many programs. In both cases, it is important for the teacher to articulate a clear rationale for the use of the computers. Teachers must recognize the effects of computers on children and know what skills they want to foster in children and how. Computers are a supplement to, not a replacement for, other materials and activities in the early learning environment.

Specific Practices. Since microcomputers arrived on the educational scene in the late 1970s, educators in growing numbers have been busy developing specific techniques for instilling computer familiarity and literacy in children. We will discuss briefly some of these techniques as they relate to a number of important concerns commonly expressed by specialists in early education. First, we will discuss the physical environment, software selections, and the use of computers in the early-childhood curriculum. Then, we will discuss computers and child behavior and classroom management.

Physical environment. As with setting up other interest centers in the classroom which involve a variety of equipment and materials, setting up a computer center is a considerable undertaking.

Charles Hohmann, Director of Computers and Early Childhood Programs for the Ypsilanti (Michigan) High/Scope Educational Foundation, recommends that two or three trapezoid-shaped tables with adjustable metal legs be used in making a computer interest center for young children. The metal adjustable legs will assure that table tops are at elbow level and screens at eye level. These tables should be arranged so that they form a half circle (see Figure 11–2) and should be located away from glare or light reflection and extreme heat or cold. One computer would be on each table facing the inside of the half circle where a group of up to four children would be able to help one another. The teacher should be where all children can be supervised properly. This requires that the children not face a wall. Power cords should be on the other side of the tables away from the children and off limits (Hohmann, 1985). If that is not possible, electrical power cords should be taped down. Roll-away carts are often used to transport computer equipment.

Other considerations in the physical environment of a computer interest or activity center include having disk drives and disk storage containers on the same side and near the teacher. That will enable the teacher to assist the child without having to move about. Although teachers should read the necessary documentation and follow the directions for operating the computer, charts with directions may be posted in convenient locations where the teacher can check at a glance for the right next step. Experience logs to keep track of the students' use of the computer and sign-up sheets should also be used.

Software selection. A second important part of getting started with computers in early childhood education is selecting the right software. This is especially important for preschoolers because, unlike their older brothers and sisters, they cannot compensate for a bad program. Teachers and parents of young children face a formidable task in this regard although some difficulties may be lessening as more, if not better, software becomes available. Software programs for children ages 2½ to 6 years have grown from 5 to more than 20 percent of the market in the past two years (Gray, 1986). Nevertheless, software selection in general has been a problem because of shortages, lack of accessibility and false advertising. We must guard constantly against false first impressions that can often result from attractive advertising and hard-sell approaches, while cultivating a more discriminating eye for software purchases. After all, software prices range up to $60. More serious than wasting money, however, is encouraging the use of poor quality software.

FIGURE 11–2

Creating a Computer Activity Center with Trapezoid-Shaped Tables with Adjustable Metal Legs

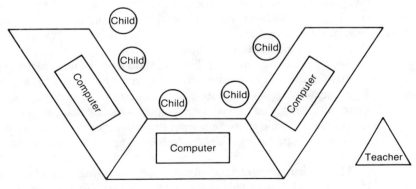

SOURCE: From Hohmann (1985)

Other guidelines entail such commonsense recommendations as being sure that software choices are machine compatible and that children are observed reacting to software selections before purchases are made. Teachers and parents who lack programming skills must be particularly careful in selecting software for children. Croft and Hess (1985) made a number of useful suggestions. According to them, among questions to ask in choosing software best-suited to young children are the following: Is the program easy to use, developmentally appropriate, and related to the child's real-life experiences? Does the program challenge the child and have the capacity to keep the child's attention for a period of time? Does the program have violent content or aversive stimulus characteristics such as loud buzzers or negative graphics? Is the program clear in its objective, fun to use, and does it allow the child to remain in control? Because often there are several games or learning activities on program disks, we might add that the percent of quality games or activities per disk be estimated, and only those disks that are worthwhile overall be selected. Finally, we might ask whether there is a built-in range of difficulty or challenge levels in the activities contained in the programs. Software should permit selecting alternative difficulty levels (Buckleitner, 1986).

Use of the computer. Third, it is necessary to develop specific uses of computers. As noted, there must be a reason for employing software and computers in the classroom or home of the young child. Realizing one's goals requires some crucial decision making. The order of presenting particular programs and activities to young children and specific strategies for interacting with children while they are using the computer are two important concerns. In addition, a great deal of thought must go into how to incorporate computer activities into other learning features of the early childhood environment.

Generally, children should begin with easy-to-use programs, such as Number Farm by DML Teaching Resources, Kindercamp by Spinnaker, or Bumble Games by the Learning Company. Initial activities will help the child gain confidence and know-how about the computer. Early computer experience must be motivating and enjoyable or should not be tried at all. Specific learning results from this early training—how to press the keys, location of on and off switches, how to restart a program. As in any other skill activity the child is expected to master, it is important that teachers or parents assist the child at first.

After using these simple programs, children can be introduced to other software that uses content of increasing levels of difficulty in such areas as problem solving, logic, memory, creativity in music, art, and design, and math and language readiness. Gradually, simplified LOGO-type languages leading to the use of LOGO should be included as the child gains confidence through experience with and command of the computer. Emphasizing the *playfulness* of computer use will encourage children to use it more.

There are important specific rules for interacting with children or groups of children as they participate in computer activities. First, adults must learn to keep one eye on the children, the other eye on the monitor screen. Adjustments are needed to feel comfortable with this modification of usual adult-child interaction. Children's reactions to games and other programs are the primary way adults find out when new challenges need to be introduced. The teacher or parent should start slowly and increase the rate of presentation as children gain confidence. Computer activities are recommended only when children are rested and wish to participate. Always stop a session while it is still fun; frequent short sessions are much better than ones that drag on. Follow-through and related activities are important complements. Focusing on the same topic, children can be encouraged to do additional work involving concrete materials or to engage in related play. Obviously, adult observational skills are basic and critical to success.

Two points may be made with respect to incorporating computer activities into the early childhood educational curriculum. First, children require information and instruction that will enable them to assimilate both "how to" knowledge and knowledge about computers and their relation to other experiences. For example, teach children about the origins of computers and why and how they are made. Being able to operate the computer and to name the parts of the computer and computer-related materials are other basic learning goals. Second, programs exist that allow for integrating microcomputers into many other traditional areas of the early childhood curriculum. For instance, Atari Notepads can be used in connection with art or creative graphics, as can Print or the program Face-Maker. The Atari program Alf is suited for science, Alf Jello for cooking. Language arts can be fostered using story dictations, and math programs such as Supermath allow children to solve problems, count, and graph; Gertrude's Secrets is another popular and useful program for promoting logical and mathematical problem-solving abilities. The program Alf and Sunburst Company's Muppets' Keyboard relate well with music. In short, there are many exciting possibilities for incorporating microcomputers with diverse activities for accomplishing traditional goals of early-childhood education.

Child and classroom management. To successfully implement microcomputers into the early childhood educational environment, rules need to be defined for children, parents, and teachers. Although these rules vary depending on the general strategy adopted, they deal with such matters as the scheduling, use, and care of microcomputers.

While parents often have time to work with their child one-to-one on the computer, teachers often introduce computer techniques, concepts, and new programs to small groups of children. This can be done either in structured small-group segments of the day or during free-play periods. For instance, one teacher with a single computer can lead a group of children; children can take turns working the keyboard, entering their responses. During free-play, computer activity can be an option for individual children. Alone or in pairs, children can enter the computer area and play a computer game or use a program. If there is a supply and demand problem, careful records should be kept of who is using the computer and when. Sign-up and tally sheets should be posted. To assure that children using the computers are not unduly disturbed by others (a common problem when computers are first introduced and are a novelty in the classroom), the computer center area can be clearly marked off. The Children's House, for instance, uses tape on the floor for this purpose. Furthermore, computer time can be used as a reward for good behavior; depriving children of computer time can be a good alternative to the usual "time-out in the quiet corner" penalty for misbehavior.

Computers and the Role of the Adult

Parents and teachers have important responsibilities in the use of computers by young children. Both need to avoid extreme attitudes about this newest form of the electronic media. Computer anxiety and avoidance are just as undesirable as romantic notions and overzealousness about its use; each often leads to "technological child abuse." Adults must remain cognizant of individual differences in the way children *think* about computers as well as in the way they *use* computers. Because there is great individual variation, a flexible and adaptable attitude is encouraged. There is no one right way to link computers, young children, and learning—the strong proselytizing one occasionally hears for specific approaches such as LOGO notwithstanding.

Second, children must be ready for computer use. Young children are concrete in their thinking and perceptually bound, limited by their own experiences and their ability to understand which is essentially prelogical in nature. Above all, adults should help children see computers as fun and valuable, in the way a good swimming instructor makes beginners feel about water. First impressions are so important. The developmental perspective then guides planning for teaching children computer skills, concepts, and applications. Both *thinking with* computers and *thinking about* computers are important early childhood educational goals. The latter is particularly important; children need to be taught how to put computers into the scheme of things.

Finally, we need to continue to design better programs and learn more about sequencing computer experiences for children. Related activity planning is very important. Eventually we will obtain a better understanding of the consequences of computer use and what, if any, are the unique contributions of computer use to children's development and well-being. Using computers to enhance development in general and play skills in particular and delineating the different ways children play with computers are two important goals.

SUMMARY

Electronic media include movies, audio- or videocassettes, records, television, radio, video and arcade games, electrical and computerized toys, and computers and their software. This chapter discussed selected forms of the electronic media in relation to children's play, highlighting television and computers as important influences on and vehicles for play.

Television exerts a profound influence on play, both because it competes for the child's time and stimulates or implants ideas for play themes and content. Research by Jerome and Dorothy Singer and others has documented how television can promote specific forms of imaginative play when used with adult intervention, and also help children distinguish reality from fantasy. However, heavy viewing and watching more violent shows (including cartoons) are inversely related to imaginative play in young children and appear to be linked to tendencies toward overt aggression. Television viewing too often can preempt play time and impede creativity.

Radio programs, movies, and video games enable children to experience fantasies; electronic and programmable toys allow them to more actively use their imaginations. Again, the adult has important roles in assisting children with play involving these diverse forms of the electronic media.

The role of computers in early childhood development is becoming increasingly important as more and more young people are coming into contact with them at home and at school. Teachers and caregivers will be better prepared to face this new challenge by recognizing the importance of developmental readiness in planning and implementing computer experiences. Cognitive more than psychomotor limitations seem to prevent early mastery of computers, and simple software and modified LOGO should precede children's programming in LOGO. In terms of the social and cognitive effects of computer use, the research reviewed indicates that fears that computers might somehow impede social development and play are unfounded, but that hopes that their use will accelerate general cognitive development are equally off the mark. Use of computers by young children can be playful or work-like and may reinforce specific mental abilities.

Finally, positions on the role of computers in the early childhood curriculum were presented: (1) the belief that computers and young children do not mix; (2) the curriculum approach; and (3) the optional activity approach. Specific practices related to the second and third position were described in terms of setting up the physical environment, selecting software, using computers, and managing the classroom. A comprehensive treatment of computers in early childhood includes emphases on *thinking with* as well as *thinking about* computers.

REFERENCES

Borgh, K., & Dickson, W.P. (1985). Two preschoolers sharing one microcomputer: Creating prosocial behavior with hardware and software. In P.F. Campbell & G.G. Fein (Eds.), *Young children and microcomputers: Conceptualizing the issues.* Reston, VA.: Reston Publishers.

Brady, E.H., & Hill, S. (1984, March). Young children and microcomputers: Research issues and directions. *Young Children*, pp. 49–61.

Brett, A. (1983, November). *Computers for young children.* Paper presented at the National Association for the Education of Young Children Annual Conference, Atlanta, GA.

Buckleitner, W. (1986). Hallmarks of quality software. *High Scope Resource*, 5(1), 12–17.

Caillois, R. (1961). *Man, play, and games.* New York: The Free Press.

Clements, D.H. (1985). Computers in early childhood education. *Educational Horizons, 63,* 124–128. 124–128.

Croft, D.J., & Hess, R. (1985). *An activities handbook for teachers of young children* (4th ed.). Hopewell, NJ: Houghton Mifflin.

Dickson, W.P. (1985). Thought-provoking software: Juxtaposing symbol systems. *Educational Research, 14,* 30–38.

Fein, G.G., Campbell, P., & Schwartz, S. (1983). *Microcomputers in the preschool: Effects on cognitive and social behavior.* Unpublished manuscript, University of Maryland.

Friedrich, L.K., & Stein, A.H. (1975). Prosocial television and young children: The effects of verbal labelling and role playing on learning and behavior. *Child Development, 46,* 27–38.

Gray, L.S. (1986, January 6). When a computer joins child's building blocks. *New York Times Education Winter Survey,* p. 8.

Greenfield, P. (1984). *Mind and media: The effects of television, video games, and computers.* Cambridge, MA: Harvard University Press.

Greenfield, P. (1982). Radio and television experimentally compared: Effects of the medium on imagination and transmission of content. *Final Report,* National Institute of Education, Teaching and Learning Program.

Hawkins, J., Sheingold, K., Gearhart, M., & Berger, C. (1982). Microcomputers in schools: Impact on the social life of elementary classrooms. *Journal of Applied Developmental Psychology, 3,* 361–373.

Hohmann, C. (1985). Getting started with computers. *High Scope Resource, 4*(3), 11–13.

Hungate, H., & Heller, J.I. (1984, April). *Preschool children and microcomputers.* Paper presented at the annual meeting of the American Educational Research Association, New Orleans.

Huston-Stein, A., Fox S., Greer, D., Watkins, B.A., & Whitaker, J. (1981). The effect of action and violence in television programs on social behavior and imaginative play of preschool children. *Journal of Genetic Psychology, 138,* 183–191.

Johnson, J.E. (1985). Characteristics of preschoolers interested in microcomputers. *Journal of Educational Research, 78,* 299–305.

Johnson, J.E., & Hoffman, T. (1984, November). *Incorporating microcomputers into the early childhood curriculum.* Paper presented at the annual meeting of the National Association for the Education of Young Children, Los Angeles.

Krasnor, L.R., & Mitterer, J.O. (1983). *LOGO and the development of general problem-solving skills.* Unpublished manuscript, Brock University, Canada.

Malone, T.W. (1984). Toward a theory of intrinsically motivating instruction. In D. Walker and R. Hess (Eds.), *Instructional software: Principles of design and use.* Belmont, CA: Wadsworth.

Mergen, B. (1982). Movies, television, and children's play. In *Play and play things: A reference guide.* Westport, CT: Greenwood Press.

Muller, A.A., & Perlmutter, M. (1985). Preschool children's problem-solving interactions at computers and jigsaw puzzles. *Journal of Applied Developmental Psychology, 6,* 173–186.

Papert, S. (1980). *Mindstorms: Children, computers, and powerful ideas.* New York: Basic Book.

Piestrup, A.M. (1981). *Preschool children use Apple II to test reading skills program.* Protola Valley, CA: Advanced Learning Technology.

Sherrod, L., & Singer, J. (1977). The development of make-believe. In J. Goldstein (Ed.), *Sports, games, and play.* Hillsdale, NJ: Erlbaum.

Silvern, S., Williams, P., & Countermine T. (1983, April). *Video game playing and aggression in young children.* Paper presented at the Annual Meeting of the American Education Research Association, Montreal.

Simon, T. (1985). Play and learning with computers. *Early Child Development and Care, 19,* 69–78.

Singer, D.G., & Singer, J.L. (1979). *Television viewing and aggressive behavior in preschool children: A field study.* Paper presented at the Conference on Forensic Psychology and Psychology. New York.

Singer, J.L., & Singer, D.G. (1980). *Television, imagination, and aggression: A study of preschoolers.* Hillsdale, NJ: Erlbaum.

Singer, J.L., & Singer, D.G. (1976). Can TV stimulate imaginative play? *Journal of Communication, 26,* 74–80.

Smith, P. (1981). The impact of computerization on children's toys and games. *Journal of Children in Contemporary Society, 14,* 73–83.

Smith-Willis, D., Riley, M., Smith, D. (1982, November/December). Visual discrimination and preschoolers. *Educational Computers Magazine,* pp. 19–20.

Talmis, Inc. (1984). *Trends in Home Computer Use.* Chicago, IL.

Teachers College Record, Summer, (1984). Entire issue.

Usitalo, D. (1981). Grandpa's Sidecar: Thirty, 15-minute radio adventures for 4- and 5-year olds at home and and school. Madison, WI: Wisconsin Educational Radio Network.

Wilson, M. (1985, June). How child care centers are using microcomputers. [Survey]. Los Angeles: Mike Wilson List Counsel, Inc.

Winn, M. (1977). *The plug-in drug: Television, children, and the family.* New York: Viking.

CHAPTER

12 Curriculum and Play

W henever an adult is responsible for a group of young children, either in a home, day care center or a preschool setting, a curriculum or plan of activities is usually arranged to meet the needs of each child. Traditionally, play has occupied a central part in any early childhood curriculum.

In this chapter we will review studies that have been done on the effects of different early childhood programs on the play of young children. Secondly, we will examine in some detail teachers' roles in three kinds of imaginative play during the preschool years, and also four current theories of imaginative play and how these theories can be helpful to the early childhood specialist. Although the emphasis will be on the roles of the teacher, there are certain aspects that would apply to the roles of the parent as well. As has been the case throughout the book, we will continue to try to derive useful suggestions from research and theory for those interested in promoting child development through the use of play.

CURRICULUM EFFECTS

A fair share of empirical research has been done over the years on the relationship between educational programs and play during the early years. Curriculum is a complex and multidimensional concept. To examine curricular effects on play, we need first to understand the ultimate goals of preschool curriculum as it is based on program structure. Program structure can be defined in terms of the extent to which the teacher assumes a major role in guiding children's behavior and the amount of emphasis on convergent activities which direct the child toward one outcome, solution, or answer (*e.g.*, use of closed-ended questions). Highly structured programs emphasize convergent learning and use more teacher directed activities, while less structured curricula for young children are marked by child centered activities and open-ended learning experiences. Another way highly structured programs are different from less structured programs is that they tend to stress content learning, external motivation, cognitive and language skills, and formal teaching. Less structured programs put more emphasis on intrinsic motivation, learning by discovery, cognitive processes, and a holistic view of the child's welfare (Hess & Croft, 1972).

In reality, educational programs in early childhood education are never purely high or low in structure. Most fall somewhere in the middle. Examples of well-known programs that are relatively high in curricular structure include DISTAR and Montessori school programs with their carefully programmed activities and didactic play materials. On the other hand, some child-centered and traditional programs encourage a variety of play experiences such as pretend games, physical exercise activities and manipulative play. Most programs for preschool children combine various amounts of less structured elements in the daily schedules, mixing formal and informal teaching practices. For kindergarten children, however, teachers nowadays seem to prefer more structure in the curriculum, in part as a response to the public's wish for greater academic preparation prior to the first grade.

The effects of an early childhood curriculum on children's play behavior and play development are complicated and impossible to assess in very precise terms because of the many concurrent and historical factors also involved. First, as we have discussed in Chapter 4, play predispositions and abilities depend on cognitive maturity and parental socialization practices and attitudes. Second, as discussed in Chapters 6 and 7, play is influenced by the child's sex and ethnic background and the child's family's social and economic standing. Third, play behavior is in part a function of materials, activities, and physical space (see Chapters 9 and 10) as well as the media (Chapter 11). On top of all of these considerations, whatever impact a program has on play is transmitted through the way a teacher manages time and space in the organization of daily activities, as well as through the more difficult to measure program atmosphere that the teachers create in part as a result of their attitudes and values. Play may be difficult to pin down, although we can say that it is intrinsically motivated, freely chosen, process-oriented, and enjoyable behavior. Nevertheless, it is also ordered behavior—the result of a host of factors that determine its form, shape, intensity, and duration. Curricular effects fall in the category of situational influences on play which operate together with or are mediated by other factors that include developmental and personality variables as well as the specific content, structure, and timing of events within the immediate physical and social environment. The preceding chapters hopefully have conveyed to the reader a sense of this mosaic of causes and have left the reader with an appreciation of some of the complexities involved in trying to understand children's play.

Studies Relating Curriculum and Play

Although it may appear that little can be expected from research on curriculum and play, putting as we just have the educational program variable into perspective within the general scheme of things that influence play, a number of

The school curriculum can have an impact on children's play patterns.

studies have been done which suggest otherwise. While the results of some of these studies may appear at first somewhat contradictory, when properly understood some conclusions can be reached.

Miller and Dyer (1975) observed 214 four-year-old children from disadvantaged homes enrolled in 14 classrooms in 10 schools representing four different types of curriculum. Although the primary focus of this study was on curricular effects on cognitive test scores, teacher ratings of children's social and play behavior were also obtained. The four types of educational programs were Montessori, Bereiter-Engelmann (patterned drill, high structure), DARCEE (language enrichment), and traditional programs (less structure). It was found that in the more structured programs there was less role play or pretend play and more manipulative play, particularly in the Montessori classrooms. Beller, Zimmie, and Aiken (1971) similarly found that children enrolled in a Montessori program engaged in less symbolic play and more practice play than children of the same age who were enrolled in less structured programs. Other researchers as well have observed little pretense and cooperative play by young children enrolled in Montessori programs (Rubin & Bryant as reported in Rubin & Seibel, 1979). Montessori children are commonly believed to be more task-oriented and less creative than preschoolers who attend less structured programs. However, as Griffing (1980) observed, middle-class black children enrolled in a Montessori kindergarten performed very imaginatively in semistructured play situations even though pretense play was not part of their regular curriculum. The effects of classroom program may pertain to performance but not ability. Again, we are reminded of the number of factors that influence children's play. One can safely assume that there would be wide variation in play skills of Montessori children just as there would be for children attending any other type of early educational program.

Huston-Stein, Freidrich-Cofer, and Susman (1977) investigated the relationship of classroom structure to social play behavior of 141 economically impoverished preschool children (average age, 4 years and 2 months). Children were enrolled in 13 classrooms. Classroom dimensions relating to curricular structure (number of teacher-led activities, teacher warmth and support, hard discipline) were rated along with children's behavior over a 5-month period using a time-sampling procedure.

Statistical analyses, taking into account differences in classroom size and children's ethnic backgrounds, showed that children in less structured classes played more imaginatively than those in highly structured classes. The authors concluded that high structure in the classroom may promote behaviors in children such as attention to tasks and conformity to authority.

There are reports from two different teams of researchers on opposite sides of the Atlantic that seem discordant at first with the above findings. Comparative observational research conducted by Tizard, Philps, and Plewis (1976) in England and Johnson, Ershler, and Bell (1980) and Johnson and Ershler (1981) in the United States failed to find results supporting the hypothesis that high structure in preschool classrooms is an inhibitor of imaginative play.

Tizard et al. (1976) investigated the free play of 109 three-and-four-year-old children attending 12 preschool classes [four classrooms representing each of three types of programs: (1) traditional English nursery schools staffed by trained teachers; (2) traditional nursery school classrooms with an added language enrichment component (high structure); and (3) nurseries without trained staff or a language enrichment component]. The play of children in the more structured classrooms differed from the play of their counterparts in less structured classrooms in two ways. First, there was a greater incidence of pretend play and less functional play in the more structured (language enriched) programs than in the traditional less structured programs. Second, preschoolers in the more structured programs exhibited more frequent use of dramatic impersonations or role play verbalizations than did children enrolled in less structured programs. Classrooms did not differ in total verbal behavior; interestingly, the two types of less structured programs (trained versus non-trained staff) did not differ in overall play level after corrections were made for differences in the ages of the children.

Johnson et al. (1980) observed for one semester the free play of 17 children enrolled in a discovery-based preschool (low structure) and the free play behavior of 18 children enrolled in a formal education preschool program (high structure). The free play periods in the two programs were similar; however, the formal program also included small, teacher-led groups where sequentially organized material was presented, while discovery program preschoolers had an additional free play period instead. The social level of play was comparable between the programs, but there were more pretense transformations during dramatic play manifested in the formal program. Observed for an additional two semesters, children in the high structure program exhibited less constructive and more dramatic play, while discovery-program children shifted from functional to constructive patterns of play (Johnson & Ershler, 1981).

To summarize, it has been found that highly structured preschools tend to reduce the range, diversity, and performance level of the play of young children (Beller, et al., 1971; Huston-Stein, et al., 1977; Miller & Dyer, 1975; and Rubin & Seibel, 1979). Imaginative play is more common in less structured programs, while constructive use of materials and goal-oriented activity are more common in highly structured programs. One might further speculate that the imaginative or dramatic play occurring in more structured programs would be more teacher-controlled and organized in contrast to the play occurring in less structured programs. Yet, in comparative research by Tizard et al. (1976) and in reports by one of the authors (Johnson, et al., 1980; Johnson & Ershler; 1981), it was found that more socio-dramatic play and transformations occurred in the more highly structured programs. It is important to note, however, that in these studies the free play of the children was not hampered by the structured components of the curriculum. In fact, the structured features of the curriculum (small group instruction stressing language arts and abstract thinking) occurring outside of free play may have actually benefited play by increasing children's representational skills. The content of a program curriculum outside free play periods may positively influence behavior during free play periods. In examining the issue of curricular effects on play, therefore, it is important to distinguish among the different types of play to discern which types are promoted, discouraged, or ignored by a given curriculum and to differentiate between component parts of the curriculum (Johnson & Ershler, 1981).

Particular curricular components may influence different forms of cognitive and social play in young children. For example, factors that maximize constructive play seem to include teacher instruction and encouragement as well as the provision of ample quantities of appropriate materials. Constructive play, on the other hand, would not be likely if conditions are distracting (too many children, not enough space, minimal adult supervision, activities too easy or too advanced) or if appropriate construction materials are scarce. Functional and dramatic play is more likely in programs which have fewer constraints. Enough time needs to be allotted for full-blown pretense to develop. Pretense flourishes in programs in which teachers encourage and model pretend activities and provide the right mix of structured and unstructured play materials. There will probably not be a great deal of make-believe in programs that restrict time and space for this type of play or in those with teachers who are disinterested in or ideologically opposed to pretense play or who mistakenly provide too many realistic, structured toys, perhaps believing them to be necessary for make-believe play. A high level of teacher direction may also decrease opportunities for the peer interactions necessary for sociodramatic and cooperative play. Since the teacher is a key element in the effects of curriculum on play, we will now discuss in some detail the role of teachers and their influence on pretend behavior in children. Pretend play is selected for this discussion since it is so highly regarded by most professionals in the field of early childhood education.

IMAGINATIVE PLAY THEMES AND THE TEACHER'S ROLE

A great variety of dramatic play can occur daily in a well-planned environment. One of the most important issues when planning play environments concerns the balance

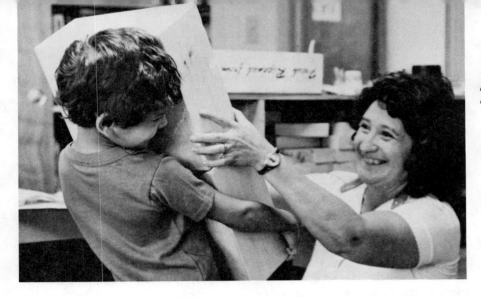

between provision for spontaneous dramatic play and encouragement of a specific sociodramatic play theme through props that suggest the theme to be acted out. Before making decisions regarding any form of dramatic play, however, teachers should first carefully examine their long-range goals for children.

Goals

A long-range goal relating to preschoolers' emotional maturity might be to help children grow in their ability to accept and handle feelings. This goal would be considered when developing programs for each individual child within the group. In dramatic play experiences, the teacher would provide ways in which children could act out, work out, and talk about feelings.

A long-range social goal might be fostering the ability to understand another viewpoint. Consideration of this goal would include ways in which the child might interact and practice communication skills. Accordingly, groups of children would be encouraged to cooperatively plan and act out familiar experiences such as housekeeping, doctor's office, or shopping. A cognitive long-range goal might be to promote mobility of thought. Make-believe requires past, present, and future references. A grocery store theme might elicit a sequence of events—going to the store, collection of groceries, checkout, putting them into the car, going home—all of which demand the child's mobility of thought. Problem solving, open-ended thinking, and symbolic representation all come into play through such activities as selection of groceries, altering actions and words to fit another player's role, and "pretending" the chair is the car. Finally, a long-term physical goal might be to encourage the child to grow in ability to match actions to words. To pretend to be a different animal, for example, requires altering body movements to fit the creature being enacted. How might different types of dramatic play foster the development of these goals?

Defining specific goals and purposes for dramatic play experiences determines its form: open dramatic play, sociodramatic play, or thematic-fantasy play (acting out stories or rhymes).

Open Dramatic Play

Spontaneous dramatic play which might develop at any given time from an external stimulus requires as much teacher planning as that needed for dramatic play centering on a specific theme. This planning must take into account the background and experiences of the children in the group. Providing props and appropriate dress-up clothes to a homemaking area or a block area might generate feelings and impulses so that the child might "act out" and express feelings without the constraints of a defined theme. Combinations of materials might stimulate imagination and invite spontaneous play. For example, after children have worked with clay for a while, the teacher would add small wooden people, cars, animals, pipe cleaners, string, flexible wire, parts of an old radio, or artificial flowers, small tree branches, some cars, and boats. After children are familiar with properties of water, the teacher could add plumbing pipes, wrenches, hats, aprons, a tool box or rubber animals, and plastic boxes.

Sociodramatic Play

When defining goals and objectives for a specific sociodramatic theme, the background experiences of the children must be considered. To be able to imitate, a child must understand to a certain extent the activity or behavior traits necessary for the role. For example, if a circus theme were selected for a group of children that had never been to the circus, the exploration of the props would be the main, if not only, focal point. Children should be allowed sufficient time to explore the props in any case, as this is an important prerequisite for successful dramatic play. There are other considerations as well. The teacher can stimulate children's interest in a given play theme through the following:

- Talk with them as they explore props. Many appropriate related activities are also possible.
- Make books, pictures, tapes relevant to the theme available.
- Tell a flannel board story, use puppets, or show a movie related to the theme.
- Plan a trip to the "site" (store, service station or post office, etc.) to refresh and expand knowledge.
- Invite a guest relevant to the theme, who may want to join the children in the play area.
- Encourage vocabulary by supplying correct labels for props, equipment, roles, and ideas as these relate to the content that the children are dramatizing.

Other practices which encourage high quality sociodramatic play include:

- Allow sufficient time in the daily schedule for children to develop dramatic play roles and themes.

- Allow for repetition throughout the week so children can experience different roles and extend knowledge.
- Encourage children to make additional props; at times the teacher or children can change or remove props.
- Invite children to become involved in setting up the center (*i.e.*, stocking grocery shelves, constructing an airplane, bus, etc.).

Ideas for several different specific sociodramatic play themes that might be relevant to children's experiences are listed in Table 12–1. One column lists a group of props that might be used to stimulate role playing. Another column suggests areas in the classroom where the props may be placed. A third column suggests mobile equipment that might be added to this area. Non-sexist roles should be emphasized. As always, developmental level and skill must be assessed before certain types of activity are promoted by the teacher.

TABLE 12–1

Sociodramatic Play Themes

Theme	Props	Area/s In Playroom	Gym or Outside Play Yard	Related Activity
Post Office	hat old stamps, seals, glue, paste mailbag mailbox letters, postcards, pens, pencils packages, paper, string paper money, coins rubber stamps cash drawer telephone sign	Set up center near homemaking center or near large blocks. Combine with library or office center	Include wagons, bikes, large boxes, (for homes/ offices)	make hats write letters make stamps construct, paint mailbox make paper money **Book Corner-Storytime** film strip, pictures, records flannel board, puzzles **Trip** post office mailbox, mail letters **Visitor** letter carrier
Grocery Store	moldable materials apron vendor's hat play money cash register food cartons, boxes	Set up center near homemaking center. Include water for washing vegetables & fruit or stack large	Include wagons bikes, wheel toys. Provide space for driving up, pickup & parking. Large boxes or triangles	Children help "stock the shelves" Make papier-mache fruits & vegetables Make money

TABLE 12-1 (continued)

Sociodramatic Play Themes

Theme	Props	Area/s In Playroom	Gym or Outside Play Yard	Related Activity
Grocery Store (continued)	pad and pencil shopping bags shelves plastic or papier-mache fruits & vegetables trucks real fruits & vegetables telephone	blocks or boxes near area. Include some dress-up clothes, billfolds, purses, shopping bags, baby buggy, stuffed animals, etc.	draped with blankets.	Design labels for empty cans Make labels for shelves **Book Corner–Storytime** pictures, records, books, puzzles **Trip** to store—make a purchase **Visitor** cashier, clerk, store manager
Police Officer	hat badge tickets license traffic signs small cards pencil and pad large cars trucks telephone	Situate center in small block area—provide small trucks & cars, small wooden people. Large block area—large trucks & cars driving wheel	Include wheel toys panel board	make badges make tickets make traffic signs make license for cars and trucks **Book Corner–Storytime** pictures, records, books, puzzles **Visitor** police officer
Space Exploration	large cartons or hollow blocks helmets panel boards rope food containers & plastic tubes	Situate near large block area	Include wheel toys, hollow tubes, hoses, rope, triangles, ladders, walkie-talkies	make helmets from ice cream cartons prepare space food **Book Corner–Storytime** film strip, movies records, pictures, puzzles **Trip** space center display **Visitor** astronomer, astronaut, airman

TABLE 12-1 (continued)

Sociodramatic Play Themes

Theme	Props	Area/s In Playroom	Gym or Outside Play Yard	Related Activity
Firefighter	hose wagon ladder rubber hatchet hat boots telephone	Setup small block area—provide small fire trucks, wooden people, street sign, doll house, etc. Large block area—driving wheel	Include wheel toys large boxes	Children make hats, ladders, badges, axes **Trip** fire station **Book Corner-Storytime** pictures, books, records **Visitor** firefighter
Sanitary Engineer	sacks ashcans wagons walkie talkie	Set-up small block area—small trucks, wooden people	Playground clean-up using wagons & wheel toys	make clean-up posters **Book Corner-Storytime** pictures, books, records record story about trip **Trip** dump—see garbage truck; playground —clean-up area **Visitor** sanitary engineer disposal plant personnel
Baker	hat pans apron rolling pin wooden spoons plastic bowls cookie cutters shelves Play-doh or raw baking materials cash register play money telephone	Set up center near homemaking center or snack tables	Sand box—add water/dishes table & chairs; or add sieves, shovels, small trucks, sticks, pebbles, shells, cupcake pans, cookie cutters, water	have a bake sale for parents write recipe make signs (pictures of baked goods clipped from magazines, etc.) play money **Book Corner-Storytime** books, pictures, flannel board,

TABLE 12-1 (continued)

Sociodramatic Play Themes

Theme	Props	Area/s In Playroom	Gym or Outside Play Yard	Related Activity
Baker (continued)				record story about trip, songs, finger plays **Trip** to bakery **Visitor** baker
Restaurant	table chairs order pad menus dishes silverware trays aprons placemats table clothes sponge napkins paper money kitchen stove kitchen sink kitchen table baking pans coffee pot refrigerator cooking hats telephone	Set up near home center or large block area. Could be combined with bakery	Set up near sand box; combine with play house or service station or painters	make picture menu make placemats prepare signs **Book Corner– Storytime** pictures, records, flannel board stories, puppets, write story about trip **Trip** to restaurant— order food observe kitchen, etc. **Visitor** waiter
Painter	cap paint brushes bucket paint overalls aprons sticks for stirring paint small stepladder towel for cleaning paint catalogues sample paint chips newspaper telephone	Devise center— large appliances boxes and tubes of colorful paint (including white) Add cans for mixing colors or shoe boxes (become blocks to build with)	Food coloring, water or paint, large appliance boxes, tubes; or wallpaper and paste, scissors, brushes	mix colors for painting **Book Corner– Storytime** pictures, books, color chart & games **Trip** painter at work **Visitor** painter (house) or artist

TABLE 12-1 (continued)

Sociodramatic Play Themes

Theme	Props	Area/s In Playroom	Gym or Outside Play Yard	Related Activity
Construction Worker	lunch bucket overalls hat pliers tape measure hammer, nails saw, screw driver wooden crate boxes sand paper tool box telephone	Large block area (include carpenter bench in area)—include wood scraps, styrofoam sheets, wall board sheets, heavy cardboard, or devise a fix-it shop using old toaster, clocks, radios, toys	Wheel toys, large boards, nails, screws, or nails, hammer, old log or workbench & table	paint finished products make tool box **Book Corner-Storytime** pictures, books, wooden or plastic construction worker figures—Lego blocks, snap blocks—flannel board **Trip** construction site **Visitor** carpenter who might prepare & build with children
Library	books records shelves table rubber stamp pad & pencils library cards chairs & tables telephone	Set up near home making center. Include pillows, shelves, lamp small table, record player		make books make check out stamp **Book Corner-Storytime** storytime in library area write story about trip **Trip** to library—check out books **Visitor** librarian
Laundromat or Cleaners	laundry basket plastic soup containers clothes dishpan clothes pins & line ironing board & iron	Set up near home center or large block area—clothes line & pins, include large trucks for delivery or add tub & water to area for "hand laundry"	2 large tubs soap clothes line pins doll clothes water	make washer/dryer from large boxes signs **Book Corner-Storytime** pictures, flannel board stories; write or tell trip experience

TABLE 12-1 (continued)

Sociodramatic Play Themes

Theme	Props	Area/s In Playroom	Gym or Outside Play Yard	Related Activity
	hangers kitchen timer cash register play money paper & pencil baskets large boxes labeled "washer," "dryer" telephone			**Trip** to laundromat—wash school soiled aprons, etc. visit cleaners—observe process visit home or schools laundry room **Visitor** owner, janitor
Doctor, Nurse Nursing Attendant	nurse's cap tape, cotton pad & pencil 2 telephones kit or bag thermometer sunglasses (without lens) unbreakable supplies (pill bottles) bandages (strips of sheeting) stethoscope baby scale tape measure or height chart white shirts eye chart examining table magazines chairs telephone	Set-up center near homemaking area Add doll beds or child size cots Make center into animal hospital—toy animals, cages, food dishes	wheel toys wagons for emergency vehicles blankets	construct an emergency vehicle (blocks on boxes) hats bandages eye chart weight & measure use plaster of paris bandages on dolls **Book Corner-Storytime** pictures, books, puppets, wooden or cardboard figures **Trips** visit hospital emergency room explore emergency vehicle **Visitor** doctor nurse emergency driver
Cowboy	hat chaps rope stickhorse neckerchief cook kit sleeping bag	Combine with snack times around fake fire and sing cowboy songs	Combine with "real" fire and cooking outdoors	make hats, vests, etc. make horses from triangles **Book Corner-Storytime** books, pictures,

TABLE 12-1 (continued)

Sociodramatic Play Themes

Theme	Props	Area/s In Playroom	Gym or Outside Play Yard	Related Activity
Cowboy (continued)	canteen firewood			flannel board, songs, finger plays, records, puzzles film strips **Trip** horse farm or rodeo **Visitor** rodeo rider
Car Wash	play money large wheel toys sponge & clothes pails plastic squeeze bottles water & soap paper towels squeegees boots garden hose telephone tickets	Set up near large block area using pretend water, etc.	Theme lends itself to outside area & warm days use water	make signs—play money **Book Corner–Storytime** picture, books, flannel board, songs **Trip** To car wash—have car washed & watch process **Visitor** wash car
Airport	cap steering wheel serving trays cockpit (packing box) walking-board wing panel board tickets food containers suitcases overalls oil cans tools ticket counter maps travel folders dress-up clothes for travel dolls & blankets telephone	Construct airplane in large block area, large truck for loading food, suitcases	Devise airplane using boxes, large block, large wheel toys, boards for ramps	make caps, badges tickets menus travel folders **Book Corner–Storytime** books, pictures, wooden figures, small airplanes, puzzles, travel folders **Trip** to airport—inspect an airplane **Visitor** pilot, mechanic, flight attendant

TABLE 12–1 (continued)

Sociodramatic Play Themes

Theme	Props	Area/s In Playroom	Gym or Outside Play Yard	Related Activity
Camping	tent cook kit firewood sleeping bags canteen flashlights camp stools	Large space or reserve for gym or outdoor activity	Add small charcoal grill with fire, roasting sticks, hot dogs, etc. or fish poles & plastic fish tub with water shovel & dirt area Maybe combine with "cowboy"	prepare food make fish poles construct camper from blocks or boxes **Book Corner–Storytime** pictures, books, puzzles, puppets **Trip** equipment area of store camp out for a day/night in park **Visitor** examine camper brought by visitor
Service Station	oil can cap flashlight rubber hose lengths rope (short lengths) sponge & bucket rubber or soft plastic tools cash register credit cards play money gas pump telephone	Set up small block area—small cars, street signs Large block area—large trucks & cars or small blocks and airplanes or large block and large airplanes	wheel toys large boxes devise a train airplane or bus using boxes, boards, triangles	make street signs, credit cards, play money construct gas pump devise train, airplane, bus, etc. **Trip** to service station airport, ride on bus **Book Corner–Storytime** pictures, books, records **Visitor** service station attendant

Source: Adapted from Johnson and Newman (1980)

Thematic-Fantasy Play

There are special teacher roles involved when attempting to stage thematic-fantasy play in the classroom or day care center. Thematic-fantasy play is based on a story or rhyme. Teachers need to make sure children understand the story or rhyme before embarking on this form of play. Teachers can prepare lists of questions in advance

for each story and can use these questions during group discussion as a form of distancing strategy (see Chapter 5). While it is important to organize questions in terms of the sequence of the plot, it is also important to vary questions from easy to difficult in terms of the cognitive processes, conceptual content, and the open versus closed nature of the inquiry. Moreover, follow up questions are as important as initial questions. To do this effectively the teacher must be a careful listener (see "Questions for Thematic Fantasy Play Stories").

During the play the teacher should manage props. Often there are too many props, and children can suffer from this material overload. Children need physical room to play, and room to use their imaginations also. Too many objects can distract from make-believe play by drawing children into sensory-motor involvement with the materials. For example, magnets on a string used as fishing poles can spoil a dramatic rendition of a fishing trip by turning the activity into a simple hand-eye coordination game.

In addition, the kinds of props should be varied. Props range from small-scale replicas of the actual objects to substitutes which are physically dissimilar. Ultimately of course, a child will not need any props but just rely on verbal reference. For example, a child might pretend to drink from an imaginary cup. Teachers should recognize the need for a mix of realistic, *constructed* materials, and abstract *construction* materials. Moldable representational materials are often great facilitators of pretend play by children over 3½ years of age (Forman & Kuscher, 1977).

In thematic-fantasy play, prop management is essential. Enacting a story can be a highly cognitive activity and too many objects can get in the way. The teacher must remember that using props is a means to an end and not an end in itself. In addition, the kinds of props chosen are important. Two main questions need to be considered: Will the prop function in the way that is required in the story? Can children use it in the prescribed manner? Physical similarity is not necessary, especially for children older than 3½ years old (see Chapter 3). However, for younger children (or children with retarded cognitive development) it is important to recognize the developmental need for realistic, concrete props at first, and then to change props so they become

QUESTIONS FOR THEMATIC FANTASY PLAY STORIES

The Three Bears

1. Where did the three bears live?
2. Why did the three bears go for a walk?
3. What did Goldilocks do first when she went into the house?
4. Who's porridge (chair) (bed) did she try first? Did she like it? Why or why not?
5. Who's porridge (chair) (bed) did she try second? Did she like it? Why or why not?
6. Who's porridge (chair) (bed) did she try last? Did she like it? How do you know? What happened to the chair?
7. What was Goldilocks doing when the bears returned? How did the bears feel? How did Goldilocks feel when she saw the bears? Why? What did she do?
8. What else might have Goldilocks done?
9. What might have happened then? Why?
10. What might you have done then if you were Goldilocks?

Cinderella

1. Where did Cinderella live? Who did she live with?
2. What chores did Cinderella do at home?
3. Why did Cinderella have to do so much housework?
4. Where did Cinderella want to go? Why didn't Cinderella's step-sisters want her to go?
5. Who came to visit Cinderella when she was left alone?
6. What did the Fairy Godmother use for horses?
7. What happened at the ball? How come?
8. What happened at midnight? How come?
9. Why did the Prince come to Cinderella's house after the ball?
10. Did you like this story? Why or why not?

Jack and the Bean Stalk

1. What did Jack's mother tell Jack to do with the cow?
2. Why did they need to sell the cow?
3. What other way might they have raised money?
4. What did Jack get for the cow?
5. How did Jack's mother feel about that? What did she do?
6. What happened then? Where did Jack go?
7. What did Jack find up on the cloud?
8. Who lived in the castle? Where did Jack hide? Where else could he have hidden?
9. What did Jack take from the Giant? Why?
10. What did Jack do then? How come? How did the story end?

Source: Adapted from Newman and Johnson (1981)

less physically similar to the reference object. For example, one would not expect a young child to pretend to place a phone call using no prop at all. Rather one would first use a realistic replica of a phone. Then one can substitute objects that look less and less like the object for which it stands (*e.g.*, a block of wood for a phone). In fact, deliberately altering a physical characteristic of a prop may heighten cognitive flexibility and help children gradually to focus more on the overall meaning of what they are doing (acting out a sequence) and less on the physical characteristics of

TABLE 12-2

Stories for Thematic Fantasy Play

Theme	Roles	Props	Setting	Related Activities

Goldilocks and the Three Bears	Papa bear
	Mama bear
	Baby bear
	Goldilocks
	Forest creatures
		table, spoons,
		  napkins, vase &
		  flowers, 3 bowls
		bonnet
		wig
		3 chairs
		3 beds
		pillows, sheets
			Arrange tables
			& chairs or other
			substitute objects
			to stand for beds,
			chairs, etc.
				Trip
				to zoo, circus, nature
				center
				
				Book Corner
				pictures, books,
				cassettes, stick-
				ons, coloring;
				draw pictures in
				small groups;
				flannel board
				story.

Little Red Riding Hood	Red Riding Hood
	Mother
	Wolf
	Grandmother
	Hunter
	Forest animals
		cape, basket, objects
		  for basket, towel
		plastic or papier-
		  mache
		fruits & vegetables
		food cartons, boxes
		rubber club
		blanket
		cap, glasses
		nose & teeth
			Set up block area
			using chairs &
			tables to designate
			locations (e.g.,
			grandma's house);
			or for outdoors,
			large boxes, play-
			ground equip-
			ment, trees,
			boards, etc. for
			houses, forest, etc.
				make hats, "food"
				  for Little Red
				  Riding Hood's
				  basket
				
				Visit
				forest ranger or
				zookeeper, zoology
				student.
				draw pictures in
				small group

Cinderella	Cinderella
	Step-mother
	Two step-sisters
	Fairy Godmother
	Prince & attendants
	Town people
	Dancers
	Queen, King
	Mice Coachman
		broom, slippers,
		  crowns, pumpkin,
		fancy dresses,
		wand, combs,
		brushes, mirrors,
		chairs, tables
			Arrange tables &
			chairs to designate
			locations in a
			section of the
			room
				preparation and
				  construction of
				  props
				types of shoes,
				cut-and-paste
				  activities
				draw pictures in
				  small groups

TABLE 12–2 (continued)

Stories for Thematic Fantasy Play

Theme	Roles	Props	Setting	Related Activities

The Three Little Pigs	Three pigs
	Wolf
		straw, wood,
		  bricks, tables
		  chairs, pot
		  for fireplace
		  sticks and scarfs
			Chairs for each
			  house with straw,
			  sticks, or brick
			  on chair to
			  designate type
			  of house;
			  chair for apple
			  tree
				weighing materials
				exploring sturdiness
				  of materials
				different types of
				  shelters: cut-outs,
				  scrap book
				draw pictures in
				  small groups
				flannel board story

Jack and the Bean Stalk	Jack
	Mother
	Seller
	Giant
	Wife
		buttons for beans
		paper for money
		doll for chicken
		chair for house
		table/platform for
		  cloud
		teacher for bean
		  stalk
		hats
			Small room or area
			  off to side—
			  set up tables &
			  chairs; or use
			  platform play
			  equipment
			  outdoors to
			  stand for cloud;
			  use wagon or big
			  wheels for Jack's
			  house
				Book Corner
				pictures, books,
				  stick-ons,
				  coloring, record
				  player; cassettes
				draw pictures in
				  small groups

Hansel & Gretel	Hansel
	Gretel
	Step-Mother
	Step-Father
	Witch
	Forest animals
	Swan
		chips for bread
		  crumbs, trees,
		  houses, tables,
		  chairs, oven,
		  box for cage,
		  rug for pond
			Arrange designated
			  locations using
			  tables, chairs,
			  and rugs
				construct props with
				  cardboard boxes
				baking gingerbread
				  cake
				
				Book Corner
				cassettes, records,
				  books
				draw pictures in
				  small groups

The Three Billy Goats Gruff	3 billy goats
	Troll
		table, large
		  blocks and plank
		  for bridge
			Small room or
			  block corner;
			  outdoors
				Book Corner
				pictures, stories,
				  cassettes of
				  animal noises,
				  coloring
				
				Visit
				goat farm
				draw pictures

TABLE 12–2 (continued)

Stories for Thematic Fantasy Play

Theme	Roles	Props	Setting	Related Activities
The Wolf and the Seven Little Kids	Mother goat Wolf Seven kids	basket, rug, chalk, flowers, furniture, tables, chairs, scissors	Section of room off to side; small room; outdoor play area	**Book Corner** books, stick-ons draw pictures flannel board story
The Big, Big Turnip	Farmer Wife Daughter Dog Cat Mouse Turnip	None	Central area of room, preferably on rug; multiple groups simultaneously enact story using large area	planting vegetables and flowers **Visit** to farm **Book Corner** stories, pictures about rural life flannel board story

Other Stories for Thematic Fantasy Play

Tom Thumb
Where the Wild
  Things Are
Snow White and the
  Seven Dwarfs
Beauty and the Beast
The Ugly Duckling
The Three Little
  Kittens
Sleeping Beauty
Jack the Giant
  Killer
The Wizard of Oz

Source: Adapted from Newman and Johnson (1981)

objects in the play setting. For example, an enterprising teacher can have a brown wig for Goldilock's hair or a blue hood for Little Red Riding Hood!

The important point is for the teacher to be *active:* Setting up, changing, and removing props to meet the changing developmental capacities of the children. In thematic-fantasy play one has a good opportunity to put this principle into practice. In addition, it is important to let children join the decision-making process as soon as possible regarding which props are needed and desirable. This can be a very valuable learning experience in problem-solving and planning.

Table 12-2 (on pp. 251–253) lists several stories that can be used for thematic-fantasy play. Each story has been analyzed into four components: Roles, Props, Setting, and Related Activities. A teacher, parent, librarian, or other adult working with young children and using thematic fantasy play should remember to adapt these suggestions to fit the situation. For example, if there are more children than parts in a story the teacher can suggest that several children play new parts that the teacher invents, such as forest creatures.

Contrasting Sociodramatic and Thematic Fantasy Play

There are a number of important differences between the teacher's role in socio-dramatic play and the teacher's role in thematic-fantasy play. These are summarized as follows:

Time
Sociodramatic play usually occurs throughout the free play period. Thematic-fantasy play, on the other hand, is normally limited to smaller time segments when the teacher can give more attention and direction to children's dramatization of stories.

Space
Sociodramatic play normally occurs in fairly large areas of the classroom often called the dramatic play center. In thematic-fantasy play, the teacher usually needs an area that is somewhat sectioned off from the rest of the children's play area. A smaller area is ordinarily sufficient compared to what is needed for sociodramatic play.

Accessibility
The play area for sociodramatic play is usually one where children are free to leave and enter at will and where new children are free to join on-going play. On the other hand, in thematic-fantasy play, the teacher often closes off the play area while the play is in progress and restricts to some extent the freedom of the children to leave and enter.

Size of group
In sociodramatic play as many children who want to partake in play are usually welcome to join in. In thematic-fantasy play, however, the number of children who can participate is constrained by the number of characters in the story.

Role assignment
Letting the children decide on roles for themselves or subtle intervention when difficulties arise is par for the course in sociodramatic play. However, in thematic-fantasy play the teacher assumes more responsibility in role assignments. The teacher will see to it that, by changing roles from day to day, the children are given the opportunity to learn the perspectives of different characters in the story.

Use of props

In sociodramatic play more extensive use of props and costuming is made, both in terms of quantity and in terms of the proportion of replica object props to substitute object props, than is the case in thematic fantasy play. For thematic fantasy play realistic props are usually kept at a minimum, and substitute or imaginary objects are employed to a greater extent in order to minimize potential distractions and thus help the children focus on the cognitive goal of the directed play session. Some realistic objects may be used at times to renew fading interest in an old familiar play theme. Costumes are used with discretion also.

Teacher direction

In sociodramatic play the teacher is more active in preparing the environment for imaginative play and is less directive while the actual play is in progress. The teacher usually joins the play when asked or intervenes when problems, questions, and/or the need for information is indicated. In thematic-fantasy play more teacher direction is involved while the story is being enacted. Often the teacher narrates while the children act out their roles, helping children who forget their parts. Many times the teacher assumes the role of one of the characters in the story. The teacher also prepares simplified versions of story plots and lists of discussion questions (see Table 12–2 and "Questions for Thematic Fantasy Play Stories").

APPLYING CONTEMPORARY THEORIES OF PLAY

Practical decisions of how to equip preschools or day care centers, how to organize play activities, how to define appropriate use of play materials, how to structure adult participation, how to interact with children, and the extent to which the curriculum should be geared toward play activities, are all questions of vital interest to early childhood education professionals. Are theoretical notions or metaphors about play of any use to teachers of young children? This section discusses four current metaphors of play and derives practical implications from each for the preschool teacher.

Transformational Theory

This familiar theory, inspired by Piaget, emphasizes the symbolic character of play in young children. Smilansky, in her famous work on sociodramatic play in so-called culturally disadvantaged children, considered the transformational aspects of play important for evaluating the level of play. (The extent of cooperation, verbal behavior, and persistence in play were other critical factors.) To judge the quality of transformational behavior, four questions are raised: (1) Is the child pretending to be someone other than who the child really is? (2) Is the child pretending that others are different from who they really are? (3) Is the child pretending that objects are different from what they actually represent? (4) Is the child pretending that the situation is different from what it really is? These types of transformations are assessed further in terms of their degree of difference from the concrete or familiar experience of the child. For example, is the child engaging in object transformation with the help of replica miniature props, substitute objects, or pretend objects? Is the play theme and content close to, or far from, the child's normal everyday life?

Metacommunication Theory

The ideas of communication, negotiation, and context are central in a second metaphor about the play of young children. Children playing together or a child playing alone must use interpersonal or intrapersonal messages to establish, maintain, interrupt, reinstate, and terminate the play event. Ethnographic researchers characterize play events in terms of frames and scripts or contexts and texts. Play does not occur in a vacuum and cannot therefore be divorced from its surroundings. Children quite easily enter and exit their play world and are always cognizant of the real world. Children at play, in other words, operate on multiple levels. While engrossed in a play episode, children are simultaneously aware of the real identities of their playmates—who they are and their standing in the peer group—as well as who they are within the play episode. The play itself and the negotiations around the play episode reflect and express the social relations that exist both within as well as outside the play episode. Duplicity of meaning is an inherent characteristic of play behavior. What takes place in the pretend world is the play proper. But play is always embedded in the actual world, revealing the dynamic relationship between the two. Anything in the actual world can become play through the communicational message "This is play." Children and adults are constantly framing and reframing their behaviors and experiences across this threshold.

Performance Theory

A related idea from Sutton-Smith (1979) is the notion that play actually involves a quadralogue. If an ordinary conversation is a dialogue, then play involves four sets of communicators—players and co-players, directors, producers, and audience. Even during solitary play the child often imagines co-players and a pretend audience. During social play, considerable coordination is required as individual children have their own ideas for how the playing should be done, or re-done, if the play does not go right the first time. This quadralogue theory or metaphor focuses on the fact that play is a staged event with multiple elements as players interact in a pretend world set up for a real or imagined audience.

Script Theory

Narrative or script theory is another recent perspective on children's play. According to this view, play content represents the child's attempt to make sense out of personal experiences. As preschoolers develop intellectually, they become better able to structure events based on experience. The content of play is an expression of the child's interpretation of experiences.

Knowledge structures activated from memory are termed "scripts." A script represents knowledge of a network of possible major subactions or "scenes" which make up a larger activity such as going to the grocery store or taking a trip to the beach. Scripts identify culturally accepted ways of acting in situations that are commonplace in the child's experience. Components of scripts include scenes, subactions, roles and relationships, the environmental objects (props) within scenes, variations of the script (e.g., going to a big supermarket or a small store), and conditions in the social world that signal the start and the ending of the script.

Children's dramatic or imaginative play viewed as script can be examined in terms of the level of narrative organization displayed in the enactments, thus providing an indicator of the child's cognitive and language development. Wolf and Grollman (1982) suggest three different levels: scheme, event, and episode. The scheme level is shown when children perform one or more brief actions which are associated with a single small event (e.g., putting a doll to bed). At the event script level, children enact two or three schemes which are parts of obtaining one goal (e.g., bathing the doll and then putting it to bed). This may also entail contoured events which involve four or more different schemes all aimed at the same end (e.g., pretending to cook hamburgers, make coffee, bake a cake, and prepare a salad). The episode level finally occurs when children perform two or more scripts directed towards a single goal (e.g., baking a pretend cake and then serving it to a playmate). Episodes may also be contoured when they involve two or more contoured events (e.g., pretending to cook a variety of food, serving them to several playmates, and then washing the dishes). Hence, the play-as-script model permits the observers to witness, appreciate, and roughly gauge both personality and self-concept disclosure, and to estimate intellectual and linguistic maturity in young children.

Implications from Theory

Teachers can apply the four theories discussed above in a number of ways. Play-as-transformation theory has been around the longest and is widely incorporated within the field. With this theory in mind, teachers are able to discern the various types of transformational behaviors implicit within pretend play episodes, and are able to measure progress in verbal, imagery, and representational abilities as shown through the child's use of realistic props, then less realistic props, and, finally, no props at all during pretend play. As a result, teachers are able to make appropriate changes in what is available in activity centers for children to use during play (such as removing or adding a realistic prop). Furthermore, teachers should be sensitive as to the apparent difficulty of enacting various roles and themes within make-believe play. For instance, themes close to the familiar everyday experience of the young child are usually chosen by children to enact before themes based on fictional roles and events (i.e., superheroes).

The play-as-metacommunication theory provides the adult with an additional lens with which to perceive play. With this theory teachers realize that during play children are engaged in communication on several levels. Children's enactments not only express the themes and plots of the play episode itself, but also reveal the social dimension of the play in context. Just as transformational theory makes the teacher more aware of the "vertical nature" of play (developmental sequences and ability levels in symbolic representation), metacommunication theory makes the teacher more aware of the "sideways nature" of play. Social relationships within play reestablish and express social relations outside the play. Witnessing play in this way, the teacher has a sensitive barometer of interpersonal relations within the classroom or day care center. Thus, this theory can be valuable in evaluating the peer status and the social development of each child, and can be used to explain some of the behaviors that take place when children are playing.

The play-as-performance theory provides yet another perspective on children's play. This theory can be useful in at least two ways. First, as with the previous theory, it brings attention to the fact that play is framed and hence consists of content and context. Either when seeking to enter the play world oneself, or in attempting to help a child join an ongoing play group, it is important to respect the play boundary that divides the child's pretend world from the actual world. Insensitivity can lead to unnecessary disruption of ongoing play. For example, overmanaging or structuring can weaken or destroy the coordinations among players, co-players, directors, producers, and audience. If a teacher feels that children would benefit from some guidance, a helpful suggestion could be made in the character of an appropriate role within the play episode instead of as an outside authority figure. For example, if the children were enacting a store scene, the teacher might take the role of a customer and make suggestions while enacting this minor role. Likewise, children having difficulty joining play groups can be coached to use appropriate social entry skills (*e.g.*, offering to take a *minor* role) and to make smooth transitions between groups. Second, the quadralogue model indicates that play is more than what it may seem at first. Children are not only players, but are also directors, producers, and the audience—real or imagined. The teacher can observe children's growing skills in these different areas. Perfection in the performance—*i.e.*, satisfaction with doing it the right way—results from those times, for instance, when children realize something new during play and want to start the sequence or cycle from the beginning again. Play directing and managing skills develop as children mature. As such, these behaviors provide an additional index of intellectual and linguistic ability in children. Furthermore, given the inevitable individual differences in these skills, teachers who examine play in this way will be in a better position to promote these skills compared to those teachers unaware of this perspective.

The play-as-script theory helps the teacher recognize and analyze differences in intellectual and linguistic abilities as well as differences in self-concept and personality. As such, this perspective enables the teacher to see the child in a new way. By observing what the child is doing during play, the teacher can evaluate what the child knows, how the child is organizing experiences and is able to express them, and what matters to the child. Lesson plans can be designed that will capitalize upon special interests of select children. Field trips and supplemental activities can be arranged; their effects can later be observed in play scripts. For example, a teacher might observe several children enacting a restaurant scene and notice that the children have rather vague notions about the roles of different restaurant personnel. A field trip to a nearby restaurant could be planned, followed by the introduction of theme related props (*e.g.,* menus). Observation of the post-trip play would reveal if conceptual growth has occurred as a result.

ROLES OF THE ADULT

Three alternative positions of play within the educational setting are: (1) All play is beneficial; (2) No play is beneficial; (3) Some types of play are beneficial. Corollaries to these positions may be derived pertaining to teacher practice and curriculum design: (1) Integrate or harmonize play with other activities (the first and third position); and (2) Segregate play from other activities (the second position). Recent play theories suggest an alternative role for the teacher in promoting play: (3) Juxtapose play with other activities. The curriculum and daily schedule can be designed in such a manner that children are allowed to benefit from play without inappropriate or unnecessary intervention on the part of the teacher.

Teachers can operate constructively to enhance child development *besides, within,* and *away from* the play frame. Communicational theory highlights the nature of play in context and the distinction between *context* and *content.* Awareness of this distinction should help teachers realize more fully the difference between operating effectively *besides,* as opposed to *within,* play.

Working Besides Play

The teacher can work effectively *besides* ongoing play by observing carefully what occurs and by waiting for appropriate times to make comments or raise questions aimed at assisting the child at play, prompting the child to think about some idea related to the play topic, or encouraging the child to consider the implication of his or her behaviors. An example of each of these three different teacher interventions would be: "Why don't you take your family to the beach?" (directed toward children who have run out of ideas playing house), "What is the difference between shoes for men and shoes for women?" (directed toward a child playing shoe salesperson), and, "Do you understand why Paul wants to give out tickets too?" (directed toward a child who has been upset and is quarreling with another child). It should be noted first that, in each case, the play frame is interrupted; whatever the child learns from the teacher intervention is not learned during play per se, but from the teacher's use of the play context—the teacher is effective working *besides* child's play. Second, the three examples reflect behaviors showing different teacher roles: structuring play, teaching during free play, and child management during free play.

Working Within Play

The teacher only works within play when the play frame is not interrupted; that is, the teacher must be a co-player. To be effective as a teacher within the play frame requires a good actor or actress who will not disrupt the play. This is an art form. The teacher has to weave the teaching message into the play itself. For example, while enacting the role of a family member, the teacher might suggest going to the beach, or the teacher might pretend to be a customer and initiate a conversation about shoes with a child who is enacting the role of the shoe salesperson.

Play structuring and teaching are conceivable within the play frame; however, it is impossible to discipline children within the play frame. This is because in those instances when children's emotional level is inappropriately high, or when children are displaying a conflict or contest of wills with another child or adult, it is necessary for the teacher to present herself or himself as an authority figure. This automatically snaps the play frame.

Working away from Play

Teacher behavior and curricular features describable as "away from" play include activities planned before as well as after free play periods. As noted, related events affect children's play. Orchestration and planning are required to make full use of the curriculum. Meaningful additions to curricular components include field trips, guests or visitors, discussions, and other activities that have the potential of enriching play experiences of children by providing content and themes which can be incorporated into children's activities during free play periods. Having children plan and discuss ahead of time what they will be doing during a given free play period, as well as having children recall and discuss what they did during the play time, can be valuable learning experiences which also can add to later play experiences. Small group instruction with intense teacher involvement aimed at fostering abstract thinking ability may pay off in improved levels of free play. As noted earlier in this chapter, high structure in a preschool curriculum must not be confused with the nature of the free play period, which may or may not include a high degree of structure.

Finally, teachers can provide specific learning activities and coaching to help children make better use of free play periods. Previous play training studies have been done with play as the independent or causal variable and with cognitive, social, and language abilities as the dependent variables or consequences. This can be turned around. For example, teachers can use various other activities to attempt to increase open-ended thinking and social skills in young children with enhanced quality of play as the goal. A possible benefit for the child would be increased effectiveness and acceptance within the peer group. For example, children could be taught to perform communication or perspective-taking tasks and subsequently be observed during free play. Now that valid and reliable observational measures of play level are available (Enslein & Fein, 1981), the impact of such tasks or activities 'away from play' on the level of play can be evaluated. If shown to be effective, structured tasks or exercises could be used advantageously by the teacher of young children to improve play skills in children.

To conclude, this section has reviewed four contemporary theories about children's play. The metaphors discussed were play-as-transformation, play-as-communication, play-as-performance, and play-as-script. The value of these theories to the teacher of young children has been described, with special emphasis given to the juxtaposition model of the relationship of children's play with early childhood educational practice. This model was discussed by elaborating upon the roles of the teacher *within, besides,* and *away from* the spontaneous play of children.

SUMMARY

In this chapter we have reviewed the research on the effects of early childhood educational programs on the play behavior of young children. We have also discussed three types of group dramatic play which teachers or parents of young children can plan: (1) spontaneous free play of a general sort; (2) sociodramatic play with particular themes; and (3) thematic-fantasy play. We have provided specific suggestions and have pointed out several ways that the three different types of dramatic play differ. We have also shown how four contemporary theories of play translate into educational practice. In so doing we have attempted to bring to the attention of the reader our approach to understanding the relationship between play and work within the context of early childhood education.

REFERENCES

Bateson, G. (1956). The message, 'This is play.' In B. Schaffner (Ed.), *Group processor: Transactions of the second conference.* New York: Josiah Macy Foundation, 145–151.

Beller, E.K., Zimmie, J., and Aiken, L. (1971). Levels of play in different nursery settings. *International Congress of Applied Psychology,* Leige.

Enslein, J. & Fein, G. (1981). Temporal and cross-situational stability of children's social and play behavior. *Developmental Psychology, 17,* 760–761.

Forman, G.E., & Kuscher, D.S. (1977). *The child's conception of knowledge: Piaget for teaching children.* Monterey, CA: Brooks/Cole.

Griffing, P. (1980). The relationship between sociometric status and sociodramatic play among black kindergarten children. *Genetic Psychological Monograph, 101,* 3–34.

Hess, R.D., & Croft, D.J. (1972). *Teachers of young children.* Boston, Houghton Mifflin.

Huston-Stein, A.: Freidrich-Cofer, L., Susman, E. (1977). The relationship of classroom structure to social behavior, imaginative play, and self-regulation of economically disadvantaged children. *Child Development, 48,* 908–916.

Johnson, J.E., & Ershler, J. (1981). Developmental trends in preschool play as a function of classroom program and child gender. *Child Development, 52.*

Johnson, J.E., Ershler, J., & Bell, C. (1980). Play behavior in a discovery-based and a formal education preschool program. *Child Development, 51,* 271–274.

Johnson, J.E., & Newman, V. (1980). Imaginative play themes and the teacher's role. *Offspring, 21,* 25–31.

Miller, L.B., & Dyer, J.L. (1975). Four preschool programs—their dimension and effects. *Monograph of the Society for Research in Child Development, 40,* Serial No. 162.

Newman, V., & Johnson, J.E. (1981). Fantasy play: Acting out stories. *Offspring, 22,* 15–29.

Rubin, K.H. & Seibel, C.C. (1979). The effects of ecological setting on the cognition and social play behaviors of preschoolers. *Annual Meeting of the American Educational Research Association,* San Francisco.

Smilansky, S. (1968). *The effects of sociodramatic play on disadvantaged preschool children.* New York: Wiley.

Sutton-Smith, B. (1979). Play as metaperformance. In B. Sutton-Smith (Ed.), *Play and learning.* New York: Gardner Press.

Tizard, B., Philps, J., & Plewis, I. (1976). Play in preschool centers—II. Effects on play of the child's social class and the educational orientation of the center. *Journal of Child Psychology and Psychiatry, 17,* 265–274.

Wolf, D., & Grollman, S.H. (1982). Ways of playing: Individual differences in imaginative style. In D.J. Pepler & K.H. Rubin (Eds.), *The play of children: Current theory and research.* Basel, Switzerland: Karger, AG.

Index

Adaptation to cultural differences, 144–145
Adcock, D., 27
Adult, roles of, 21–43, 65–66, 85–87, 105–106, 123–125, 142–145, 182–184, 216–217, 230, 259–261. *See also* Teachers
Advantaged child, imaginative play of, 130–135
Adventure playgrounds, 201–202
Aggression, spatial density and, 189
Aiken, L., 236
Ammar, H., 136, 137
The Anthropological Association for the Study of Play, 138
Approval of adult, 23–24
Arousal modulation theory of play, 9
Arrangement of space, 191–194
Art in play, 117, 119, 192, 196
Associations serving toy and hobby industries, 178
Attention, 92
Attitude cultivation, 142–143
Axline, V., 13

Baer, D.M., 122
Bakeman, R., 49
Bandura, A., 92
Barnett, L.A., 14, 37, 83
Bateson, G., 9, 10
Bateson's theory of play, 9–10
Beasley, R.R., 199, 201, 202

Beckwith, J., 205
Behavior, 44, 143–145, 189
Behavior reinforcement, 91
Bell, C., 115, 237
Beller, E.K., 236
Berger, C., 221
Berk, L.E., 123, 125, 191, 194
Berlyne, D.E., 9, 51
Berndt, R., 57
Bhavnani, R., 76, 114
Bishop, D., 83
Bloch, M.N., 137
Blocks, 117, 118, 173–176, 192, 196
Book areas, 192, 197
Borgh, K., 221
Boyatzis, C.J., 199
Boy-boy or boy-girl interactions, 112
Boys, gender differences in play and, 109–128
Brady, E.H., 218, 219
Bragdon, N., 133
Brainerd, C.J., 17, 103
Brett, A., 219
Brophy, J.E., 49, 113, 151
Brown, N.S., 7
Brownlee, J.R., 49
Bruner, J.S., 6, 8, 10, 15, 16, 25, 83
Bruya, L.D., 203

Also Available from
Scott, Foresman and Company
Good Year Books

Good Year Books are reproducible resource and activity books for teachers and parents of students in preschool through grade 12. Written by experienced educators, Good Year Books are filled with class-tested ideas, teaching strategies and methods, and fun-to-do activities for every basic curriculum area. They also contain enrichment materials and activities that help extend a child's learning experiences beyond the classroom.

Good Year Books address many educational needs in both formal and informal settings. They have been used widely in preservice teacher training courses, as a resource for practicing teachers to enhance their own professional growth, and by interested adults as a source of sound, valuable activities for home, summer camp, Scout meetings, and the like.

Good Year Books are available through your local college or university bookstore, independent or chain booksellers, and school supply and educational dealers. For a complete catalog of Good Year Books, write:

Good Year Books
Department PPG-T
1900 East Lake Avenue
Glenview, Illinois 60025